Beyond Hellenistic Epistemology

Beyond Hellenistic Epistemology

Arcesilaus and the Destruction of Stoic Metaphysics

Charles E. Snyder

BLOOMSBURY ACADEMIC
LONDON • NEW YORK • OXFORD • NEW DELHI • SYDNEY

BLOOMSBURY ACADEMIC
Bloomsbury Publishing Plc
50 Bedford Square, London, WC1B 3DP, UK
1385 Broadway, New York, NY 10018, USA
29 Earlsfort Terrace, Dublin 2, Ireland

BLOOMSBURY, BLOOMSBURY ACADEMIC and the Diana logo are trademarks of
Bloomsbury Publishing Plc

First published in Great Britain 2021
This paperback edition published 2023

Copyright © Charles E. Snyder, 2021

Ryan McInerney has asserted his right under the Copyright, Designs and
Patents Act, 1988, to be identified as Author of this work.

For legal purposes the Acknowledgments on p. vi constitute an extension of
this copyright page.

Cover design: Charlotte Daniels
Cover image © Baivector / Shutterstock

All rights reserved. No part of this publication may be reproduced or transmitted
in any form or by any means, electronic or mechanical, including photocopying,
recording, or any information storage or retrieval system, without prior permission
in writing from the publishers.

Bloomsbury Publishing Plc does not have any control over, or responsibility for, any
third-party websites referred to or in this book. All internet addresses given in this
book were correct at the time of going to press. The author and publisher regret any
inconvenience caused if addresses have changed or sites have ceased to exist,
but can accept no responsibility for any such changes.

A catalogue record for this book is available from the British Library.

Library of Congress Cataloging-in-Publication Data
Names: Snyder, Charles E., author.
Title: Beyond hellenistic epistemology: Arcesilaus and the destruction of
stoic metaphysics / Charles E. Snyder.
Description: London, UK; New York, NY, USA: Bloomsbury Academic, 2021. |
Includes bibliographical references and index. |
Identifiers: LCCN 2021004549 (print) | LCCN 2021004550 (ebook) | ISBN
9781350202375 (hb) | ISBN 9781350202382 (epdf) | ISBN 9781350202399 (ebook)
Subjects: LCSH: Stoics. | Arcesilaus, of Pitane, 316 or 315-240 B.C.
Classification: LCC B528 .S57 2021 (print) | LCC B528 (ebook) | DDC 188–dc23
LC record available at https://lccn.loc.gov/2021004549
LC ebook record available at https://lccn.loc.gov/2021004550

ISBN: HB: 978-1-3502-0237-5
PB: 978-1-3502-0240-5
ePDF: 978-1-3502-0238-2
eBook: 978-1-3502-0239-9

Typeset by Deanta Global Publishing Services, Chennai, India

To find out more about our authors and books visit www.bloomsbury.com
and sign up for our newsletters.

Contents

Acknowledgments		vi
Introduction		1
1	The Structure of Early Stoic Metaphysics	27
	Disciplinary Holism	28
	Epistemological Part	39
	Philosophical Historiography	46
2	The Ontology of Early Stoic Apprehension	55
	Representations of the Real	55
	Indiscernible Beings	66
	Reconstructing ἀκαταληψία and ἐποχὴ περὶ πάντων	82
3	Total Inaction and the Impossibility of Stoic Ethics	101
	The Ontology of Stoic Virtue	103
	The Abyss of Stoic Nature	115
	Minimal Eudaimonism	127
4	The Old Academy's Traditional Hierarchy of Goods	135
	Polemo on Happiness	137
	The Basic Explanatory Framework of Old Academic Ontology	144
	Bipolar Notions of Nature	162
Concluding Analysis		181
	Cicero's Genealogy of the Academy	182
Bibliography		189
Index of Subject		202
Index of References		209

Acknowledgments

I would like to thank the Department of Philosophy at the New School for Social Research, especially Dmitri Nikulin, Cinzia Arruzza, Richard Bernstein, and Simon Critchley. Debts are owed to Giuseppe Veltri, Racheli Haliva, Daniel Davies, Karolin Berends, and Maria Wazinski at the Maimonides Centre for Advanced Studies, Jewish Skepticism, University of Hamburg, and the Deutsche Forschungsgemeinschaft for my time there as a Junior Fellow. I would also like to thank the wonderfully gifted students in my 2019 summer seminar on Plato and ancient metaphysics at Eastern Correctional Facility in Napanoch, New York. Parts of this book have appeared in preliminary form in a number of journals, and I am grateful to the editors at *The Review of Metaphysics* and *Études platoniciennes* for permission to draw on this material here.

Introduction

For every image of the past that is not recognized by the present as one of its own concerns threatens to disappear irretrievably. Walter Benjamin, *"Theses on the Philosophy of History"*

An attractive consensus has emerged in the historiography of Hellenistic philosophy. Proponents of the consensus advance the general claim that the Academic Arcesilaus of Pitane (c. 316–240 BCE) set out to attack Stoic "epistemology." These scholars moreover contend that the epistemic possibility of Stoic κατάληψις ("apprehension") is the principal target of attack. The notion of epistemic possibility is integral to the consensus that Arcesilaus opposed the theoretical prospect of human beings acquiring knowledge through "apprehension."[1] The denial of epistemic possibility is typically associated with the belief "that *we* view the world through a kind of epistemological veil." One proponent informs readers, using the vernacular of current scholarship on Hellenistic philosophy, that the so-called epistemological veil implies that our "sense-impressions are of their nature unreliable," or "that *our* senses are

---

[1] For a notable example of this approach to the attack, see Charles Brittain, "Arcesilaus," in *Stanford Encyclopedia of Philosophy*, ed. Edward Zalta (Fall 2008), https://plato.stanford.edu/archives/fall2008/entries/arcesilaus/. Other examples include: Hans Joachim Krämer, *Platonismus und hellenistische Philosophie* (Berlin: De Gruyter, 1971), 9–10; Jonathan Barnes, "Medicine, Experience and Logic," in *Science and Speculation: Studies in Hellenistic Theory and Practice*, ed. Jonathan Barnes, Jacques Brunschwig, Myles F. Burnyeat, and Malcolm Schofield (Cambridge: Cambridge University Press, 1982), 43; LS 1, 445; Woldemar Görler, "Älterer Pyrrhonismus, Jüngere Akademie, Antiochus aus Askalon, § 47 Arkesilaos," in *Die Philosophie der Antike 4: Die hellenistische Philosophie*, ed. Hellmut Flashar (Basel: Schwabe, 1994), 819; R. J. Hankinson, *The Sceptics* (London: Routledge, 1995), 77; Malcolm Schofield, "Academic Epistemology," in *The Cambridge History of Hellenistic Philosophy*, ed. Keimpe Algra, Jonathan Barnes, Jaap Mansfeld, and Malcolm Schofield (Cambridge: Cambridge University Press, 1999), 323–31; Michael Frede, "The Sceptics," in *Routledge History of Philosophy*, vol. 2, ed. David Furley (London: Routledge, 1999), 263; Baron Reed, "The Stoics' Account of the Cognitive Impression," *Oxford Studies in Ancient Philosophy* 23 (2002): 148; Anna Maria Ioppolo, "Arcésilas dans le *Lucullus* de Cicéron," *Revue de Métaphysique et de Morale* 57, no. 1 (2008): 22; Simone Vezzoli, *Arcesilao di Pitane: L'origine del platonismo neoaccademico* (Turnhout: Brepols, 2016), 105 (hereafter Vezzoli followed by fragment number or *Arcesilao* with page number). For early expression of this approach, see Eduard Zeller, *Die Philosophie der Griechen in ihrer geschichtlichen Entwicklung*, pt. 3, vol. 1, 5th ed. (Leipzig: O. R. Reisland, 1923), 509–10.

poor judges of them" (italics added).² Among the more obvious indicators, the collective pronouns signal the prevailing discourse of epistemology in the historiography of Hellenistic philosophy. The discourse of epistemology ascribes to Hellenistic philosophers a fundamental interest in the project of investigating what is required of us, *qua* subjects capable of making judgments about the world, to know the world beyond the so-called veil. In the terminology of another influential proponent, the "center-piece of Hellenistic epistemological theories" is the concern over what it is that "*we* need to find" in order to circumvent the veil of perception and justify *our* claims to knowledge.³

The framework of epistemology, as currently applied in the historiography of Hellenistic philosophy, narrows the field of research by assuming what is herein called a humanistic viewpoint. In the context of this study, a historiographical framework is humanistic in focus if it takes for granted that human beings are the focal point, or "center-piece," of the reconstructed theses and arguments originally formulated in the ancient texts.⁴ Whether or not proponents of the framework of epistemology in the historiography of Hellenistic philosophy appeal to such collective pronouns, they almost always invoke a vague conception of the human as a hypothetical epistemic subject for the purpose of placing the hypothetical subject, and the epistemic possibility relative to this subject, at the

---

² George Boys-Stones, "Plutarch on the Probable Principle of Cold: Epistemology and the *De primo frigido*," *Classical Quarterly* 47, no. 1 (1997): 230. Boys-Stones is a proponent of an expanded version of the epistemological approach. This iteration of the epistemological approach is more expansive as it refers more generally to Academic attacks on Stoic epistemology. Other examples taking an expanded approach include: Myles F. Burnyeat, "Antipater and Self-Refutation: Elusive Arguments in Cicero's *Academica*," in *Assent and Argument: Studies in Cicero's Academic Books*, ed. Brad Inwood and Jaap Mansfeld (Leiden: Brill, 1997), 279; Tobias Reinhardt, "To See and to Be Seen: On Vision and Perception in Lucretius and Cicero," in *Roman Reflections: Studies in Latin Philosophy*, ed. Gareth D. Williams and Katharina Volk (Oxford: Oxford University Press, 2016), 78, who frames Book 2 of Cicero's *Academica* (Lucullus) as a debate between Academics and Stoics "over the Stoic theory of knowledge"; and Gisela Striker, "*Ataraxia*: Happiness as Tranquility," *Monist* 73 (1990): 106, who holds that Hellenistic Academics (*inter al.*, Arcesilaus and Carneades) were wiser than Pyrrhonists for "limiting themselves [in criticizing Stoics and Epicureans] to the field of epistemology."
³ Gisela Striker, "The Problem of the Criterion," repr. Striker, in *Essays on Hellenistic Epistemology and Ethics* (Cambridge: Cambridge University Press, 1996), 151. See also the reconstruction of Brittain, "Arcesilaus," §3: Zeno "argued that *we* ought to restrict *our* assent to just cognitive or kataleptic impressions" (italics added).
⁴ To further clarify, the following exposition of the humanistic application of epistemology to ancient philosophical arguments has notable affinities with Louis Althusser's critical analysis of "une philosophie de l'homme" (i.e., a philosophical humanism or a philosophy of man) and the species of philosophical humanism Althusser refers to as "abstract" humanism. Louis Althusser, *Pour Marx*, avant-propos de Étienne Balibar (Paris: La Découverte, 2005), 234–8, 253–5. For the English translation, see Louis Althusser, *For Marx*, trans. Ben Webster (London: Verso, 2005), 227–31, 242–4. Moreover, for an account of "humanism" in conformity with this delineation of a humanistic focus, see Reiner Schürmann, "Adventures of the Double Negation: On Richard Bernstein's Call for Anti-Anti-Humanism," *Praxis International* 3 (1985): 284: "Humanism will turn out to designate those conceptual strategies in the 'soft sciences' that refer all possible topics to man."

center of their reconstructions.⁵ With respect to the historiography of the Stoic-Academic debates, the notion of epistemic possibility governs the humanistic interest.

In response to this humanistic concern for epistemic possibility, it is said that Zeno and the successors of his Stoic school appeal to a special kind of impression, the so-called "apprehensive impression" (φαντασία καταληπτική). This kind of impression is supposed to secure the possibility of knowledge for human beings. It is worth specifying that the Stoic conception of the human is not, *sensu stricto*, the "rational animal" (*animal rationale*), for god (viz. Zeus) is likewise considered a rational animal. It is therefore more accurate to say that, for the Stoa, the human is the "mortal animal partaking in reason" (Cicero, *Acad.* 2.21: *si homo est, animal est mortale, rationis particeps*).⁶ The hypothetical subject presupposed by the notion of epistemic possibility in the dispute over Stoic epistemology can more appositely be designated the "mortal animal partaking in reason." Yet, proponents of the consensus prefer to make abstract references to "us" *qua* epistemic subjects rather than specify the content of the Stoic conception of the human. Retrojecting an abstract and ahistorical concept of the epistemic subject for the purpose of reconstructing this ancient, epistemological debate, the basic task of specifying the Stoic conception of human animality is expelled by the conceptual regimentation of epistemological reconstruction. For present purposes, it suffices to say that from the perspective of this framework the debate seems primarily epistemological, and it appears to concern *our* epistemic possibility.⁷

Specialists in this arena of ancient philosophy regularly employ the term "epistemology" to classify and specify the content of the arguments and doctrines of the Hellenistic schools.⁸ It is now standard to use the term to delineate a major field of ongoing research in contemporary philosophy. With the conceptual resources of this field of philosophical research currently in wide professional circulation, it is perhaps no surprise to find ancient specialists associating

---

⁵ Reed, for example, relies on the collective pronoun "us" and the hypothetical "subject" throughout, though the latter is the dominant preference. Reed, "Cognitive Impression," 148, 159–61. For a critical analysis of the subject-object framework, see Sean Kirkland, *The Ontology of Socratic Questioning in Plato's Early Dialogues* (Albany: State University of New York Press, 2012), 3–22.
⁶ For discussion of the notion of *animal rationale* in relation to Stoicism, see Thomas Bénatouïl, "*Logos et scala naturae* dans le Stoïcisme de Zenon et Cleanthe," *Elenchos* 23, no. 2 (2003): 297–300.
⁷ Hankinson, *Sceptics*, 106: "So the Sceptics may in good faith suppose that the Stoics were committed, in so far as they propound the theory of cataleptic impressions as a criterion of truth and reality, to an internalist definition of them: not merely can *we* know things on the basis of such impression, but *we* can know that *we* know them. Indeed the Stoic texts seem to support that impression" (italics added).
⁸ E.g., John Sellars, *Hellenistic Philosophy* (Oxford: Oxford University Press, 2018), 32–57.

the Hellenistic age with an "epistemological turn."[9] The term "Hellenistic" conventionally refers to a historical period extending from the death of Alexander the Great (323 BCE) to the defeat of Mark Anthony and Cleopatra at the Battle of Actium (31 BCE). Indeed, "Hellenistic philosophy" normally refers to the views of philosophers who lived during this period. To quote a standard view, which remains largely unchallenged, "it is generally agreed that the Hellenistic period is 'the great age of ancient epistemology.'"[10] According to this agreement, while philosophers prior to this "great age" tended to reflect upon the possibilities and limits of human knowledge, negative assessments declaring the impossibility of human knowledge remained peripheral and isolated in comparison with the more centralized assumptions of realist theories of knowledge governing ancient philosophical reflection. Realist assumptions involve the belief that humans can know things and facts in themselves, including the world itself. Moreover, realist assumptions in epistemology usually presuppose a monistic view of reality, that is, a view that things themselves exist within a single, unified whole: for example, the finite totality that Zeno and later Stoa call "the world" (κόσμος/*mundus*). In the terminology of Stoic philosophy, the predicates "true" and "false" convey the assumption that true and false refer to propositions that are true and false of "a real objective world," or "a common objective world, external to ourselves and comprising things with a nature of their own."[11] On this view, the inclination of ancient philosophers, "from Parmenides onward," was to reflect not on how the mind "can be in touch with anything at all, but how it can fail to be." The "deep hold of realism" begins to unravel, or so it is claimed, in the early fourth century, around the time of the so-called great age of ancient epistemology. Around this time, as specified by the humanistic focus of Striker and Brunschwig, philosophers begin to submit the theme of knowledge to a more radical form of questioning whereby the very possibility of human knowledge takes center stage. Previously, pronouncements of epistemological doubt on the part of pre-Hellenistic philosophers were nothing more than minor episodic expressions of a peripheral tendency to declare truth and knowledge unavailable; however, with early Hellenistic figures such as Pyrrho, his disciple Timon, and the Academic Arcesilaus, the question concerning the possibility of human knowledge becomes "the *primary question* to which every philosophical school had to

---

[9] Jacques Brunschwig, "Introduction: The Beginnings of Hellenistic Epistemology," in Algra et al., *Cambridge History*, 229; Striker, "Problem of the Criterion," 150 (see n3 above for full reference).
[10] Brunschwig, "Introduction," 229.
[11] Myles F. Burnyeat, "Idealism and Greek Philosophy: What Descartes Saw and Berkeley Missed," *The Philosophical Review* 91, no. 1 (1982): 18–20, 25. Leo Groarke, *Greek Skepticism: Anti-Realist Trends in Ancient Thought* (Montreal: McGill-Queen's University Press, 1990), 19–20.

provide an answer" (italics added).¹² Contemporary scholars are as accustomed to providing historiographical reconstructions of "Academic epistemology," or "the critical epistemology of Arcesilaus," as they are to providing reconstructions of Stoic epistemology.¹³

In taking the framework of epistemology as self-evident or unproblematic—or by uncritically reiterating the claim that Arcesilaus and his Academic successors in the Hellenistic age attacked Stoic epistemology—scholars are susceptible to endorsing the view that Arcesilaus "refused metaphysical speculations" in favor of pursuing epistemological skepticism.¹⁴ The selective framing of epistemology in the historiography of Hellenistic philosophy, which this study rejects on philosophical grounds as the appropriate framework for reconstructing Arcesilaus's opposition to Stoic philosophy (including his opposition to Stoic ethics), is, for ease of reference, hereby designated *epistemological centrism*. In the context of reconstructing Arcesilaus's opposition to the early Stoa, epistemological centrism refers to the historiographical approach guided by the humanistic assumption that the core of the dispute is a concern over the epistemic possibility of apprehension. Working from this assumption, it seems uncontroversial to state that Arcesilaus limited his criticism of Stoic philosophy to the "field of epistemology," or that his attack on Stoic epistemology functioned to undermine

---

¹² Brunschwig, "Introduction," 230.
¹³ Brad Inwood and Lloyd P. Gerson, eds., "Introduction," in *The Stoics Reader: Selected Writings and Testimonia* (Indianapolis, IN: Hackett Publishing Company, 2008), xi. Schofield, "Academic Epistemology," 323–31. Baron Reed states the assumption governing the usage of the modern term "epistemology" in the historiography of Hellenistic philosophy: "The debate between the Stoics and Academics has considerable interest for modern epistemology as well. Indeed, in many respects the positions that emerged over the course of this debate are quite similar to theories currently prominent in epistemology." Reed observes that "this similarity has been noted by modern epistemologists who draw upon the views of the ancient philosophers," and by scholars who claim that the Stoics' view of the cognitive impression "can best be understood in the light of recent developments in epistemology." Reed, "Cognitive Impression," 149.
¹⁴ Radek Chlup, *Proclus: An Introduction* (Cambridge: Cambridge University Press, 2012), 9–11. See also Lloyd P. Gerson, "Plotinus and the Platonic Response to Stoicism," in *The Routledge Handbook of the Stoic Tradition*, ed. John Sellars (London: Routledge, 2016), 47–8, for the thesis that Plotinus is the first to develop an explicitly Platonic attack on Stoic ontology. On the other hand, some scholars suggest that Arcesilaus's attacks on the epistemic possibility has underlying Platonic motivations, as part of an attempt to revive and reinterpret a Platonic dualism between sensation and reason (e.g., in Vezzoli, *Arcesilao*, 101–35), or a Platonic version of the dualism between δόξα and ἐπιστήμη (e.g., in Franco Trabattoni, "Arcesilao platonico?," in *L'eredità platonica: studi sul platonismo da Arcesilao a Proclo*, ed. Mauro Bonazzi and Vincenza Celluprica (Naples: Bibliopolis, 2005), 22–8). These scholars assume that Academic attacks on Stoic epistemology are inspired by Platonic dialogues of a metaphysical resonance. See, e.g., Carlos Lévy, "Platon, Arcésilas, Carnéade: Réponse à J. Annas," *Revue de Métaphysique et de Morale* 2 (1990): 298–300, 305–6, and Carlos Lévy, "La Nouvelle Académie a-t-elle été antiplatonicienne?," in *Contre Platon I. Le platonisme dévoilé*, ed. Monique Dixsaut (Paris: Vrin, 1993), 141–9, and Carlos Lévy, *Les philosophies hellénistiques* (Paris: Librairie Générale, 1997), 186–8. Despite overt appeals to the alleged metaphysical roots of Arcesilaus's polemic, Lévy and Vezzoli uphold a humanistic viewpoint by reconstructing Arcesilaus's attack on Stoic apprehension as an attack on the *epistemic possibility* of Stoic apprehension.

the epistemological basis of Stoic ethics. Either way, the "critical epistemology" of the Hellenistic Academy would obviously involve an argumentative strategy aimed primarily at refuting Stoic epistemology. Such views continue to circulate unchallenged, as the taxonomic application of "epistemology" remains firmly entrenched in the mainstream of current Hellenistic scholarship.

Scholars occasionally issue brief statements of caution regarding the unjustified application of the concept of epistemology in the reconstruction of ancient philosophy. Such statements acknowledge the inextricable connections between the field that contemporary philosophers neatly classify as epistemology and the domain of physics, for example, or the connections between the epistemological and the area of ethical inquiry.[15] As shown herewith (Chapter 2), epistemological centrists occasionally refer to the Stoic principle of the identity of indiscernibles, issuing *obiter dicta* on the importance of this metaphysical principle for the Stoic defense of apprehension. To date, however, such passing references to the significance of this principle fall far short of specifying the content of this principle vis-à-vis the general structure of Stoic metaphysics, and the metaphysical tenets regarding individual bodies in particular. The structural connection of Stoic "apprehension" to the metaphysics of individual bodies is a theme that recent historiographers continually ignore.

The aim of this study is twofold, namely, to foreground what epistemological centrism routinely suppresses, while defending an alternative, theoretical scheme for rationally reconstructing the metaphysical premises at stake in the dispute.[16] This study does not purport to provide an exhaustive textual analysis of the evidence for the dispute or of Hellenistic epistemology more generally. It is intended, instead, to motivate a new philosophical framework for the ongoing interpretation of key ancient sources, thereby thematizing the metaphysical issues routinely muted in the dominant discourse, focusing in particular (but not exclusively) on select passages from the works of Sextus Empiricus and Cicero. As a first approximation of a core thesis of this revisionist, rationally reconstructive approach, the present study introduces the following claim.

---

[15] Nicholas P. White, "Plato's Metaphysical Epistemology," in *The Cambridge Companion to Plato*, ed. Richard Kraut (Cambridge: Cambridge University Press, 1992), 291–2. John Glucker, *Antiochus and the Late Academy* (Göttingen: Vandenhoeck & Ruprecht, 1978), 62, denies a sharp distinction between ethics and epistemology for Arcesilaus and his successors. See also Jean-Baptiste Gourinat, "L'épistémologie stoïcienne," *Lexicon Philosophicum: International Journal for the History of Texts and Ideas*, Special Issue (2018): 124.

[16] By "metaphysics," I mean the study concerned with articulating what kind of being (or beings) grounds other kinds of being. This type of study is also comprehensive or ontological insofar as it aims to articulate the structure among the entire range of beings that are or come to be. The aim of such an enterprise is a certain sort of systematic explanation of the entire range of beings. See Chapter 1 for further clarification of these terms.

Arcesilaus's opposition to Zenonian philosophy reveals—independent of questions concerning what Arcesilaus took himself to be opposing—that the general structure of Stoic metaphysics is committed to a metaphysics of individual bodies whereby each and every body is inapprehensible and, therefore, unknowable. The displacement of epistemological centrism in the study of Arcesilaus's opposition to early Stoic philosophy serves to situate Arcesilaus's anti-Stoic arguments within the framework of the ontology of knowledge. Owing to this reframing, the epistemic possibility of Stoic apprehension is shown to depend on further conditions of possibility, which are grounded in the metaphysics of individual bodies. In sum, Arcesilaus's anti-Stoic arguments contest the ontological conditions of the conditions of epistemic possibility. Thus the prevailing humanistic focus on epistemic possibility controlling historiographical reconstruction is decentralized, and the possibility of apprehension is thematically integrated into the more comprehensive structure of Stoic metaphysics. In the framework of the ontology of knowledge, the purported epistemic subject *qua* mortal animal partaking in reason is just one variable within a structural nexus of individual beings. This framework is anti-humanistic owing to its explicit criticism of, and refusal to follow, the modern historiographical partiality granting priority to a dehistoricized epistemic subject as the centralizing focus of historiographical specification. Briefly, allow me to summarize four conceptual consequences of this approach.

The first result of this new historiographical approach is the specification of the metaphysical content of ἀκαταληψία ("inapprehensibility").[17] Although the thesis of "inapprehensibility" does contradict the Stoic view of the possibility of human knowledge, the thesis more fundamentally involves requalifying the relative disposition of bodies in Zeno's etiological conception of apprehension. In other words, the notion of inapprehensibility is metaphysical insofar as it qualifies a particular mode in which bodies are disposed as individual beings. According to the metaphysical formulation of this thesis, individual bodies obtaining in a particular space at a particular time are relatively disposed—given the overall structure of Stoic ontology (i.e., *metaphysica generalis*)—to being inapprehensible for a particular class of individual beings. The arguments from

---

[17] I follow the convention of using the English term "inapprehensibility" for ἀκαταληψία and the English term "inapprehensible" for ἀκατάληπτος. Translations of ἀκαταληψία are governed by the translation of the Stoic terms κατάληψις, which is most commonly rendered "cognition" or "apprehension," and καταληπτικὴ φαντασία, standardly translated as "apprehensive impression" or "cognitive impression." For discussion of the advantages and disadvantages of the customary English translations, see R. J. Hankinson, "Stoic Epistemology," in *The Cambridge Companion to the Stoics*, ed. Brad Inwood (Cambridge: Cambridge University Press, 2003), 60 n1. Unless otherwise noted, translations of Greek and Latin are my own.

indiscernible beings demonstrate that Zeno's causal conception of apprehension is committed to the view that the individual beings generating impressions are inapprehensible for mortal animals partaking in reason. (Whether or not historiographers are further entitled to ascribe to Arcesilaus himself the view that Zeno's causal conception of apprehension is fatally committed to a metaphysical notion of inapprehensibility is not the relevant point.)

Impressionism is fundamental to Zeno's causal conception of apprehension. As David Lachterman observes, Zeno's canonical impressionism consists in the view that apprehending "is a transaction between bodies sufficiently apparent to make an impression and bodies" that are "apt to being excited by such an impression."[18] Individual bodies leave their impressions on the embodied souls of mortal animals partaking in reason in the guise of representations. Some of these representations purport to penetrate the so-called epistemological veil, thereby placing within the epistemic grasp of mortal animals with reason what in fact obtains. To preempt a potential misunderstanding of this reformulation of ἀκαταληψία, allow me to stipulate that the content of the metaphysical notion of inapprehensibility defended below is *not* equivalent to the claim that inapprehensibility is an *intrinsic* property of individual bodies. The content of the notion is, nevertheless, reducible to the claim that each and every individual body is *relatively disposed* to some other class of bodies in virtue of its transactional relation to some other class of being in Stoic ontology. By "relatively disposed," I mean to identify within this context the metaphysical status that individual beings have in virtue of their relation or lack of relation to some other being or beings.[19] For example, being a lover of Zeno the Stoic founder is the property of being relatively disposed to loving the individual Cypriot denominated "Zeno." The lover is thus relatively disposed in a certain way toward the individual Zeno. Hence, relative dispositions can be positive. In Stoic ontology, the relative disposition of inapprehensible bodies is negative because the property "being

---

[18] David Rapport Lachterman, *The Ethics of Geometry: A Genealogy of Modernity* (New York: Routledge, 1989), 99.

[19] For the distinction between the property of the having of a relation to some group and the property of the having of a relation to one thing, see George Edward Moore, *Some Main Problems of Philosophy*, repr. ed. (London: Routledge, 2013), 324: "But just as we may have a property which consists in the having of a relation to some one group or collection, so we may have properties which consist in the having of a relation to some one thing, which is *not* a group or collection." To clarify, this is not to say that Zeno (or any other Stoa before Chrysippus) had a clearly formulated notion of the metaphysical aspect of a given body as πρός τί πως ἔχον ("relatively disposed"). For discussion of πρός τί πως ἔχον, as well as the historical development of this notion in early Stoicism, see Stephen Menn, "The Stoic Theory of Categories," *Oxford Studies in Ancient Philosophy* 17 (1999): 227–36. See also LS 1, 165–6, for discussion of the so-called categories understood as the fourfold "classification of the metaphysical aspects under which a body can be viewed."

inapprehensible" holds for them in virtue of their lack of disposition relative to a certain class of individual beings. Indeed, this lack of disposition relative to certain classes of being is considered impure when it consists in not having a particular mode of disposition relative to one thing or being.[20] With regard to the individual in love with Zeno, being disposed as a lover in this way constitutes an impure, relative disposition, which is positive because it consists in having a disposition relative to an individual, namely, Zeno the Cypriot. By contrast, consider relative dispositions to be pure when the dispositions of individual beings themselves consist in the having of a relation to some class of beings. Within the structure of Zeno's ontology, the relevant class of beings in relation to which any given individual body is inapprehensible is the group of mortal animals partaking in the power of giving or withholding assent, a capacity assigned to this class of mortal animal. The negativity of inapprehensibility consists in two indissociable aspects: a negative metaphysical thesis concerning the way in which certain beings *themselves* are disposed in relation to mortal animals partaking in reason; and the restricted, epistemological thesis concerning the impossibility of infallible assent for mortal animals partaking in reason.[21] The notion of inapprehensibility inevitably entails the overlap of metaphysical and epistemological theses.

Given that Zeno's understanding of moral progress depends upon the causal conception of apprehension, the beings (or bodies) assigned the power of making apprehension possible are the same substantial beings invested with the power of making Stoic virtue (understood as an epistemic disposition to live in accordance with nature) possible. Imposing an alternative framework, the present study proceeds to show that Arcesilaus's anti-Stoic arguments venture beyond the question of epistemic possibility by posing higher-level questions regarding the ontological conditions presupposed by Zeno in his causal accounts of apprehension, knowledge, and virtue. Instead of associating the aim of Arcesilaus's critical opposition with a part, or subpart, of the early Stoic

---

[20] Expanding upon the distinction given by Moore, Edward J. Khamara, "Indiscernibles and the Absolute Theory of Space and Time," *Studia Leibnitiana*, Bd. 20, H. 2 (1988): 144–6, argues that pure properties include intrinsic (non-relational) properties and certain relational properties, that is, properties that individuals have in virtue of their relations or lack of relations not to some particular individual, but to one or another class of individual beings.

[21] The commentary of Long and Sedley (LS 1, 446), despite otherwise adhering to the framework of epistemology in reconstructing Arcesilaus's opposition as an attack on Zeno's "empiricist theory of knowledge" (see n1, *supra*), alludes to the metaphysical claim of ἀκαταληψία, as argued for in this study: "*I* [where *I* is the proposition that 'all things are incognitive'] is the proposition most distinctive of the whole New Academy." For similar allusions to the object or thing within the framework of epistemology, see Anna Maria Ioppolo, *La testimonianza di Sesto Empirico sull' Accademia scettica* (Naples: Bibliopolis, 2009), 35–6; Vezzoli, *Arcesilao*, 25.

tripartition (i.e., the epistemological), on the ensuing anti-humanistic account Arcesilaus's critical opposition to early Stoic philosophy reflects an attack on the coherence of the Stoic conception of the world as a structurally coherent whole. Now, to further clarify the revised meaning of ἀκαταληψία, consider briefly the view that Sextus associates with the followers of the Academic Philo of Larissa (c. 159/8–84/3 BCE). Sextus Empiricus writes, "The followers of Philo declare that as far as the Stoic criterion is concerned, that is, the apprehensive impression, things are inapprehensible (ἀκατάληπτα εἶναι τὰ πράγματα), but that as far as the nature of things themselves (τὰ πραγμάτων αὐτων) are concerned, they are apprehensible" (PH 1.235 (= LS 68T)).[22] Elsewhere, Sextus states that in conformity with the followers of Philo noted above, Arcesilaus had already argued that "all beings," according to the Stoic formulation of the criterion in the causal account of apprehension, "are inapprehensible" (M. 7.155 (< LS 41C, F 87 Vezzoli)). Arcesilaus's arguments refer, then, to the "beings" or "things" posited by Zeno's causal formulation of the criterion. However, unlike the followers of Philo, it remains unclear from this passage whether Arcesilaus issued any philosophical claim, or espoused any definite view, about the nature of beings themselves independent of his critical examination of early Stoic premises. To be sure, Cicero, for one, seems to have some insights into Arcesilaus's reasoning vis-à-vis the "obscurity of things themselves" (earum rerum obscuritate, Acad. 1.44). Nonetheless, one should proceed with caution here; for Cicero refrains from saying that Arcesilaus himself asserted a specific claim of his own, to the effect that things themselves are obscure; nor does he state that Arcesilaus himself compared the scope of his ignorance to that famously espoused by Socrates. As argued in the Concluding Analysis, Cicero is engaged here and elsewhere in the Academica in the task of defending Arcesilaus's polemic on the basis of his own selective understanding of the history of the ancient Academy and of Arcesilaus's seminal role in the rise of the so-called New Academy (Acad. 1.46). Cicero is

---

[22] See Numenius apud Eusebius, Praep. ev. 14.7.15 (= F 124 Vezzoli) for a similar distinction between things that are "unclear" and things that are "inapprehensible." In this passage, it is said that Carneades diverged from Arcesilaus on the universality of the suspension of assent. Harald Thorsrud, "Arcesilaus and Carneades," in The Cambridge Companion to Ancient Scepticism, ed. Richard Bett (Cambridge: Cambridge University Press, 2010), 72, construes the distinction in Eusebius in terms of epistemic possibility, taking the passage to refer to the "impressions" (of some agent) as "inapprehensible" or "unclear." However, the passage in Eusebius makes no explicit reference to impressions, or, for that matter, to impressions as inapprehensible. I take it that reference to impressions is implied by the explicit reference to things as inapprehensible, in consideration of the fact that for the Stoics an impression is a particular kind of thing. Cf. Praep. ev. 14.8.3–4 (< F 126 Vezzoli), for a rebuke of Arcesilaus "on account of the total destruction of things" (διὰ τῆς ἀπαξαπάντων ἀναιρέσεως χρημάτων).

careful to avoid ascribing the views uncovered through his reconstruction of Arcesilaus's reasoning to Arcesilaus himself.

The second upshot of this new historiographical framing is the specification of the metaphysical content of ἐποχὴ περὶ πάντων ("suspension [of assent] about all things"). Epistemological centrists suppress the metaphysical content of this notion by conceptualizing its content exclusively in terms of the epistemic access human subjects may or may not be able to secure, given the psychological faculties implied by the technical notion of assent in Zeno's theory of knowledge. With such conceptualization, proponents of epistemological centrism fail to specify, or acknowledge, that those subjective faculties already implicate certain metaphysical commitments. On the epistemological construal, the notion of inapprehensibility is held to be equivalent to the thesis that there are no apprehensive impressions. That is to say, no impression qualifies as apprehensive, a proposition from which scholars typically infer what seems (on their humanistic view) to be the core of inapprehensibility: that no human knowledge is possible.[23] Inapprehensibility is simplified into a humanistic thesis about impressions and the non-epistemic access associated with the faculty of apprehension in Stoic epistemology. Put differently, proponents of epistemological centrism tend to reduce the thesis of inapprehensibility to the negative epistemic thesis of non-apprehension. This reduction is a result of an unconscious effort to assign a measure of metaphysical neutrality to Arcesilaus's attack, as the hierarchical order and structure of Stoic reality are extirpated from the purview of critical focus. The arguments against Stoic philosophy are thus presented as metaphysically neutral insofar as they concern the possibility of epistemic access for a certain kind of being, namely, the human subject. The epistemic notion of non-apprehension is therefore conceptually austere given its limited analytical focus on the deficiency of the faculties of epistemic subjects, which in turn eliminates from specification the qualification of the beings that make apprehension possible. From this reduction of the content of inapprehensibility to non-apprehension, epistemological centrists can then try to claim that inapprehensibility entails that "nothing can be known." Armed with

---

[23] Brittain, "Arcesilaus," § 3; Schofield, "Academic Epistemology," 325–6, esp. n10; Luca Castagnoli, "Dialectic in the Hellenistic Academy," in *Dialectic after Plato and Aristotle*, ed. Thomas Bénatouïl and Katerina Ierodiakonou (Cambridge: Cambridge University Press, 2019), 192. Castagnoli equates the conclusion of ἀκαταληψία with the proposition "that no impression is cognitive (ἀκαταληψία, 'Inapprehensibility')"; Diego E. Machuca, "Scepticisme, *apraxia*, et rationalité," in *Les raisons du doute: études sur le scepticisme antique*, ed. Diego E. Machuca and Stéphane Marchand (Paris: Classiques Garnier, 2019), 53, identifies "l'ἀκαταληψία universelle" (= l'inappréhensibilité) with the simplified epistemic formulation of "l'affirmation de l'impossibilité de toute connaissance." The universality of inapprehensibility is meant here to qualify the impossibility of *all* human knowledge.

this claim, proponents of epistemological centrism are positioned to reduce—in correspondingly austere terms—the notion of "suspension [of assent] about all things" to a specification that is just as metaphysically neutral. For the latter also conceals the notion's metaphysical qualification of Stoic things *qua* individual bodies and incorporeals, about which suspension may be the appropriate response. Proponents of the epistemic formulation of inapprehensibility typically restrict the universality of suspension to assent or belief, such that the thesis is understood simplistically as the concern to suspend *all* acts of assent or *all* beliefs.[24] The problem with the thesis that associates the universality of suspension only with the faculty of assent or belief is that it once again eliminates from specification the relative disposition of those things grounding the possibility of giving or withholding assent in the causal conception of Stoic apprehension. In so doing, scholars revoke the metaphysical aspects associated with the universality of suspension. The Stoic conception of efficient beings *qua* bodies is left undetermined and the original Academic criticism of Stoic philosophy is thereby conceptually curtailed. On the basis of the epistemic notion of non-apprehension, proponents of epistemological centrism construe ἐποχὴ περὶ πάντων as the simplified, humanistic thesis that the alleged subject partaking in reason ought to totally suspend the psychic faculty of assent or belief. The explicit reference to "all things" is removed from the notion of the "suspension [of assent] about all things" in favor of the reductive epistemic specification of ἐποχή as the outright suspension of the faculty of assent. Again, the epistemic specification promotes metaphysical neutrality insofar as it suppresses the status of the Stoic conception of causally efficacious bodies in the humanistic formulations of non-apprehension and total suspension. According to the new framework, however, the content of suspension (of assent) about all things is specified not in terms of the thesis that the Stoic sage ought to suspend all assent, but rather in terms of the thesis that the Stoic sage ought to suspend assent about all the beings that contribute to generating (true and false) impressions. This includes, first and foremost, the identity of each and every individual body that presents itself. However, it further includes incorporeal individuals, which obtain by means of bodies in a causal network owing to the causal efficacy of bodies.

Epistemic notions of non-apprehension and total suspension continually attract scholars to the supposition that Arcesilaus inaugurated a kind of "epistemological skepticism." Accordingly, the notions of non-apprehension

---

[24] Robert W. Sharples, *Stoics, Epicureans and Sceptics: An Introduction to Hellenistic Philosophy* (London: Routledge, 1996), 27; Lloyd P. Gerson, *Ancient Epistemology* (Cambridge: Cambridge University Press, 2009), 117.

and universal suspension jointly coordinate the core components of Arcesilaus's skeptical orientation. The Greek term σκέψις means "investigation," and scholars often use the English term "skeptic" in the sense of an open-ended investigation in the course of characterizing what is distinctive about Arcesilaus's role as scholarch of the Academy (although they are aware that he did not employ this term to refer to himself or his distinct mode of philosophical investigation). When scholars refer to Arcesilaus as a skeptic, they almost always refer to him as a philosopher who continually submitted to investigation doctrines concerning the possibility of human knowledge, in the course of which he either denied or more modestly refused to affirm the positive doctrine of epistemic possibility under investigation.[25] One might suppose that without the relevant epistemological framework governing the reconstruction of Arcesilaus's dispute with Stoic philosophy—which is to say, a framework according to which it can be said that "*we* have sensory and non-sensory impressions to which *we* take attitudes of acceptance, rejection, or suspension" (italics added)[26]—Arcesilaus's critical orientation against the early Stoa would be incomprehensible. This study is designed to break the spell of this distorting supposition.

Proponents of epistemological centrism engage in the historiographical model of making *de dicto* specifications of ascribed commitments. Historiographical ascriptions of *de dicto* specification aim to specify the arguments and beliefs of an historical figure in a way that would be recognized and acknowledged as specifications of those arguments and beliefs by the one whose beliefs they are. For instance, in the context of Arcesilaus's dispute with Zeno, *de dicto* specifications aim to specify precisely what Arcesilaus took himself to be doing or not doing in formulating arguments against the epistemic possibility of Stoic knowledge. Moreover, proponents of epistemological centrism engage in the historiographical model of making *de re* specifications of ascribed commitments.[27] Historiographical ascriptions of *de re* specification are not restricted to the commitments or beliefs that the historiographer thinks that historical figures themselves would have recognized and acknowledged. Rather, *de re* interpretations aim to specify what a given historical figure or author is

---

[25] For this understanding of an epistemological skeptic, see Hankinson, *Sceptics*, 15. For a humanistic specification of this attitude as the attitude of "epistemological pessimism," see Charles Brittain, "Middle Platonists on Academic Scepticism," in *Greek and Roman Philosophy 100 BC–200AD*, 2 vols., ed. R. W. Sharples and Richard Sorabji (London: Institute of Classical Studies, 2007), 297.

[26] Katja Maria Vogt, "Hellenistic Academy," in *The Routledge Companion to Ancient Philosophy*, ed. James Warren and Frisbee Sheffield (New York: Routledge, 2014), 1157.

[27] Cf. the distinction between *de dicto* and *de re* models of historiographical interpretation in Robert Brandom, *Tales of the Mighty Dead: Historical Essays in the Metaphysics of Intentionality* (Cambridge, MA: Harvard University Press), 94–111.

really arguing for or against, independent of any considerations regarding what the historical figure believed, or would have acknowledged believing, about the content of those actions. Application of the term "skeptic" to Arcesilaus's philosophical orientation involves this model of *de re* interpretation.

The task of specifying Arcesilaus's skeptical orientation is conventionally entangled with the separate task of settling the question concerning whether Arcesilaus *qua* epistemological skeptic took himself to be committed to non-apprehension, total suspension, or some other view. Proponents of epistemological centrism remain divided on this question. One popular way of presenting Arcesilaus *qua* epistemological skeptic is to claim that he took his investigative method (and would have acknowledged his arguments) as entirely destructive and *ad hominem*. To this end, Arcesilaus—proceeding destructively against all philosophical claims to knowledge, not just the claims and beliefs defended by Zeno and his followers—refused to commit himself to any positive view about the epistemic possibility of knowledge. Epistemic notions of non-apprehension and total suspension are understood as the conclusions of his anti-Stoic arguments, which Arcesilaus deduced from Stoic premises and then attributed to Stoic epistemology without thereby committing himself to those conclusions. Indeed, because Arcesilaus is not personally invested in defending Stoic premises outside the context of oral argumentation *contra* Stoic epistemology, one might conclude that the notions of non-apprehension and total suspension represent conclusions that Arcesilaus himself attributed to Stoic epistemology, while refusing to affirm them as his own beliefs.

Another common presentation of Arcesilaus *qua* epistemological skeptic holds that the epistemic notion of total suspension represents Arcesilaus's "point of view," or "the state of mind in which the Academic [Arcesilaus] finds himself" from the continual opposition of two contradictory theses. Consequently, the universality of suspension is for Arcesilaus himself the unavoidable manifestation of *aporia* at an epistemological level, which is to say, he finds himself "incapable of asserting or denying that there is knowledge."[28] Arcesilaus strives to force the Stoics to accept his own "state of mind" (i.e., ἐπέχειν, "to suspend judgment") as the only available option for the Stoic sage, given the deduction of the epistemic notion of non-apprehension. The *de re* specification of Arcesilaus *qua* skeptic often reverts to *de dicto* interpretation with the contention that Arcesilaus took himself to be committed to suspending

---

[28] Anna Maria Ioppolo, "Arcesilaus," in *Skepticism: From Antiquity to the Present*, ed. Diego E. Machuca and Baron Reed (London: Bloomsbury, 2018), 42.

judgment or belief prior to his attack on Zeno's epistemology. The various proponents of epistemological centrism carry on this debate by proffering disparate *de re* specifications in the hope of eventually settling the question regarding whether Arcesilaus upheld as his own view the epistemic thesis of universal suspension, or whether the view is tendered as a *reductio ad absurdum* of Stoic epistemology. One influential proponent stipulates, in clear terms, the criteria of this ongoing entanglement of *de re* and *de dicto* interpretations: "We can infer that the Academics themselves were committed to those conclusions only if there is good reason to think that they accepted the Stoic epistemological framework their arguments depend on—the Stoic theories of thought, belief, perception, apprehension, rationality, etc.—or had other independent grounds for maintaining their conclusions."[29]

Instead of taking epistemological centrism as the frame of reference for the historiographical specification of theses or ascribed commitments, this study proceeds with an analysis of Arcesilaus's arguments against Zeno's causal conception of apprehension and the ontology presupposed by the causal conception.[30] This approach aims to specify what *really* follows from the arguments made against the claims and presuppositions of the causal conception. Similar to the reconstructions of epistemological centrism, this mode of reconstruction is interested in making correct *de re* specifications of what *really* follows from Arcesilaus's arguments against Zenonian impressionism.[31] However, specifications of the content of those arguments in the present study are made independent of determining what Arcesilaus himself really believed, or what he would have acknowledged about his philosophical beliefs and argumentative methods in response to questions of clarification and extension.

---

[29] Charles Brittain, "Introduction," in *Cicero: On Academic Scepticism*, trans. Charles Brittain (Indianapolis, IN: Hackett Publishing Company, 2006), xxiv.

[30] The premise of this study is that Arcesilaus argued against early Stoic philosophy. The argument constructed from this premise sets aside the controversy of determining whether Arcesilaus took himself to be arguing purely dialectically, that is, without commitment to the anti-Stoic arguments or conclusions, or whether he took himself to be arguing with some level of theoretical commitment to the negative arguments and conclusions more generally, as passages in Cicero (*Acad.* 1.45 (< LS 68A, F 45 Vezzoli), *De orat.* 3.67 (< F 35 Vezzoli)) and Numenius (*Praep. ev.* 14.8.1–10 (F 125, 126 Vezzoli)) are regularly taken to suggest. On the distinction between so-called strong and weak commitment, as well as a defense of Arcesilaus's weak assent, see Michael Frede, "The Sceptic's Two Kinds of Assent and the Question of the Possibility of Knowledge," in *The Original Sceptics*, ed. Myles Burnyeat and Michael Frede (Indianapolis, IN: Hackett Publishing Company, 1997), 127–51. Cf. Casey Perin, "Making Sense of Arcesilaus," *Oxford Studies in Ancient Philosophy* 45 (Winter 2013): 313–40.

[31] The model of *de re* interpretation may center on the "claims made" by an author, regardless of the author's opinion about the matter; the *de re* model of interpretation in the present study centers on the *arguments* made by Arcesilaus regardless of his beliefs about those arguments and about the views he provisionally accepts in making those arguments.

To reiterate, *de re* specification is, in this context, unrestricted to the beliefs and commitments that the historiographer posits as having been recognized and acknowledged by Arcesilaus.

Allow me to further clarify the approach taken herein. When the arguments of Arcesilaus provisionally concede the first and second conditions of Zeno's understanding of apprehensive impressions, such provisional acceptance concedes not only the Stoic claim that there are true and false impressions, as epistemological centrists routinely assume; such acceptance also grants the associated metaphysical claims of Zeno's canonical impressionism: for example, that impressions often derive from individual bodies obtaining in a real causal network of a particular space at a particular time.[32] The task of specifying what is *really* entailed by, or what *really* follows from, the attack on the metaphysical conditions of early Stoic impressionism is independent of any consideration regarding what Arcesilaus really believed about the content involved in provisional acceptance, or what he would have acknowledged about the strategic aims of his polemical method in response to various requests for clarification and elaboration.

To differentiate the methodology another way, the present study is not in the business of offering *de dicto* specifications of what Arcesilaus committed himself to, or would have acknowledged about his arguments and beliefs. Resembling a many-headed "hydra," Arcesilaus reportedly argued on both sides of a particular thesis, not distinguishing or acknowledging the arguments and beliefs representing his own view on the matter (Eusebius, *Praep ev.* 14.6.1–3 (< F 122 Vezzoli)). The present study aims to illuminate the range and scope of his anti-Stoic arguments and what the arguments *really* accomplish, independent of specifying his actual state of mind or what his acknowledged beliefs would have been to historiographical requests for clarification and elaboration. In the course of showing that his anti-Stoic arguments challenge the presupposed metaphysical conditions of Stoic apprehension—not just the epistemological aspects of Stoic teaching in relative isolation from the metaphysics of individual bodies, which undergirds early Stoic impressionism—it should become clear how his arguments confront Zeno's conception of individual beings generally,

---

[32] On provisional acceptance, see Harald Thorsrud, "Arcesilaus: Socratic Skepticism in Plato's Academy," *Lexicon Philosophicum: International Journal for the History of Texts and Ideas*, Special Issue (2018): 202 (esp. n16), and 204. According to this account of provisional acceptance, when one makes an argument against an opponent by provisionally accepting "some proposition," the inferences in the argument are guided by such acceptance, "regardless of whether" one also believes, and thus is "inclined to feel, that the proposition is true." One might "accept a proposition as a basis for further investigation without ever coming to believe or disbelieve it."

namely, individual bodies and the individual incorporeals. A fortiori, Arcesilaus challenged the very structure of reality on the Stoic account. Arguments from indiscernibility extend beyond a humanistic focus on the purportedly deficient non-epistemic faculties of human subjects. From the historiographical perspective of the ontology of apprehension/knowledge, the portrayal of Arcesilaus as an epistemological skeptic is at the very least incomplete. In view of his arguments against the ontological conditions of apprehension/knowledge, it makes better sense of the polemics to specify his mode of investigating as the kind of investigation that *really* shows how the philosophical commitments of early Stoicism themselves entail a species of ontological skepticism.[33] This species of skepticism essentially involves questioning the apprehensibility of causally efficacious bodies, and thereby the knowability of the world as a living being itself. That is, the arguments of Arcesilaus show that, when put to the test, the Stoic ontology of apprehension entails the absurd view that both the world and the bodies that present themselves therein are fundamentally obscure and inapprehensible. The orientation of Arcesilaus's mode of critical questioning is not primarily concerned with the question of whether agents have epistemic access to what lies beyond the veil, or with the question of whether agents have the capacity to acquire knowledge that this or that is thus-and-so. Arcesilaus's arguments, rather, contest the posited truth-making conditions that according to Zeno constrain a mortal animal's rational grasp of the world (itself being a living animal), conditions in virtue of which mortal animals partaking in reason make claims when arriving at some belief, whether this pertains to the world as a whole, or to an individual object therein.

Arcesilaus's accusation holding "nature" responsible for the general obscurity of things constitutes yet another reason for understanding his arguments from the perspective of an ontology of apprehension. In one response to the Stoic "inaction" (ἀπραξία) objection—as it is later articulated by Cicero's Lucullus (*Acad.* 2.31–2, cf. *Acad.* 2.39, *omnem actionem tollit e vita*)—Arcesilaus blames the agency of what Zeno conceptualized as "nature" for the obscurity of things. The humanistic interpretation of epistemological centrism diminishes the accusation against nature itself by specifying the target of the accusation as the nature of *our* rational faculties (sensation, impressions, assent, etc.). But as I argue: this is not an accurate specification of the passage in Cicero. From Cicero's Lucullus, readers learn that Arcesilaus offered a seemingly "hopeless"

---

[33] The distinction between epistemological and ontological skepticism is made by Hankinson, *Sceptics*, 12–16. Cf. Mauro Bonazzi, "Plutarch on Pyrrhonists and Academics," *Oxford Studies in Ancient Philosophy* 43 (Winter 2012): 291.

response to the inaction objection. Arcesilaus's response provisionally accepts the deduction of ἀπραξία as a Stoic conclusion, hence as a problem for the Stoa that follows from the absurdity of Zeno's impressionism. The response turns the objection against Zeno by provisionally accepting the agency of Stoic *natura* ("nature") only to immediately accuse nature of actively concealing the truth of things, rendering it impossible for mortal animals partaking in reason to act virtuously. Arcesilaus's accusation against nature is representative of his critical use of Zeno's Stoic premises, but this time to undermine the coherence of his ethical outlook. This is the third result of the historiographical shift from epistemological centrism to the anti-humanistic framework of the ontology of knowledge. Given that Zeno's theory of virtuous action presupposes that nature makes real individual bodies apprehensible in relation to mortal animals partaking in the rational power of assent, arguments undermining nature and the metaphysical conception of individual bodies ought to be understood as arguments that fatally undermine Zeno's idealization of virtue. The metaphysical specifications of ἀκαταληψία and ἐποχὴ περὶ πάντων entail the impossibility of acting in pursuit of Stoic virtue.

At this point, allow me to step back and articulate a structural overview of the arguments presented thus far. The first stage of the reconstruction (Chapter 1, "The Structure of Early Stoic Metaphysics") explicates the general structure of early Stoic metaphysics. This stage is propaedeutic to the application of the framework of the ontology of Stoic apprehension at the next stage of analysis. The second stage (Chapter 2, "The Ontology of Stoic Apprehension") commences with a preliminary discussion of the historical emergence of modern epistemology to prepare for the central task of the book: reconstructing Arcesilaus's indiscernibility arguments within the framework of the ontology of knowledge. For scholars today, indiscernibility arguments represent Arcesilaus's concerted effort to refute the epistemic possibility of Stoic apprehension. However, I argue that by introducing counterfactual conditions into the polemic, indiscernibility arguments mount a broader attack against the metaphysical conditions of Stoic apprehension. Indiscernibility arguments introduce counterfactual conditions that challenge not only the epistemic possibility of apprehensive impressions, but also the metaphysical possibility of the identity of individual bodies. Zeno's conception of apprehension is informed by supplementary convictions about individual beings and the totality of individual beings, totalizing views about what there is, what there could be, or what there could have been. These supplementary views control all attempts at justifying Stoic apprehension. The attack on Zenonian impressionism, and its conception of apprehension, undermines the ground of *epistemic access to what there is* for mortal animals partaking in reason, and calls into question the knowability of *what there is*.³⁴

The central argument of this stage of the reconstruction identifies the weakness of the Stoic response to arguments from indiscernibility. The weakness involves an unwarranted supposition of absolute difference. Absolute difference is, in this context, the supposition that each and every body is unique and individually distinct from every other body (or incorporeal). The metaphysical supposition of the unique identity of individual bodies assigns each and every body the causal power of effectively motivating the response of κατάληψις. Relevant to this conception of individual bodies, Theodor W. Adorno specifies the content of absolute difference, stating: "the thought of identity always already presupposes total comprehensibility and familiarity."³⁵ The problem with "identity thinking," on Adorno's account, is not merely that it presupposes the comprehensibility and familiarity of a given object or body, but that it further assumes the comprehensibility and familiarity of an "absolute conception" of reality. Zeno presupposes an "absolute conception" of reality, according to which the world itself is a unified totality that is there *anyway*, namely, independent of the representations and actions of mortal beings partaking in reason. Zeno's conviction that a true account of the structural totality of the real is possible rests upon the most basic assumption of metaphysical realism: that the world as a unified whole is itself knowable, which entails for Zeno and his canonical followers that the constituent individual bodies according to which the Stoic world is structured are apprehensible. On the Stoic variety of metaphysical realism, the world is a unified whole or totality structurally comprised of real individual bodies that are causally efficacious and apprehensible. In view of this "absolute conception" of the world, all representations are then to be analyzed for their success or failure.³⁶ In other words, the metaphysical principle of the

---

[34] Nicholas P. White observes the overlap between metaphysics and epistemology in Plato's dialogues, addressing "Plato's disinclination to separate epistemological and metaphysical issues in the modern way," which takes the humanistic role of perspective in the faculty of judgment to be of paramount importance. White continues: "From an epistemological point of view the role of perspective in a judgment can seem paramount, whereas the role of the *circumstances of the object* seems like a different kind of consideration, involving the nature of the property that one is ascribing" (italics added). White, "Plato's Metaphysical Epistemology," 291–2.

[35] "Mit Axiomen wie dem von Vollständigkeit und Lückenlosigkeit setzt Identitätsdenken eigentlich immer schon totale Überschaubarkeit, Bekanntheit voraus." Theodor W. Adorno, *Zur Metakritik der Erkenntnistheorie. Studien über Husserl und die phänomenologischen Antinomien* (Frankfurt am Main: Suhrkamp, 1971), 40. For a slightly different English translation of this passage, see Theodor W. Adorno *Against Epistemology: A Metacritique*, trans. Willis Domingo (Cambridge, MA: Polity Press, 2013), 32.

[36] For discussion of the "absolute conception" of reality, see Bernard Williams, *Descartes: The Project of Pure Enquiry* (London: Routledge, 2005), 49–52, 196–7, 230–2. See Chapter 1 for analysis of Zeno's metaphysical realism.

identity of indiscernible bodies has in view the comprehensibility of each and every possible body in space and time, as well as the difference between bodies and individual incorporeals, which depend metaphysically upon bodies for their discrete manifestations within a causal network.

The argument of Chapter 2 demonstrates that a methodological distinction between *our epistemic access to what there is* and *what there is* controls the framework of epistemology. Philosophers specializing in the field of epistemology address a host of problems centered on *our epistemic access to what there is*. In accordance with this methodological distinction, as well as the primacy assigned to the humanistic question of *our* epistemic access, historiographers prioritize the question of *our* epistemic access in the reconstruction of Hellenistic philosophy and isolate Stoic epistemology from its metaphysical conditions of possibility. In other words, proponents of epistemological centrism in the reconstruction of Arcesilaus's dispute with Zenonian philosophy persistently thematize problems associated with *our* epistemic access and obscure the conceptualization of the structure of what there is, which as a whole conditions epistemic access for mortal animals partaking in reason. As a result, historiographers continually reproduce simplified epistemological specifications of ἀκαταληψία and ἐποχὴ περὶ πάντων. This chapter rejects two of the most common epistemological specifications of ἀκαταληψία, relying mainly on the ancient evidence to confirm the metaphysical dimensions of ἀκαταληψία and ἐποχὴ περὶ πάντων.

The regular effacement of early Stoic physics from the reconstruction of Academic polemics with Stoic impressionism is part of a historiographical effort to reduce the historical distance of past figures and schools from current epistemological concerns. Carrying out such effacement, epistemological centrists reproduce doxographical accounts of Stoic and Academic epistemology. Rather than attend to the strangeness of the Hellenistic past, which may help philosophers question the concerns and assumptions dominating philosophical research today, current doxographies tend to reinforce the timely pretensions of present epistemological assumptions.[37] As Michael Frede and Richard Rorty argue, the doxography of past philosophy imposes a conceptual framework on the past without undertaking the additional task of defending the assumed framework. Modern doxographies are not only selective in that they focus on well-known philosophers, or philosophical schools, from the past; in addition, they precipitately presume the legitimacy of using certain conceptual resources

---

[37] Bernard Williams, "Descartes and the Historiography of Philosophy," in *The Senses of the Past: Essays in the History of Philosophy*, edited with an introduction by Myles Burnyeat (Princeton, NJ: Princeton University Press, 2006), 259, 263–4.

from modern or contemporary philosophical discussion in the specification of the views and arguments of philosophers bygone.³⁸ When the framework of epistemology is taken to be the autoexplicable starting point of the historiography of Hellenistic philosophy, historiographers abandon the important task of illuminating the peculiar strangeness of the early Hellenistic period. An autoexplicable starting point is, on my definition, what is taken to be self-evident such that it demands neither justification nor explication on the part of the historiographer as the relevant philosophical framework for the study of ancient Greek and Roman philosophy. Moreover, modern doxographies obscure the indisputable fact that the concept of "epistemology" and its corresponding professional domain of inquiry have histories of their own. The focus on epistemic possibility in the historiography of early Hellenistic philosophy tends to manufacture what Rorty refers to as a "cream-skimming picture" of the past. By focusing the analysis almost entirely on the humanistic question of epistemic access, epistemological centrism is poised to skim the cream off the substance of Arcesilaus's attack on early Stoic philosophy.³⁹

The third stage of the reconstruction (Chapter 3, "Total Inaction and the Impossibility of Stoic Ethics") examines Arcesilaus's response to the Stoic inaction objection, and the implications of this response for Stoic physics. The analysis begins with the ancient report that Arcesilaus deracinated the Stoic notion of appropriate action. Because Zeno's theory of virtue presupposes that real individual bodies are apprehensible in relation to mortal animals partaking in reason, arguments undermining the metaphysical conception of individual bodies and the psychological power of giving assent are interpreted here as arguments that undermine Zeno's account of appropriate action. Zeno defends a notion of appropriate actions (τὰ καθήκοντα) in which the sage's perfect appropriate actions and the imperfect appropriate actions of mortal animals generally represent smaller aspects of a grand and more comprehensive rational order. For human animals, appropriate action is supposed to involve the sort of action that is responsive to rational considerations. In the particular case of non-virtuous, imperfectly rational animals, appropriate actions are nonetheless extensionally equivalent to the actions of a perfectly virtuous mortal animal. The difference in ranked value between perfect and morally inferior actions consists

---

[38] Michael Frede, "Doxographie, historiographie philosophique et historiographie historique de la philosophie," *Revue de Métaphysique et de Morale* 97, no. 3 (1992): 324. Richard Rorty, "The Historiography of Philosophy: Four Genres," in *Philosophy in History: Essays on the Historiography of Philosophy*, ed. Richard Rorty, J. B. Schneewind, and Quentin Skinner (Cambridge: Cambridge University Press, 1984), 62–3.

[39] Rorty, "Historiography of Philosophy," 66.

in the varying dispositions from which human beings regularly act. For the virtuous, a particular course of action is both virtuous and appropriate owing to its being performed on the basis of a true and unwavering system of assents vis-à-vis the world, or some part of it. Appropriate action begets a harmony between the mortal animal partaking in reason and the absolute conception of the world *qua* rational, finite totality. Therefore, it can be said that Zeno and the early Stoics idealize a so-called Grand End account of appropriate action. The "Grand End" account of appropriate action maintains that the rationality of mortal animals in their perfect or imperfect actions is the kind of rationality that is responsive by means of apprehension to a rationally organized world. Appropriate action is supposed to lead to, and even sustain, the dispositional knowledge of living in perfect conformity with the normative properties exhibited rationally by the world itself.

Now, reconsider the polemics of Arcesilaus. Arguments in support of the thesis of inapprehensibility subvert Zeno's Grand End account of action and the possibility of such harmony. In lieu of any such Grand End, Arcesilaus invokes a non-metaphysical, or minimalist, notion of right action. The concluding chapters of this study re-examine the anti-Stoic arguments in the light of his polemical introduction of a revised, minimalist notion of right action.[40] The thread uniting the fourth stage (Chapter 4, "The Old Academy's Traditional Hierarchy of Goods") of this study with the Concluding Analysis is a sustained argument against the Epistemological Novelty Thesis: the historiographical claim advanced by proponents of epistemological centrism that the Academy's change, or skeptical turn, under Arcesilaus is primarily epistemological. The argument against the Epistemological Novelty Thesis is the fourth and final consequence of this new historiographical framing. The premise of the Epistemological Novelty Thesis associates Arcesilaus's Socratic revival of oral contentiousness first and foremost with his attack on the knowledge-claims of his Stoic contemporaries. Scholars infer from this premise that Arcesilaus brings about a pessimistic "change of outlook" in epistemology. The Epistemological Novelty Thesis restricts the historiographical investigation of the Academy prior to Arcesilaus, that is, the so-called Old Academy, to the centrality of epistemology. Epistemological centrism expunges from its historiographical reconstructions the ethical views of the Academy prior to Arcesilaus, thereby neglecting to identify the metaphysical

---

[40] On *minimal* eudaimonism, see Chapter 3. I adapt Brad Inwood's use of the term *minimal* in his account of what later came to be known as the unorthodox kind of Stoicism associated with Zeno's pupil, Ariston of Chios (*fl.* 260 BCE). Brad Inwood, *Stoicism: A Very Short Introduction* (Oxford: Oxford University Press, 2018), 14–15.

principles upholding the tradition of Academic ethics, from Speusippus's eudaimonism to the variety of eudaimonism upheld by Arcesilaus's predecessor, Polemo of Athens. Arcesilaus's disaffiliation with the tradition of Academic ethics accordingly disappears from historiographical reconstruction.

There is a considerable body of transmitted evidence summarizing the doctrines of the early Academic successors of Plato, most notably Speusippus and Xenocrates. The evidence testifies to an unwavering Academic commitment to metaphysical realism. According to Speusippus and Xenocrates, the world itself has a systematic unity with principles and constituent parts, and the inherent structure of this unity supposedly enables a systematic explanation of the constituent parts and principles of the whole, including the order and rank of ethical goods. Academic varieties of metaphysical realism originally affirmed by Speusippus and Xenocrates entail a particular sort of disciplinary holism. Contrary to the sort of holism later formulated by Zeno, sensible and composite beings depend on the intelligibility of noncorporeal beings (mathematicals, ideal numbers and figures, or forms) and the unqualified simplicity of some first principle ("the One" or the "Monad"), even when the first principle is held to be beyond οὐσία or goodness. Disciplinary holism is based on the general assumption that the arrangement and structure of this whole can be systematically studied and understood, but what makes Academic holism distinct from the Stoic sort is the appeal to the metaphysical priority of the intelligible over the sensible. Although it remains unclear to what extent Polemo embraced the explanatory project of disciplinary holism, it is nevertheless clear from his idea of happiness that he preserved the metaphysical priority of the noncorporeal in his account of virtue. By adhering to a standard Academic/ Peripatetic hierarchy of ethical goods, Polemo and the Socratic legacy of his ethical approach continued to uphold the Academic tradition of arranging the goods of the world into three categories, ranking psychic goods superior to both external and bodily goods. As argued in Chapter 4, Polemo's Academic conception of ethical eudaimonism is informed by the metaphysical priority of the noncorporeal. Among other ideas, such metaphysical priority guides his cursory dismissal of Zenonian ethics. The otherwise disparate eudaimonist views of the so-called Old Academy, from Speusippus and Xenocrates to the early Hellenistic Academy of Polemo, are premised on the metaphysical priority of the noncorporeal, which in turn governs the hierarchical classification of goods traditionally upheld by Plato's successors.

Against the backdrop of this Academic tradition, Arcesilaus's destruction of Stoic metaphysics and the counterproposal of a revised notion of appropriate action should appear rather innovative. Expanding upon his arguments for the metaphysical theses of ἀκαταληψία, ἐποχὴ περὶ πάντων, and the consequent impossibility of Stoic virtue, Arcesilaus introduces a metaphysically deflated notion of appropriate action. This deflated sense of appropriate action departs from the core explanatory principle governing the Academic tradition of identifying and ranking a plurality of goods.[41] Simply put, with the revised version of appropriate action sketched by Arcesilaus, the fundamental assumptions of disciplinary holism and the explanatory principles of metaphysical realism governing Academic and Stoic ethics are no longer fundamental. Arcesilaus's arguments overturn Zeno's view that a structural understanding of the world is possible for mortal animals partaking in reason, while the introduction of a revised notion of appropriate action lays the theoretical groundwork for an account of virtuous action that defies the standard metaphysical principles of Academic ethics. Against the Epistemological Novelty Thesis, the concluding argument of this study specifies the novelty of his Socratic revival against the backdrop of the Academy's metaphysical hierarchy of goods. Independent of considering what Arcesilaus took himself to be doing with the introduction of this revised notion, or with the arguments against the causal conception of Zeno's apprehension more generally, the outline of a revised notion of appropriate action represents Arcesilaus's departure from an Academic tradition of identifying and metaphysically ranking, according to a systematic understanding of the world as a whole, a hierarchy of goods as they really are.

The main title of this study is denominated *Beyond Hellenistic Epistemology* for three reasons. In Chapters 1 and 2, I defend the view that Zeno's causal theory of apprehension entails certain metaphysical beliefs about what there is as a whole and what grounds what. This view regarding the relation between the structure of early Stoic metaphysics and the causal theory of apprehension is used to criticize the humanistic "cream-skimming" pictures created by the widespread application of the historiographical framework of Hellenistic epistemology. The titular construction, then, is an allusion to this form of metaphysical entailment as it applies to the content of the arguments both for and against Zeno's causal conception of apprehension. In another sense, and less controversially, "beyond"

---

[41] At some point, in the course of considering the validity of the argument against the Epistemological Novelty Thesis, readers will surely wonder about Plato. For the limited purposes of this study, I assume that Plato, founder and head of the Academy, presented views and philosophical positions in a literary form that is well suited to concealing the content of his commitments, and so this study explores what happens when historiography marginalizes the difficult task of specifying the content of his so-called doctrines, as they appear in both literary form and in the later testimonies regarding his so-called unwritten teachings, while prioritizing Arcesilaus's relation to the Old Academy and the revival of Socratic education in the Academy under Polemo.

might be taken to refer to the inextricable connection between Stoic ethics and the causal conception of apprehension. In other words, as the ontology of Stoic apprehension comes under attack, so does Zeno's ethical theory. Chapter 3 advances the argument that, if the ontology of Stoic apprehension is incoherent (as indiscernibility arguments purport to demonstrate), then the Stoic conception of virtue is unrealizable. Finally, entitling the book thus constitutes the kind of call to attention that is needed to broaden the focus of the current historical frame. To this end, the pre-Hellenistic and early Hellenistic phases of the Academy are included, so that a proper philosophical contextualization of the continuity and break in the early Hellenistic Academy's philosophical orientation from Polemo to Arcesilaus can be assessed. Chapter 4 and the Concluding Analysis are designed to inspire historiographers of Hellenistic philosophy to consider more holistically the philosophy of the Academy prior to Arcesilaus when seeking to specify the Academy's change of direction in the early Hellenistic period.

1

The Structure of Early Stoic Metaphysics

In the early third century BCE, the Academic Arcesilaus opposed a complex metaphysical worldview, which the Stoic founder formulated to describe the fundamental relations of reality as a whole. Early canonical followers of Zeno (334–263/2 BCE) understood "the all" (τὸ πᾶν) as an aggregate of the four elementary concentric spheres (earth, water, air, fire or aether), which make up the finite "totality" or "the world" (τὸ ὅλον = τὸ κόσμος) and the infinite void surrounding the world.[1] As a finite totality, the world is an object of investigation and moral emulation. One early Stoic conception of the rationality of the sage not only entails that there is such a world but also that such rationality consists of a general body of knowledge, in virtue of which the world itself as a unified structural totality is known as natural, supremely rational, and the best of all that Zeus has created (Cicero, *De nat. deor.* 2.21, Sextus, *M.* 9.104 (= *SVF* 1.111)). Although the sage disposes of a body of knowledge in virtue of which she has a general understanding of the overall structure of the world, it is important to emphasize that the sage's knowledge of the world does not mean that she knows or is required to know all the facts relevant to a particular situation or experience. As will be shown, the rationality of the Stoic sage is consistent with the "partial ignorance" of suspending assent in certain circumstances, and the "partial ignorance" of not always knowing the consequences of her decisions in particular situations.[2] Venturing beyond the fashionable humanistic framing of

---

[1] Sextus, *M.* 9.332 (= LS 44A), Plutarch, *Comm. not.* 1074b–c, Stobaeus, *Ecl.* 1.19 (= *SVF* 1.99). For discussion of this view of totality as one of the widely accepted principles of Stoic ontology and physics, see Keimpe Algra, "The Early Stoics on the Immobility and Coherence of the Cosmos," *Phronesis* 33, no. 2 (1988): 158. For a detailed reading of Stobaeus, *Ecl.* 1.19 in relation to Zeno in particular, see Serge Mouraviev, "Zeno's Cosmology and the Presumption of Innocence: Interpretations and Vindications," *Phronesis* 50, no. 3 (2005): 236–40.

[2] Michael Frede, "Introduction," in *Rationality in Greek Thought*, ed. Michael Frede and Gisela Striker (Oxford: Clarendon Press, 1996), 16–17, reconstructs the reasoning behind the Stoic rejection of omniscience. For defense of this reasoning alongside an examination of the ancient evidence, see René Brouwer, *The Stoic Sage: The Early Stoics on Wisdom, Sagehood and Socrates* (Cambridge: Cambridge University Press, 2014), 33–4.

Stoic epistemology, it should become increasingly evident that the arguments of Arcesilaus impair the supreme rationality of the world as it is conceived by Zeno and his canonical followers. One task of this chapter is to retrieve an image of the early stages of this Hellenistic dispute that is concealed by the conformism of current doxographical trends in the study of Hellenistic epistemology.

Disciplinary Holism

As a young adult, Zeno immigrated from the Cypriot city of Citium to Athens, pursuing forthwith a life of philosophy. Studying initially under the tutelage of Crates the Cynic, Zeno was inspired to repudiate conventional social norms in the pursuit of an alternative conception of the good life. But soon after Zeno moves on to study with Polemo of Athens, head of the Platonic Academy, and at some point with the Megaric philosopher Stilpo. In studies with Academic associates in particular, Zeno may have found a more congenial institutional setting for the development of his own distinct views on the world as a whole and on philosophical knowledge as a complex system.[3] Eventually, he would supplement his vision of the world with a formulation of the ethical *telos*: τὸ ὁμολογουμένως τῇ φύσει ζῆν ("living in accordance with nature," D.L. 7.87, cf. Cicero, *De fin*. 4.14), or his shortened formula τὸ ὁμολογουμένως ζῆν ("living in consistency," Stobaeus, *Ecl*. 2.75.12), both resembling ethical doctrines concerning the *telos* promoted by the Academics Polemo and Xenocrates (*De fin*. 4.3, 14–18, 61, Clement of Alexandria, *Strom*. 2.22). In fact, more than one ancient source ascribes the same *telos* to Aristotle (*De fin*. 4.15) and Theophrastus (*De fin*. 4.3, Plutarch, *Comm. not*. 1069e–f). Zeno however develops his own ideal of "living in consistency" while preserving the Cynic ideal of virtue's self-sufficiency (*De fin*. 5.79), integrating both tenets with his own fundamentally (but not strictly) empiricist thesis, according to which apprehensive impressions supply the criterion of truth. His renunciation of conventional bodily goods

---

[3] Cicero (*De fin*. 4.3) and Sextus (*M*. 7.16–19) ascribe a tripartite division of philosophy to Aristotle and the Peripatetics. Aristotle (*Top*. 1.14, 105b19–25) presents a similar division, but his division applies to "propositions" in general, not philosophy per se or a λόγος that belongs to philosophy because it belongs to the structure of the world. Cicero, in what is a controversial transmission of the historical views of the division espoused by Antiochus of Ascalon (*De fin*. 4.3–6, cf. *Acad*. 1.19), provides the only text ascribing this division to Xenocrates, Speusippus, Polemo, Aristotle, and Theophrastus. For Antiochus's idiosyncratic adoption of the tripartite division, see Malcolm Schofield, "Antiochus on Social Virtue," in *The Philosophy of Antiochus*, ed. David Sedley (Cambridge: Cambridge University Press, 2012), 173–6.

(such as health or physical strength) as genuine goods suggests that he sided with Stilpo's ethical doctrine that whatever bodily illness or weakness a body incurs, or whatever other external advantages (wealth or poverty) human beings happen to acquire or lose, conditions of physical health, strength, and other external advantages ought to be excluded from the category of the good (and bad). And from his training with the dialectician Diodorus Cronus, it seems that Zeno started to refine his own distinct set of views in the disciplines of logic and dialectic, further enabling the clarification of his own pioneering vision of philosophical λόγος as a comprehensive elaboration of wisdom.

Zeno's own foundational work in philosophy spans three main parts, corresponding to his tripartite division (τριμερῆ) of philosophical discourse into logic, physics, and ethics (D.L. 7.39–41 (= LS 26B), Cicero, De fin. 4.4–5, Aëtius 1 proem. 2 (= SVF 2.35), Sextus, PH 2.13).[4] It is said by more than one source that Xenocrates first articulated this tripartite division of philosophy (Cicero, Acad. 1.19, Sextus, M. 7.16). The ascription is difficult to verify. More confidently, it can be said that in the division of philosophical discourse developed by Zeno and elaborated by his canonical followers, for the first time it is conceived that "no part of philosophy is preferred over any another" (οὐθὲν μέρος τοῦ ἑτέρου προκεκρίσθαι), as all three of its parts are conceived as "blended" (μεμίχθαι, D.L. 7.40).[5] With this conception of the parts of philosophical discourse, one might suppose that Zeno's followers believed that his original conception of the tripartitioning entails that the parts are not only "blended" but "inseparable"— depending inter al. on how each follower would conceive of the organic coherence of the blending, whether it is conceived as similar to the unity of a living animal, an egg, a garden, or a beautiful city (D.L. 7.40).[6] Regardless of whether it was Zeno or his canonical followers who first expressed such blending, the unity of these parts involves commitment to a type of disciplinary holism that radically revises the hierarchical classifications of disciplinary holism promoted by

---

[4] D.L. 7.41 gives more than one Stoic division of logic. Zeno originally divided logic into rhetoric and dialectic (Cicero, De fin. 2.17, Sextus, M. 2.7 (= SVF 1.75)), whereas other followers (possibly Chrysippus) added a subpart on definitions and another on canons and criteria. In what is perhaps another Stoic division of logic (D.L. 7.43), the subpart dialectic is further partitioned into two smaller fields or topics: significations and utterance. "Impressions" are classified under significations.

[5] Following the emendation of προκεκρίσθαι as it appears in Tiziano Dorandi, Diogenes Laertius: Lives of Eminent Philosophers (Cambridge: Cambridge University Press, 2013), 500. The standard translation of D.L. 7.40 (e.g., Jaap Mansfeld, "Zeno and the Unity of Philosophy," Phronesis 48, no. 2 (2003): 120–1) is misleading for following Cobet's editorial conjecture of ἀποκεκρίσθαι.

[6] A different account of this passage worth considering is given by Ian G. Kidd, "Posidonius and Logic," in Les stoïciens et leur logique, ed. Jacques Brunschwig (Paris: J. Vrin, 2006), 30.

philosophers in the schools of Plato and Aristotle.[7] By disciplinary holism, I mean the general view that no area of philosophical study can be fully comprehended apart from a systematic understanding of the ontology of beings as a whole. In ancient philosophy, and in one form or another, disciplinary holism presupposes a commitment to some variety of metaphysical realism. Metaphysical realism involves the generic assumption that judgments are true and false in virtue of a real "objective world" existing independently of the activities of any knowing, acting beings. For both the Academics and Zeno, the fundamental assumption of metaphysical realism is that reality, or the world, has a complex unity, and that a systematic understanding of the world as a unified whole is possible. The immediate successors of Plato in the Academy—Speusippus and Xenocrates—maintain a variety of metaphysical realism with the idea that judgments are true and false in virtue of the way the world is structured independent of the activities of any individual human souls. Both Academic and early Stoic orthodoxy affirmed different varieties of the dogma that the real objective world is a unity in the sense that its constituent parts are really related and relatively disposed to being known by the epistemic powers of human being. Thus doctrines specific to the area of ethics or epistemology are inextricably connected with doctrines specific to other partitioned areas because the principles (whether corporeal or noncorporeal) enabling the formulation of doctrine in one area are related to principles enabling the formulation of doctrine in another.[8] Chapter 4 explores the function of disciplinary holism in relation to the Academy's traditional hierarchy of goods and Arcesilaus's appeal to a non-metaphysical notion of right action. In the case of Zeno and his early followers, the disciplinary holism associated with their metaphysical system holds that one and the same *Logos* is responsible for producing the world and the epistemic faculties of mortal animals partaking in reason, which are expressed in speech and exercised in action. In the succinct formulation of Pierre Hadot: "La physique a donc pour objet le Logos de la nature universelle, l'éthique le Logos de la nature raisonnable humaine, la logique ce même Logos s'exprimant dans le discours humain. D'un bout à l'autre, c'est donc la même réalité qui est à la fois Nature créatrice, Norme de la conduite et Règle du discours" ("The subject of physics is therefore the *Logos* of universal nature, the subject of ethics the *Logos* of rational human

---

[7] Pierre Hadot, "Les divisions des parties de la philosophie dans l'Antiquité," *Museum Helveticum* 36 (1979): 208–12. Cf. Max Pohlenz, *Die Stoa: Geschichte einer geistigen Bewegung* (Göttingen: Vandenhoeck & Ruprecht, 1959), 34–6; Émile Bréhier, *Histoire de la philosophie*, vol. 1 pt. 2 (Paris: Presses Universitaires de France, 1961), 208; *The History of Philosophy: The Hellenistic & Roman Age*, trans. Wade Baskin (Chicago: The University of Chicago Press, 1965), 36–8.
[8] Cf. Lloyd P. Gerson, "What Is Platonism?," *Journal of the History of Philosophy* 43, no. 3 (2005): 260.

nature, and the subject of logic that same *Logos* expressed in human speech. From one end to the other, it is one and the same reality which is at the same time creative nature, norm of action and ruler of discourse or argument"). *Logos* is, therefore, the active (corporeal) principle of reality, what Zeno in his treatise *On Substance* (Περὶ οὐσίας, D.L. 7.134) identified as an everlasting "god," the artificer of each and every individual body throughout all matter.

The study of impressions is originally situated within the disciplinary study of logic, more specifically within the subpart dialectic (D.L. 7.43). The logical subpart of rhetoric, by contrast, is "the science of speaking well with respect to rational discourse in narrative form" (D.L. 7.42); the compactness and brevity of the apprehensive impression, illustrated by Zeno in the clenching grip of a fist, correspond to the "compactness and brevity" of dialectic (Sextus, *M.* 2.7 (= *SVF* 1.75)). The discipline of logic is thus bifurcated into dialectic and rhetoric. In the process of clarifying the tripartition, from Zeno's early formulations to Chrysippus's explications a generation later, logic remained the partitioned area of study designed to yield the criteria or standards of justification that non-virtuous mortal animals partaking in reason must learn in order to advance from the ordinary performance of imperfect appropriate action to the perfect right actions of the idealized sage. Expert proficiency in the subject matter of Zenonian logic entails proficiency in the science of dialectic.

Stoic dialectic is, therefore, integral to the cultivation of a virtuous disposition. The following epitome of Stoic dialectic is commonly considered Zeno's early formulation: "the science of conversing correctly with respect to rational discourse in question and answer form" (περὶ τὸν ἐν ἐρωτήσει καὶ ἀποκρίσει λόγον, D.L. 7.42).[9] Although early formulation of this science already demands, in principle, the ability to distinguish what is true from what is false, Zeno's successors embark on a more ambitious explication of "rational discourse." A more comprehensive formulation of Stoic dialectic reflects this ambition: "the science of things true and false and neither true nor false."[10] The sage's mastery of dialectic extends over a range of content built in to Zeno's early formulation,

---

[9] τὴν [ἐπιστήμην] διαλεκτικὴν τοῦ ὀρθῶς διαλέγεσθαι περὶ τὸν ἐν ἐρωτήσει καὶ ἀποκρίσει λόγον. The text of the passages of Diogenes Laertius is taken from the edition of Tiziano Dorandi, *Diogenes Laertius: Lives of Eminent Philosophers* (Cambridge: Cambridge University Press, 2013). Dorandi (*Diogenes Laertius*, 501) adopts the correction *supra lineam* 49 in manuscript B², reading τὸν [. . .] λόγον instead of τῶν [. . .] λόγων. The accusative singular τὸν λόγον ("rational discourse") underscores the systematically unified nature of the subject matter (λόγος) under examination in question and answer form.
[10] D.L. 7.42: ὅθεν καὶ οὕτως αὐτὴν ὁρίζονται, ἐπιστήμην ἀληθῶν καὶ ψευδῶν καὶ οὐδετέρων. Cf. Anthony A. Long, "Dialectic and the Stoic Sage," in *Stoic Studies* (Berkeley: University of California Press, 1996), 85–9.

principally, the representational content of impressions (i.e., the purported realities signified by rational discourse), which includes the subjects and predicates forming the representational content of propositions, and inferences, the valid use of which depends on the representational content of apprehensive impressions—what Victor Brochard aptly designates "the vital node" ("le nœud vital") of Stoicism.[11] The ethical significance of Zeno's formulation of dialectic undergoes greater elaboration as well. The virtues later assigned to this subpart of logic are tacitly implied in the view that dialectic is peculiar to the sage (D.L. 7.83, Alexander, *In Top.* 1.8–14), the ideal of perfect rationality and complete virtue. As scholars are prone to recognize, Zeno was the first to promote the ideal that the mastery of dialectic is peculiar to the sage.[12] From its inception, the study of logical validity and the forms of inference (the basic elements that comprise a dialectical ability to converse correctly) was an indispensable component of Stoic education (D.L. 7.45–8).

Verbatim quotations from the few treatises on physics that Zeno reportedly authored (such as Περὶ τοῦ ὅλους, *On the Whole*) are scarce in later sources and testimonies.[13] Later sources often report Stoic doctrine without discriminating the physical doctrines of Zeno from what later became the canonical doctrines of early Stoicism (namely, the doctrines of Zeno and his followers), making it impossible in all but a few cases to distinguish the founder's original doctrines from the conceptual nuances advanced by his successors, especially Chrysippus (279–206 BCE). For example, Sextus Empiricus reports that it is the Stoics (οἱ μὲν ἀπὸ τῆς Στοᾶς φιλόσοφοι, *M.* 9.332 (= LS 44A)) who conceive of the world as a finite totality, with the externally surrounding void constituting the all. Questions surely remain: is this Zeno's view of the all? Should one infer that Zeno himself, perhaps in his work *On the Whole*, originally made such a distinction between the totality and the all? A passage from Diogenes Laertius reports that Zeno considered in that work the world to be "one" (D.L. 7.140-2), and testimony from Arius Didymus (Stobaeus, *Ecl.* 1.19, *SVF* 1.99) does make it seem that Zeno himself conceived of an infinite void surrounding the world.[14] Moreover, in what appear to be quotations and translations of Zeno's doctrines

---

[11] Victor Brochard, *Les sceptiques grecs* (Paris, 1887), 106.
[12] Luca Castagnoli, "How Dialectical Was Stoic Dialectic?," in *Ancient Models of the Mind: Studies in Human and Divine Rationality*, ed. Andrea Nightingale and David Sedley (Cambridge: Cambridge University Press), 167–9.
[13] Regarding the difficulties of tracing physical doctrines back to Zeno himself, see Jaap Mansfeld, "Zeno of Citium: Critical Observations on a Recent Study," *Mnemosyne* 31 (1978): 156–67; Keimpe Algra, "Zeno of Citium and Stoic Cosmology: Some Notes and Two Case Studies," *Elenchos* 24, no. 1 (2003): 9–28; Mouraviev, "Zeno's Cosmology," 232–49.
[14] Adopting the analysis of Mouraviev, "Zeno's Cosmology," 240–9.

in Cicero, it seems that the Stoic determination of the world as a living being and the greatest of all living beings originates with Zeno. At *De nat. deor* 2.22, Cicero claims that Zeno argued for the identification of the world as a living being from the premise that the world has parts that are themselves alive; also, it is stated that Zeno argued from the additional premise that the world gives birth to animate creatures with *logos* to the conclusion that the world-whole itself has *logos*.

Zeno apparently grants no special place for metaphysics in the division of philosophical discourse. But as Jacques Brunschwig observes, from its inception Stoic philosophical investigation entailed the investigation of "any and every object in the world from a certain point of view ('*qua* being', and also *qua* such and such type of being)," including, I might add, the world itself.[15] Brunschwig defends the legitimacy of a long historiographical tradition in which scholars reconstruct the metaphysics of Stoic philosophy. Still, one might be more restrictive with the designation of "metaphysics" and challenge the view that Zeno and early canonical Stoics were motivated to address the defining question of metaphysics, the "question of what it means to say of any object that it is."[16] This designation of metaphysics assumes that the study of metaphysics is largely, if not entirely, regulated by a single guiding question: again, the question of what it means to say of any object that it is. To pursue a less centralized and more systematic view of metaphysics, I maintain that one of the more important tasks of metaphysics is to articulate the order or structure among the beings that are, to say what kind of being or beings grounds other kinds of beings, thus offering a unified framework for the explanation of the entire range of beings in the world.[17] Such explanatory frameworks are meant to give human beings the conceptual resources to explain that which is not self-explanatory in terms of first principles, what may be called the "autoexplicable" stopping points of explanation.[18] The explanatory framework enables the inquirer to address the many questions

---

[15] Jacques Brunschwig, "Stoic Metaphysics," in Inwood, *Cambridge Companion*, 206–9.
[16] Katja Maria Vogt, "Sons of the Earth: Are the Stoics Metaphysical Brutes?," *Phronesis* 54, no. 2 (2009): 144–5. Given an apparent lack of motivation on the part of Zeno and the Stoics to address this defining question, Vogt reasons that the ascription of metaphysics, or ontology, to the research program of the Stoic system is warranted only in a "weak" sense.
[17] For a condensed version of this account of Stoic metaphysics, see Charles E. Snyder, "Arcesilaus and the Ontology of Stoic Cognition," *The Review of Metaphysics* 73, no. 3 (2020): 458–61.
[18] Lloyd P. Gerson, *From Plato to Platonism* (Ithaca, NY: Cornell University Press, 2014), 16–17, 105 n24; D. T. J. Bailey, "The Structure of Stoic Metaphysics," *Oxford Studies in Ancient Philosophy* 46 (2014): 255–7, associates this explanatory task with the study of metaphysics, and rightly ascribes the task to Zeno and his orthodox followers. In the course of this study, I adopt for convenience of expression Bailey's tactic (257, esp. n15, n16) of avoiding the terms "exist" and "existence" in the context of explicating Stoic metaphysics, favoring instead descriptions of the different *ways to be* in Stoic ontology.

that arise over the course of experience in a coherent and systematic fashion: for example, a philosophical account of the nature of human action (ethics), of the visible motion of the heavens (physics), and the inferential relations among certain propositions (logic). Moreover, the task of saying something about what grounds what often involves the additional task of saying something about the order or structure of the totality of beings. The assumption that there is such a totality is perhaps the most profound legacy from Presocratic natural philosophy to influence and orient the explanatory projects of the Old Academy, Aristotle and his early predecessors, as well as the early Stoa.[19] The project of determining the structure of the totality of beings is a more precise formulation of what Martin Heidegger means when he associates traditional metaphysics with the "question about beings as such and as a whole."[20] In conformity with this specification of the project of traditional metaphysics, Brunschwig defends two ways in which it is legitimate to speak of the task of Stoic metaphysics. In one sense, canonical Stoicism classified within the domain of physics specific topics that philosophers and historiographers traditionally associate with the province of metaphysics: such as bodies, first principles, elements, god(s), as well as limit, time, place, and void (D.L. 7.132). Bodies are for Zeno metaphysically primary; they are considered the only things in the world capable of acting or of being acted upon.[21] It is worth noting that our sources do not attribute the properties of "resistance" (Galen, *Qual. inc.* 19.483 (= *SVF* 2.381, part)) and "three-dimensionality" (D.L. 7.135 (= *SVF* 3 Apollodorus 6, part, LS 45E)) to Zeno's original notion of body. Scholars generally agree, however, with Jaap Mansfeld in holding that Zeno's conception of body implied such attributes.[22] Available evidence is limited on the topic of time. Sources do not attribute the doctrine that time is an "incorporeal" specifically to Zeno. There are, though, two sources stating that Zeno affirmed that "time is the interval of motion, this being the measure and mark of speed and slowness of each thing" (Stobaeus, *Ecl.* 1.8, Simplicius, *ad. Cat.* 80a4 (= *SVF* 1.93)). Given this definition of time and its

---

[19] In fact, the assumption that there is such a totality still informs the research of one strand of contemporary analytic metaphysics. For example, see Jonathan Schaffer, "The Action of the Whole," *Proceedings of the Aristotelian Society,* Supp. Vol. 87 (2013): 67–87.
[20] Martin Heidegger, "Die onto-theo-logische Verfassung der Metaphysik," in *Identität und Differenz* (GA 11), ed. Friedrich-Wilhelm von Herrmann (Frankfurt am Main: Vittorio Klostermann, 2006), 76; "The Onto-Theo-Logical Constitution of Metaphysics," in *Identity and Difference,* trans. Joan Stambaugh (Chicago: University of Chicago Press, 2002), 70.
[21] Cicero, *Acad.* 1.39 (= *SVF* 1.90, LS 45A), Eusebius, *Praep. ev.* 15.14.1 (= *SVF* 1.98, LS 45G), cf. D.L. 7.134 (< *SVF* 1.85), Sextus, *M.* 10.218, Plutarch, *Comm. not.* 1073e.
[22] Mansfeld, "Critical Observations," 163; Jean-Baptiste Gourinat, "The Stoics on Matter and Prime Matter," in *God and Cosmos in Stoicism,* ed. Ricardo Salles (Oxford: Oxford University Press, 2009), 55–6.

dependence on the speed and slowness of things and bodies, it is likely that Zeno had already considered time (along with the void) some sort of being or thing, but not an individual body capable of acting or being acted upon.

These Stoic topics correspond to what is later identified as the discipline of *metaphysica specialis*. Zeno and his canonical followers grant certain topics within the study of physics a privileged status in the explanatory framework of Stoic philosophy. Therefore, the task of articulating the order and structure of beings depends in part on identifying the topics that belong to the domain of physics. The classification of the void within the domain of physics suggests that one issue for natural investigation is the topic of "the all," and the relation of the extra-cosmic void to the cyclical expansions and contractions of the world. In a more generic sense, the domain of physics is assigned the task of articulating the order and structure of things in general. A generic specification of physics includes a list of three topics of investigation (1. the totality or whole, 2. the elements, 3. the search for causes, D.L. 7.132).[23] A focal issue of physics in the generic sense is thus the manifest organization of the whole with respect to the elements and causes of the whole, including each individual body within the whole. The task of metaphysics more closely associated with this generic sense of physics is what will later be called *metaphysica generalis*, or what is often referred to as *ontology*, which concerns articulating the order or structure of beings in general.

As a philosophy of nature, canonical Stoicism rests on two assumptions: (1) that there is a world, and (2) that the constituents of this totality are relatively disposed to being known. The classification of specific and generic topics within physics may not have originated with Zeno, but what is indisputable is that his most industrious followers (Cleanthes and his student Chrysippus) take up the concepts and definitions that Zeno first formulated and advance those initial proposals by further clarifying an explanatory system originally designed by Zeno to determine the ontological status of each thing in relation to all other things. In addition to a theory of the whole as it relates to the all, Stoic metaphysics involves a basic division of each and every *some thing* (τὸ τι) into either the corporeal (e.g., the soul, wisdom, truth) or the incorporeal (e.g., place, time, void, sayables) way of being. The basic division entails an account of a third way to be, the way in which incorporeals take on some manifest relation to individual bodies. For early Stoic ontology, a unifying explanatory

---

[23] On the recurrence of "elements" in the generic and specific classifications, see Brunschwig, "Stoic Metaphysics," 208.

framework requires an account of the following ways to be: (1) the way of being (εἶναι) of individual bodies in possession of the power to act or be acted upon; (2) the way of being of incorporeals which subsist (ὑφιστάναι), such as place, time, void, and sayables; and (3) when an individual body is spatiotemporally present, or causally networked in a certain way relative to what subsists, incorporeals are said to "obtain" (ὑπάρχειν).[24] Taking this sense of "obtaining" to imply that a causal body is spatiotemporally manifest or present, the Greek infinitive ὑπάρχειν denotes a way of being that Zeno illustrates with his hand; grasping an individual thing (and the representational content that belongs to the thing), as a fist grasps some individual body, is possible because a body is spatiotemporally present (*Acad.* 2.145 (= LS 41A)).[25] The activity of grasping some individual (and its content) implies that the body grasped is manifest in the manner of being here and now spatiotemporally present for the one doing the grasping.[26] Hence, in conjunction with the Stoic conception of bodies as the fundamentally real, there is a general theory of subsistence as a way of being that is required for bodies to alter over the course of time, emerge at a particular place, and for mortal creatures partaking in reason to successfully verify and falsify the propositions which pertain to the bodies that manifest themselves. And within the general theory of subsistence as a distinct way of being, there is an account of "sayables" as a particular way in which some beings subsist. The account of "sayables" attests to the fact that in Stoic ontology the incorporeals ultimately depend on the efficient causality of bodies for them to obtain. Before analyzing the Stoic conception of "sayables," it is worth reiterating a relevant historiographical point in relation to Zeno. A general theory of incorporeal beings which one can reliably ascribe to the Stoic founder himself remains elusive.

---

[24] Bailey summarizes this view in the following way: "Bodies *are*; incorporeals as such *subsist*; and when the former are configured in such-and-such ways . . . the latter can be said to *obtain*. Effectively, these three ways to be are the radical alternative to Aristotle's matter/form metaphysics, and the receptacle/Form-participation view of Plato's *Timaeus*." For a more thorough articulation of this structure, see Bailey, "Structure of Stoic Metaphysics," 256–76. On the obscure metaphysical status of universals (species and genera, such as man, horse, animal) for Zeno and his followers (Stob., *Ecl.* 1.136, D.L. 7.61 (= *SVF* 1.65, part)), see Victor Caston, "Something and Nothing: The Stoics on Concepts and Universals," *Oxford Studies in Ancient Philosophy* 17 (1999): 145–213; and for a different account, Bailey, "Structure of Stoic Metaphysics," 285–305. Against Caston, Bailey argues that the Stoics thought that there are universals, but still excluded them from their widest genus of being 'something' (τὸ τί), that is, to be some *individual* thing. Cf. Brunschwig, "Stoic Metaphysics," 220: "to be something is to be *some* thing; that is, some *particular* thing."

[25] For a persuasive defense of Zeno's causal model of experience that brings out the implicit metaphysical connotations of Zeno's phrase ἀπὸ ὑπάρχοντος ("from what is [spatiotemporally] present"), see Pavle Stojanović, "Zeno of Citium's Causal Theory of the Apprehensive Appearances," *Ancient Philosophy* 39, no. 1 (2019): 160–9.

[26] Pierre Hadot, "Zur Vorgeschichte des Begriffs 'Existenz': ὑπάρχειν bei den Stoikern," *Archiv für Begriffsgeschichte* 13 (1969): 121–3, esp. n33, for discussion of τὸ ὑπάρχον in Zeno's definition of the apprehensive impression.

It is far from certain that Zeno ever articulated such a theory, even if one takes Cicero at his word that Zeno himself denied that what is non-bodily could have casual efficacy (*Acad.* 1.39). Ancient sources suggest that the gradual emergence of canonical Stoicism develops largely as a result of his immediate successors, Cleanthes and Chrysippus, clarifying and extending Zeno's association of the fundamentally real with the efficient causality of bodies, and his corresponding denial of the efficient causality of non-bodily or incorporeal things. In other words, it seems uncontroversial to say that Zeno articulated views about the whole structure of reality that his orthodox successors continued to refine in the holistic spirit that the school founder originally proposed. Therefore, it can be said with Brunschwig et al. that Zeno and his canonical followers raised a host of metaphysical questions not only about topics specific to physics, but also about topics associated with the other parts of the core division of philosophical discourse, such as virtue *qua* body (in the domain of ethics), the void *qua* incorporeal (in the domain of physics), and predicates and propositions *qua* incorporeal (in the domain of logic).

Clarifying each internal part of Zeno's tripartition, his canonical successors elaborated in a certain way on what he had conceived as linguistic items, coining the term λεκτόν, or the "sayable"—the incorporeal thing that is thought "to subsist in correspondence with a rational impression" (D.L. 7.63 (= LS 33F), Sextus, *M.* 8.70 (= LS 33C)). "Sayables" are held to be the kind of thing that subsists independently of actually being expressed or thought by a mortal animal partaking in reason.[27] For instance, take the predicate ". . . to wail" as an example of what Zeno's successors understood as a deficient, incomplete sayable. The deficiency of such a sayable consists in its incomplete expression, for the sayable in this case has been detached from the complete linguistic function that a predicate is able to fulfill when combined with a subject term, for example, the (complete) sayable "Oedipus is wailing." The complete sayable is the (true or false) proposition expressed by a complete declarative sentence. Moreover, the Stoics distinguished within the species of the complete sayable particular propositions in which the supplied subject yields a complete sayable by means of a referring term, such as "Oedipus wails," from particular propositions involving ostensive reference, such as "This one wails." The proposition "This one wails" is an instance of a complete "definite" sayable, while "Oedipus wails" is an

---

[27] On "sayables" as subsisting independently of thought and language, i.e., the minds of mortal animals partaking in reason, see Jean-Baptiste Gourinat, "Stoic Dialectic and Its Objects," in *Dialectic after Plato and Aristotle*, ed. Thomas Bénatouïl and Katerina Ierodiakonou (Cambridge: Cambridge University Press, 2019), 142–56.

instance of a complete sayable that is predicative or middle. The proposition "Someone wails" is an example of another subspecies of the complete sayable: the indefinite. Evidently, for indefinite complete propositions to express something true, a corresponding definite proposition ought to be found as true (Sextus, *M.* 8.98 (= *SVF* 2.205, LS 34H)), and if none of the relevant individual bodies obtain or manifest as wailing, the indefinite sayable "Someone wails" cannot be true. The definite proposition is said to obtain whenever the relevant predicate obtains for the individual body indicated (*M.* 8.100 (= *SVF* 2.205, LS 34I)). If definite (and indefinite) propositions depend on the availability of a referent in the form of an individual body to be true or subsist, then it seems correct to infer that the species of complete sayables has a certain priority among sayables as a genus. Complete sayables also enjoy a certain priority among subsisting incorporeal beings, for all the other incorporeal beings (place, time, void) bring with them the subsistence of sayables, since true and false propositions are said about each incorporeal. Consider this asymmetric relation in the other direction; the subsistence of complete sayables does not bring with it the other incorporeals.[28] In this limited sense, the subsisting incorporeals of place, time, and void are comparable to bodies in a way that complete sayables are not, that is, in the sense that each and every individual body brings with it the subsistence of true and false propositions.

The ontology of early Stoic philosophy stands in stark contrast to the way that Academics (Speusippus, Xenocrates) and Peripatetic philosophers (Aristotle, Theophrastus) in their own respective ways take up and advance the same Presocratic legacy informing Zeno's worldview. To reiterate, the legacy of Presocratic philosophy involves the belief that there is such a thing as a world or totality. And Zeno's philosophy, as noted above, rests on the belief that there is such a cosmic unity, one in which the constituents of the world are really related, that is to say, independent of the representations or actions of mortal animals partaking in reason. By contrast, the leading philosophers of the Old Academy (and the Peripatetic school) promote an explanatory approach to the systematic study of the totality of beings that is hierarchical and fundamentally noncorporealist. According to this approach, the simple precedes the complex or composite, and the intelligible or noncorporeal precedes the sensible. The precedence of the noncorporeal refers to an explanatory priority and to what grounds what in the order of being. The explanatory framework is based on

---

[28] Bailey, "Structure of Stoic Metaphysics," 278: "If there are times, places, and the void, then there are true and false propositions about times, places, and the void."

the commitment that an understanding of the complex phenomena of sensible bodies depends on an understanding of the unqualifiedly simple and intelligible, just as the complex phenomena of sensible bodies themselves depend on the simple and intelligible for their mode of being.[29] In contrast to the corporeality of principles and elements of Stoic metaphysics, the simplicity of a first principle takes priority in the Academic task of explaining, for instance, the goal of human action, given the irreducibility of soul to the corporeal and the irreducibility of intellect to soul. Just as the action of an individual human soul is explained in accordance with the priority of the intellect/intelligible over the psychical, so the psychical takes precedence over the corporeal in determining a hierarchy of ethical goods. In agreement with an ontological framework that closely associates the simple and noncorporeal with the irreducibility of the divine, the Academic hierarchy of intelligible being is the cornerstone of an ethics of εὐδαιμονία ("happiness") that ranks goods of the soul (i.e., the virtues) higher than goods external to the soul.

Epistemological Part

One of the central tasks of this study is to undermine the view that the arguments of Arcesilaus, Polemo's most well-known pupil in the Academy, principally attack Zeno's epistemology. To accomplish this task, it is important to identify the domain of epistemology within Zeno's comprehensive view of philosophy. First of all, I find it instructive to consult a recent summary of "Stoic logic" that recognizes a discrepancy between what "we" traditionally think of as the problem-areas of epistemology and the Stoic topics which roughly correspond to the problem-areas widely recognized in the field today. The summary reads:

> Epistemological issues were a concern of logic, which studied *logos*, reason and speech, in all of its aspects, not, as we might expect, only the principles of valid reasoning—these were the concern of another division of logic, dialectic. The epistemological part, that concerned with canons and criteria, belongs to

---

[29] I take it that the last lines of *Meta.* Λ 10 (1076a2–6) suggest that Aristotle embraces the task of determining the first principles of the whole of beings. At *Meta.* Λ 6–7, Aristotle argues for a simple first principle of the whole. Cf. 1072a31–5 for his understanding of that which is simple and primary among beings: "Now the intellect is moved by the intelligible, and things which are intelligible in virtue of themselves are in one of the two columns of opposites; and of these, substances are primary, and of substances, that which is simple and in actuality is primary. Oneness is not the same as the simple; for 'one' signifies a measure, but that which is 'simple' signifies the manner in which something is."

logic conceived in this broader way because it aims to explain how *our* mental capacities make possible full realization of reason in the form of wisdom, which the Stoics, in agreement with Socrates, equated with virtue and made the sole sufficient condition for human happiness (italics added).³⁰

The summary situates epistemology within the domain of logic, or, more exactly, it situates "the epistemological part" within a domain of logic conceived more broadly than it is at present. Stoic epistemology, or "the epistemological part" of Stoic philosophy, is not, strictly speaking, a main "species" (εἶδος/γένος) or "part" (μέρος) of the tripartite division, nor is it an identifiable "field" (τόπος, D.L. 7.43) within the original partition of logic into the subparts of dialectic and rhetoric.³¹ Although such an epistemological part is unspecified as a "part" by Zeno, or by any other later Stoic, I assume for the sake of *de re* specification that one can legitimately identify such a humanistic sub-domain of inquiry in Stoic philosophy, which currently involves investigating various epistemic capacities within the broader investigation of Stoic *logos*. The identification of an epistemological part, in accordance with the framework of epistemology in the reconstruction of Arcesilaus's polemic with early Stoicism, takes for granted that one can extract and isolate without any residual complication a set of humanistic problem-areas belonging to, or having some close association with, a sub-domain within logic not exactly equivalent with either the subpart of Stoic dialectic or Stoic rhetoric. It should be clear, at any rate, that when modern scholars adopt epistemological centrism in making the claim that Arcesilaus criticized or attacked Zeno's epistemology, they often mean that his arguments first and foremost attack the canons and criteria allegedly available to epistemic subjects for the realization of Stoic wisdom.

Epistemology is nowadays considered a major branch of philosophy. In contemporary philosophy, epistemologists tend to acknowledge at least four major problem-areas rendering epistemology its own branch of research and theories of knowledge a distinct type of philosophical theorizing. First, there

---

[30] James Allen, "Stoic Epistemology," in *A Companion to Epistemology*, 2nd ed., ed. Jonathan Dancy, Ernest Sosa, and Matthias Steup (Oxford: Blackwell Publishing, 2010), 750–3. I single out this summary because it is one of the few studies to situate, and discuss, "Stoic epistemology" in relation to the tripartite division of philosophy. Other well-known treatments, such as Julia Annas, "Stoic Epistemology," in *Companions to Ancient Thought* 1: *Epistemology*, ed. Stephen Everson (Cambridge: Cambridge University Press), 184–203, Hankinson, "Stoic Epistemology," 59–84, and Michael Frede, "Stoic Epistemology," in Algra et al., *Cambridge History*, 295–322, set aside the tripartite system from the explication and specification of Stoic epistemology.

[31] For an illuminating discussion of the alternative terms the Stoics used to describe both the parts and subparts of philosophical discourse, see Katerina Ierodiakonou, "The Stoic Division of Philosophy," *Phronesis* 38, no.1 (1993): 61–7.

is what is often called the analytic problem concerning the meaning of the concept of knowledge, and the distinct meaning of that concept in relation to other associated concepts one uses to describe mental activity, such as belief, justification, and ignorance. A second problem concerns the scope or limits of human knowledge, given the mental capacities a particular theory of knowledge attributes to human beings. Thirdly, there are a host of issues associated with the question of method. The question of method pertains, more broadly, to the question of how human knowledge is to be sought and acquired, and whether there is one or more ways of properly conducting the search—given the relevant kind of knowledge in question, namely, the kind of knowledge associated with the natural sciences, or the kind(s) associated with human or social sciences. Finally, there is for the traditional epistemologist a problem concerning how to effectively respond to worries about whether knowledge is at all possible. This problem is typically construed as the question concerning knowledge of the world that exists independent of knowing or acting subjects. The problem is standardly expressed as a particular sort of skepticism, that is, skepticism about the external world.

It is worth reflecting on the obvious fact that the term "epistemology" is a relatively recent term for classifying such problems under a distinct branch of research. As late as the end of the eighteenth century, no single term widely circulated for gathering under one field the problems now setting the research agenda of epistemology.[32] In 1769, Alexander Baumgarten proposed the word *gnoseologia* for such problems, but that term would soon be eclipsed in the wake of Eduard Zeller's 1862 "Über Bedeutung und Aufgabe der Erkenntnistheorie." The compound noun *Erkenntnistheorie* ("theory of knowledge") quickly became the preferred term. In his *Institutes of Metaphysics* (1854), James E. Ferrier had already introduced the term "epistemology" to mark a distinction between it ("theory of knowledge") and "ontology" (theory of Being or the totality of what there is). According to Ferrier, insoluble problems stem from philosophers indulging in the "preposterous" procedure of predicating anything about Being before having clarified what knowledge is. On this view, the method of epistemology ought to preclude questions about *what there is*. Ferrier was not

---

[32] For a concise historical account of epistemology and an extensive bibliography, see Jan Woleński, "The History of Epistemology," in *Handbook of Epistemology*, ed. Ilkka Niiniluoto, Matti Sintonen, and Jan Woleński (Dordrecht: Springer, 2004), 3–54. In a more recent study, Pasnau states: "Today the study of knowledge is one of the foundational subjects of philosophy. But this has not always been so—indeed, for long periods of time, epistemology can appear not to have been an important subject at all, let alone a foundational one." Robert Pasnau, *After Certainty: A History of Our Epistemic Ideals and Illusions* (Oxford: Oxford University Press, 2017), 1.

alone, nor was he as innovative in proposing such a methodological procedure as it might appear from these brief remarks.

The recent history of this type of theorizing supports the widespread view among historiographers that the project of Cartesian metaphysics marks a turning point in the historical emergence of this new branch of research. Prior to Descartes, according to this view, philosophical inquiry was largely oriented and guided by metaphysical questions, by the sort of questions Ferrier sought to forestall on methodological grounds, at least until the question of knowledge is answered. A gradual shift allegedly began with (but mostly after) Descartes, such that questions of human knowledge assume methodological priority. Although Descartes may belong to a pre-Cartesian way of pursuing metaphysics as first philosophy, considering the solutions he offers to certain problems of knowledge, and the fact that they arise "only in the context of engaging with the two metaphysical issues" of God's existence and the distinction of the soul from the body, the truth of existence ("I am") is secured on Descartes's view by an act of epistemological certainty that discovers "I am thinking."[33] Rather than set out straightaway to grasp beings, or the totality of beings as such, post-Cartesian philosophy likewise embarks on a new course of investigation that first turns to *our* thinking capacities and *our* epistemic access to what there is as a foundation of knowing what other beings there are, or could be. Modern philosophy is, or at least becomes, largely an attempt to replace ontology with epistemology as the new *prima philosophia*. Not long after Descartes, the distinction that becomes increasingly prominent is one concerning *our access to what there is* and *what there is*. John Locke, for example, provides a rather clear articulation of this methodological distinction, nearly two centuries before Ferrier, with his statement that "the first step towards satisfying several Enquiries" is to take a "Survey of our Understandings, examine our own Powers," and so until "that was done I suspected we began at the wrong end, and in vain sought for Satisfaction in a quiet and secure Possession of Truths, that most concern'd us, whilst we let loose our Thoughts into the vast ocean of *Being*."[34]

After this proposed methodological turn toward the investigation of *our* mental capacities, a tradition of epistemology emerges in which a realm of mental capacities is distinguished and isolated from a metaphysical realm of beings or things as mind-independent. The distinction retained a certain prominence

---

[33] Desmond Clarke, "The Epistemology of Descartes," in *Epistemology: The Key Thinkers*, ed. Stephen Hetherington (London: Continuum, 2012), 101.

[34] John Locke, *An Essay Concerning Human Understanding*, ed. Peter H. Nidditch (Oxford: Oxford University Press, 1975), Book 1, Chapter 1, §7.

throughout the twentieth century. For the influential naturalist W. V. O. Quine, the investigation of *what there is* (ontology) becomes a matter of investigating the structures of *our* conceptual scheme, which grant us access to what there is. That is to say, logical relations among certain observation sentences are treated as the storehouse of evidential support for *our access to what there is*. Quine's naturalistic interest in investigating the "flow of evidence from the triggering of the senses to the pronouncements of science" maintains the methodological prioritization of epistemology over ontology.[35]

The project of investigating the conceptual structure of *our access to what there is* (via epistemically privileged propositions) adheres to the assumption that with the correct foundational epistemology human beings gain access to *what there is*, and for some thinkers that includes access to everything that there is. The latter is often conceptualized as the world, "everything that is the case," or, in Ludwig Wittgenstein's phrase, "the totality of facts."[36] Martin Heidegger famously challenges the assumption motivating the epistemological problem concerning how knowledge of the world is possible.[37] According to his existential analytic, the problem-areas of epistemology emerge as the result of "skipping-over" the genuine issue of the world phenomenon,[38] as concepts such as knowledge, justified true belief, and the so-called external world command the attention of traditional epistemology. The "skipping-over" consists in the fact that epistemologists overlook how it is that mental capacities are already embedded within the world, for *our* access to everything that is the case is as much something that is the case as anything else. That is to say, mental access to what there is must also be part of what there is. The methodological priority of epistemology over ontology is, in other words, already an ontology of knowledge insofar as it presupposes that there is a world independent of the mental capacities to grasp what is the case, a world comprised of beings or things structured by real relations and properties already there independent of our access to them. However, traditional epistemology does not reflect on the underlying metaphysical conditions of the world, nor does it reflect on how

---

[35] W. V. O. Quine, "Three Indeterminacies," in *Perspectives on Quine*, ed. Robert Barrett and Roger Gibson (Oxford: Basil Blackwell, 1990), 3.
[36] John McDowell, *Mind and World* (Cambridge, MA: Harvard University Press, 1998), 27, refers to Wittgenstein's concept of the world as "everything that is the case," or "die Gesamtheit der Tatsachen" ("the totality of facts"). Cf. Ludwig Wittgenstein, *Tractatus Logico-Philosophicus*, trans. D. F. Pears and B. F. McGuinness (London: Routledge and Kegan Paul, 1961), § 1, 1 and 1.1.
[37] Martin Heidegger, *Sein und Zeit*, 11th ed. (Tübingen: Max Niemeyer Verlag, 1967), §§ 19–21, 90–9, and §§ 43–4, 200–30; trans. Joan Stambaugh, revised and with a Foreword by Dennis J. Schmidt as *Being and Time* (Albany, NY: SUNY Press, 2010).
[38] Heidegger, *Sein und Zeit*, §14, 63–6 at 65, and §21, 93–9 at 98–9.

such a mind-independent world could give rise to epistemic subjects and the mental capacities enabling such beings to reflect on such access to the world. The methodological detachment of epistemology from ontology is often the first and most decisive step in the adoption of a naive ontology of knowledge. The ontological presupposition of the world in epistemology is in no way self-evident or autoexplicable. Rather, it is a judgment from a certain perspective and it can be contested, like any other judgment. When such a judgment is presumed true, rather than examined and tested, then the unreflected ontology becomes naive. Heidegger's analysis, by contrast, reflects on the underlying presuppositions motivating the epistemological problem of *our* access to the world and the corresponding judgment that the world is, initially, a world without observers. In lieu of such a judgment, Heidegger pursues an analysis of being-in-the-world, according to which observers in the mode of *Dasein* find themselves and the environment that they determine with the same right as they find plants, stones, atoms, the starry heavens, and so on. On his view, the existential analytic compels these beings to ask in what sense the judgment that isolates a world of beings independent of and preceding observers is at all justified. Simply put, is it justified for such a being to refer to the world as if it were essentially independent of any reference to it?[39] Or perhaps one should consider, setting off in a different direction than Heidegger's analytic, that "mind" (*Geist*) and the givenness of preceding beings (*Vorfindlichkeit von Seiendem*) are essentially mediated by one another, such that mind can be as little isolated from the givenness of the world as the givenness of the world from mind?[40]

With these different directions in view, one can more easily distinguish between epistemology and the ontology of knowledge. An ontology of knowledge takes its primary orientation from the notion of the being of the world as inclusive of a totality of relations posited by a given philosophical theory. The being of the world is typically presupposed in the framework of epistemology as an ontological correlate preceding judgments about what is the case.[41] From the perspective of an ontology of knowledge, epistemologists are prone to issuing certain ontological judgments not only about what is methodologically primary

---

[39] See Markus Gabriel, *An den Grenzen der Erkenntnistheorie. Die notwendige Endlichkeit des objektiven Wissens als Lektion des Skeptizismus* (Freiburg: Aber, 2008), §3, 64–5, for a fuller discussion of the principal difficulties that follow from starting out with the assumption that the world is independent of the fact that we refer to it.

[40] Adorno, *Erkenntnistheorie*, 32.

[41] For a similar use of this distinction, see Markus Gabriel, "Zum Außenweltproblem in der Antike: Sextus' Destruktion des Repräsentationalismus und die skeptische Begründung des Idealismus bei Plotin," *Bochumer Philosophisches Jahrbuch für Antike und Mittelalter* 12 (2007): 33.

to investigate, but also about the world of beings beyond the veil which certain mental capacities may or may not be able to access. Rather than first assume a humanistic focus on the problem-areas concerning what human knowledge might be, or the conceptual structure of *our* access to the world, an ontology of knowledge examines the ontological conditions of a given theory of knowledge. The latter first thematizes the being of the world and its structure, and proceeds with an investigation of how it is possible for the world to generate its own doubling into mind, or mental access, on the one hand, and external things, on the other, such that some beings are capable of reflecting on their possible knowledge of external things as they really are. The ontology of knowledge is thus primarily oriented by the anti-humanistic concern over the structure of beings as a whole, such that knowledge of the world of beings could even become an issue and a possibility for rational animals, or mortal animals partaking in reason. How does this anti-humanistic approach to the order and structure of beings relate to the historiography of the dispute between Arcesilaus and the canons of early Stoic philosophy? From the perspective of an ontology of knowledge, I venture the following answer: that Zeno and his followers were unable to articulate a theory of apprehension, knowledge, or virtue without proposing an ontological structure in those theories, a structure conditioning the epistemic conditions of apprehending the causal beings supposedly preceding and presenting themselves to mortal animals partaking in reason.

The distinction between the traditional framework of epistemology and an ontology of knowledge is key for understanding the philosophical scope of the dispute between Arcesilaus and Zeno. Let me reiterate that something akin to a subpart of epistemology, or an "epistemological part," within Zeno's tripartition can be reconstructed through *de re* interpretation, as proponents of epistemological centrism generally assume.[42] Granting the validity of historiographical projects aimed at reconstructing Stoic epistemology, philosophical historiographers should nevertheless specify that this Stoic part (or subpart) entails some conception of "correspondence" between the power of apprehension and the properties

---

[42] The assumption of a compartmentalized and circumscribed field of Stoic epistemology has been called into question. See, for example, Emidio Spinelli, "Ancient Stoicism, 'Robust Epistemology', and Moral Philosophy," in *Thinking about Causes: From Greek Philosophy to Modern Physics*, ed. Peter Machamer and Gereon Wolters (Pittsburgh: University of Pittsburgh, 2007), 40. Frede, "Stoic Epistemology," 296, challenges any neat compartmentalization of Stoic epistemology, but more indirectly. He states that "Stoic epistemology amounts to a complex hypothesis as to how nature has endowed us with the means to attain knowledge and wisdom." In other words, the articulation of how knowledge is possible cannot be detached from the articulation of complex views about nature and virtue.

"required of the real or possible object" of apprehension.⁴³ For precisely this reason, reconstructions of the conceptual battleground in the Hellenistic period that isolate a part or subpart of epistemology from the ontological conditions of epistemic possibility in the Stoic account of apprehension distort the scope of Arcesilaus's anti-Stoic arguments. As a brief overview of the conclusions in later chapters, this study maintains that in raising counterfactual possibilities associated with pairs of indiscernible beings, Arcesilaus's anti-Stoic arguments demonstrate that the ontology articulated in the causal conception of Stoic apprehension is a result of a set of judgments that can be effectively contested. Those arguments reveal that the epistemic possibility of Stoic apprehension depends on questionable ontological conditions. Indiscernibility arguments challenge Zeno's causal conception of apprehension, but not in isolation from other parts and subparts of philosophy/philosophical discourse, or from the way that Zeno conceives of the world as a coherent whole.

Philosophical Historiography

To clarify what proponents of epistemological centrism mean by the oft-repeated claim that Arcesilaus opposed Stoic epistemology, I introduce *de re* and *de dicto* models of interpretation in the historiography of philosophy. With *de dicto* ascriptions of past ideas and arguments, the historiographer aims to specify what a past figure took it that she was committing herself to by making a certain argument, and what that figure would have regarded as evidence for and against those commitments.⁴⁴ Ascriptions of *de dicto* interpretation thereby aim to specify how the historical figure or author under examination understood the content of what they were arguing or doing in making an argument. To adapt a phrase that Bernard Williams uses to describe the history of ideas, in opposition to the history of philosophy, the direction of attention for the historiographer of ideas specifying *de dicto* ascriptions is to "look sideways to the context of a philosopher's ideas," which is to say, to seek a determination

---

⁴³ Jacques Brunschwig, "Epistemology," in *Greek Thought: A Guide to Classical Knowledge*, ed. Jacques Brunschwig and Geoffrey E. R. Lloyd with the collaboration of Pierre Pellegrin, trans. Catherine Porter (Cambridge, MA: Harvard University Press, 2000), 74. On the overlap of Stoic epistemology with other parts of the Stoic system, cf. Jacques Brunschwig, "The Conjunctive Model," in *Papers in Hellenistic Philosophy*, trans. Janet Lloyd (Cambridge: Cambridge University Press, 1994), 82.

⁴⁴ Brandom, *Mighty Dead*, 98: "One engaged in this sort of interpretation [*de dicto* specifications of ascribed commitments] is trying to specify the contents of commitments in a way that would be recognized and acknowledged as specifications of those contents *by* the one whose commitments they are."

of what a past philosopher was trying to say with those assertions in that particular context.[45] The history of ideas, in this sense, resembles what Michael Frede calls "historiographie historique" ("historical historiography"): "Car c'est seulement l'historiographie historique qui peut déterminer avec toute l'exactitude possible la position dans son contexte historique et les raison pour lesquelles elle fut avancée" ("For it is only historical historiography that is able to determine with all possible accuracy the position in its historical context and the reasons why it was advanced").[46] Unlike "historiographie philosophique" ("philosophical historiography"), that is, the attempt to reconstruct and record the history of philosophy from the point of view of a certain philosophical framework, historical historiography of philosophy is primarily interested in *de dicto* specifications of the content of the ascribed commitment. In the present case, *de dicto* specifications often involve taking the ancient doxographies and secondhand reports of later philosophers either as evidence for what the primary figures themselves said and believed, or as partial evidence that the doxography or secondary source is quite liberal in reporting the propositional content of the primary figure's beliefs. One difficult task of *de dicto* ascription is to come up with ways of reliably tracking when a given testimony ventures beyond what the primary source author or figure intended to argue. It is worth noting that for each and every attempt to specify *de dicto* the conceptual content of an historical text or fragment in Hellenistic philosophy, the historiographer is not able to convey the specification without undertaking some evaluative stance in choosing one specification of the propositional content in a given source as inherently more plausible than some other specification of that same content.

By contrast, *de re* interpretation specifies what *really* follows from certain arguments independent of any consideration of what the given historical figure took it that she was committing herself to when formulating the argument. Specifications *de re* are not restricted to the beliefs that the philosophical historiographer takes it would be acknowledged and recognized by the figure(s) in question. This sort of specification may identify particular arguments (e.g., Arcesilaus's anti-Stoic arguments) or views of a historical figure (Zeno's beliefs concerning apprehension), but do so with the aim of setting those arguments or views in a new conceptual context, which serves the philosophical historiographer in determining what *really* follows from the attested arguments or views. It is worth noting that the idea of pure *de re* interpretation is as

---

[45] Williams, "Historiography of Philosophy," 257.
[46] M. Frede, "Doxographie," 323–4.

problematic as the idea of pure *de dicto* interpretation. In order to assess the truth of what a historical figure said independent of considering the figure's belief about a matter, the philosophical historiographer engaged in making *de re* specifications must first presume to have identified the content of a specific argument or belief correctly, or at least plausibly, prior to isolating the content of the claim from the authorial context and evaluating it by means of the new conceptual context, that is, the chosen framework upon which the historiographer purports to determine what *really* follows from the claim. Without the supplemental basis of some suitably accurate *de dicto* specifications and ascriptions, the *de re* interpreter risks overlooking the strangeness and originality of the approach of the historical figure(s) under reconstruction. Just as with *de dicto* ascriptions, the historiographer making *de re* specifications is obliged, prior to setting the views or arguments in a new conceptual context and reflecting on what *really* follows from certain arguments, to interpret the text or source in accordance with their own evaluative stance concerning what is plausible to identify as the figure's arguments or views. The historiographer engaged in ascribing *de dicto* specifications must first presume to have understood, according to some idea of what is valid, the content of a specific claim, prior to ascribing the content of the claim to the figure in question and assessing whether the figure believes that content to be true. In any event, the tasks of *de re* and *de dicto* specification cannot be totally separated from one another, as each relies to some varying extent on the model of interpretation involved in the other. For present purposes, the most relevant point is that the model of *de re* specification in the historiography of philosophy requires laying out and justifying, alongside the views and arguments extracted from a text or source, an auxiliary framework that the philosophical historiographer takes to be true, so that the specification and evaluation of what *really* follows from the views and arguments can legitimately proceed.

Moreover, there are two historiographical variants of the *de re* model of specifying propositional content. The first is considered immediate *de re* specification. Herein the commitments delineating a new conceptual context from which additional premises are drawn are the commitments acknowledged by the historiographer without any reference to a mediating tradition. The second variant is the one adopted throughout this study. It involves acknowledging a mediated *de re* specification of content, a variant designated *de re* interpretation *de traditione*. In this variant, the commitments defining the conceptual context are mediated by "further claims made by others whom the interpreter, but not necessarily the authors [or figures] involved, retrospectively sees as engaged in a common enterprise, as developing common thoughts or concepts."[47] Integrating the content from the source with the content of claims made by other authors and figures, the *de re* interpreter *de traditione* engages in a common enterprise by implicitly adopting the perspective of some tradition of common thoughts or concepts. From this perspective, the historiographer interprets past philosophy by acknowledging a certain mediating tradition of philosophical thought. By offering readings *de traditione*, the *de re* interpreter adopts an explicit evaluative stance toward the validity of what is claimed, undertaking commitments concerning the relations of various sources and texts. *De re* historiography may lay claim to seeing retrospectively that a given author or historical figure engages in a tradition that is unacknowledged as a tradition by that author or figure. Additionally, the *de re* interpreter *de traditione* is often concerned to associate a past philosopher's views or arguments with present problems and current formulations of those problems in present philosophical discussion. In taking up a tradition, the historiographer brings to bear on a historical text/figure a framework of auxiliary premises that often serve, from the point of the view of the historiographer, as the context for specifying and evaluating the arguments of the historical text(s) or figure(s). The interpretation of the dispute between Arcesilaus and early Stoic philosophy defended in this study is one version of retrospective *de re* interpretation *de traditione*. Proponents of epistemological centrism offer another version of retrospective *de re* interpretation *de traditione*. In taking up a humanistic framework, proponents of epistemological centrism are far less concerned with the task of arguing for the *de dicto* specification that early Stoics took themselves to be defending the "epistemological part" against Arcesilaus than they are with imposing the perspective of a mediating tradition, the tradition of epistemology that is unacknowledged *as* a tradition by Zeno. One might argue, in accordance with the model of *de dicto* specification, that in response to questions of clarification and extension, Zeno or some other early Stoic dogmatist would have acknowledged their commitments to formulating what we today call the "epistemological part" of Stoicism, and that in response to questions of clarification and extension, Arcesilaus himself, the first "epistemological skeptic" in the Academy, would have acknowledged that he was committed to attacking principally Stoic "epistemology" because he believed that epistemology to be false. But to be clear: *de dicto* specification is not the core of what the proponents of epistemological centrism in the historiography of Stoic-Academic debates seek to provide. Recall that the interpreter engaged primarily

---

[47] Brandom, *Mighty Dead*, 107.

in *de dicto* interpretation aims to specify the contents of beliefs from the past in a way that would be recognized and acknowledged as specifications of those contents by the past historical figures. The ascription of "epistemology," on the other hand, makes the content of Stoic views on knowledge worth reconsidering in the light of a mediating tradition that is relevant to present philosophical discussion. What the Stoics themselves reportedly designated by logic and its parts is not the relevant focal point of epistemological centrism. Take Michael Frede, who states that for Zeno and the Stoa "epistemology is treated as a part" of logic.[48] The Stoics evidently developed terminology for designating the main parts of Stoic discourse, as well as the subparts within each main part of the Stoic tripartition. In situating epistemology within the part of Stoic philosophy that the Stoa themselves referred to as logic, Frede is not primarily concerned with what the Stoa themselves reportedly said about "parts" and "subparts" of philosophical discourse. His concern, rather, is to supplement an uncontroversial *de dicto* specification, namely, that Zeno and his canonical followers themselves identified logic as one part of philosophical discourse, with a widely used term in modern and contemporary philosophy.

In any case, for the two versions of *de re* specification in the historiography of philosophy, the interpreter is charged with the task of justifying what she takes to *really* follow from the arguments and claims of the historical figures as they function in the new conceptual context, which is introduced to assess and evaluate the content of the claims being specified. I have already acknowledged adopting the mediating tradition of metaphysics in the reconstruction of Arcesilaus's dispute with the early Stoa. One reason for favoring this mediating tradition as the proper framework of philosophical historiography over the tradition of epistemology as it is conventionally applied stems from the naive ontology that traditional epistemology and epistemological centrism presuppose without justification. Just as traditional epistemology neglects to reflect on the metaphysical presuppositions associated with the distinction between *what there is* and *our access to what there is*, epistemological centrists in the historiography of Stoic-Academic debates neglect to specify the metaphysical conditions that make it possible, on the Stoic view, for mortal animals partaking in reason to receive true impressions.

Notice that when *de re* specification of propositional content abandons the task of defending the collateral commitments that come from the new inferential framework as the proper commitments for assessing what *really* follows the

---

[48] Frede, "Stoic Epistemology," 298.

arguments in the historical record, the work of reconstructing the views of the past on the basis of that framework can take the form of doxography, especially when the adopted conceptual context is one that remains so firmly entrenched in present philosophical discussion that the additional task of justifying the entrenched framework is conventionally considered unnecessary. The task of doxographers is to report the views of past philosophers, and to do so in a way that makes the propositional content of those views worth reconsidering in the light of present philosophical discussion. The doxographer is not primarily concerned with the actual historical sequence in which views of the past were put forward and defended. Nor is the doxographer typically concerned with rationally reconstructing the reasoning for certain claims, or defending their inferential framework that supposedly led past philosophers to certain beliefs and reject others as the correct framework. At any rate, let it be granted that in reproducing the beliefs of past philosophers, one cannot totally avoid a certain degree of anachronism, especially when they belong to philosophers from a very distant past. Doxographical reportage of past philosophical views is presented in a manner that is more readily intelligible to a contemporary audience, and this kind of presentation often involves the use of language and terminology that is foreign to the language and terminology of the past philosopher whose views are being reconstructed. The doxographer may claim to present the true intention of the philosopher in the light of present philosophical knowledge, even when inclined to attribute to the past philosopher an intention that the doxographer is aware that such an intention could not have been the intention of the past philosopher, given the historical context in which the past figured lived and thought. From the critical perspective of the historiographer concerned first and foremost with *de dicto* specifications of past philosophical beliefs, the doxographer is bound to articulate those beliefs in a manner that exceeds an acceptable degree of anachronism, for in making the concepts of the past intelligible to a contemporary audience the doxographer is obliged to translate those concepts into the technical language of present philosophical discussion, to adapt them to the new conceptual framework. To the historiographer making *de dicto* ascriptions, doxography to a considerable extent disguises the beliefs and arguments of the past by isolating the conceptual content from the historical context. From the critical perspective of the historiographer primarily concerned with *de re* specifications of past philosophical views, doxography is bound to seem conceptually inadequate, for the doxographer makes little or no attempt to reconstruct, independent of any consideration of what the dead philosopher would have said in response to questions of clarification and extension, what *really* follows from the claims or arguments made by a dead philosopher.

When one thinks of the doxography of ancient philosophy, one usually thinks almost immediately of Diogenes Laertius. His *Lives of the Eminent Philosophers* blends biographical anecdotes with reportage of past philosophical views. There is a modern variation on this kind of doxography, which emerged near the end of the nineteenth century, around the time the study of Plato and Aristotle experienced a kind of renaissance.[49] Julia Annas, in an influential overview of ancient ethics, acknowledges that her monographic study is just this: a modern variation of doxography. Annas states that the study gives "an account of past theories, from a present viewpoint which is inevitably selective both as to which theories are still philosophically live and as to which terminology will be best understood."[50] Ancient doxographers, by contrast, tended to assume that all or almost all the views of some exceptional philosopher of the past is worth considering in light of some present philosophical viewpoint. The modern doxographer tends to be "selective"; from another perspective, however, such selectivity is a conventionally acceptable way to construe a form of historiographical skimpiness.[51] Either way, in this new form of doxographical writing, the modern doxographer dispenses with biographical reportage in favor of appropriating certain conceptual resources from present philosophical discussion for the reconstruction of arguments of past philosophers deemed perennial from some present viewpoint. Proponents of epistemological centrism can easily devolve into this style of doxographical reportage, using the humanistic language and terminology of the specialized branch of epistemology. As with interpreting *de re*, doxographical proponents of epistemological centrism do not take themselves to be restricted to the commitments that the modern doxographer might take dead authors or figures to have acknowledged regarding the conceptual content being interpreted. With the term "epistemology" qualifying one part or subpart of Stoic philosophy, epistemological centrists revive a form of doxography to specify that Arcesilaus disputed Stoic "epistemology" independent of determining what Arcesilaus took himself to be critically questioning when confronting the views and arguments of the Stoic school. In doxography, the additional premises constituting the new conceptual framework are those adduced by the doxographer, but little, if any, reason is given for holding those commitments as the true commitments that the interpreter should undertake in specifying the content of past philosophy.

---

[49] Frede, "Doxographie," 323–5.
[50] Julia Annas, *The Morality of Happiness* (Oxford: Oxford University Press, 1993), 3 n1.
[51] Rorty, "Historiography of Philosophy," 65.

In harmony with its ancient precursors, epistemological centrism as a form of modern doxography tends to suppress the actual historical development that has given rise to the entrenched concepts and problem-areas of its own conceptual framework. The guiding assumption is that the present viewpoint of epistemology is intrinsically credible on philosophical grounds, or at least sufficiently conventional, "live," and familiar that it requires little in the way of additional reflection or justification as the relevant framework for supplying the language and terminology for the presentation of historiographical reconstruction. As a result, epistemological centrism helps to reconstruct and present the views and arguments of the Hellenistic schools as if the conceptual framework of "epistemology" lies outside the scope of philosophical reflection.

To summarize, the main problem with epistemological centrism is not anachronism, nor is it the retrojection of a language and terminology that conceals *de dicto* specifications uncovering the originality in Arcesilaus's anti-Stoic arguments or in a given Stoic doctrine. The problem stems from taking on a particular viewpoint while failing to reflect on the ontological conditions mediating Stoic epistemology and governing the epistemic possibility of knowledge. As a consequence of this lack of reflection, epistemological doxographers neglect to specify what *really* follows from the arguments and views in the dispute between Arcesilaus and the early Stoa. The most immediate conceptual by-product of this failure, and the main topic of the next chapter, is the myopic simplification of ἀκαταληψία ("inapprehensibility"), which specifies its content with the proposition that knowledge is impossible. From the perspective of a mediating metaphysical tradition, there are evidentiary grounds for specifying the content of ἀκαταληψία in a much different way.

2

The Ontology of Early Stoic Apprehension

I begin by stating the main argument of this chapter. Arcesilaus was the first philosopher in antiquity to oppose Zeno's causal conception of apprehension. Imposing a different conceptual framework, the reconstruction shows that the defense of the causal conception of apprehension depends on a number of contestable metaphysical judgments. Arguments from indiscernibility reveal that the epistemic possibility of apprehension depends on questionable views about the world and its purported ontological structure. Indiscernibility arguments attack Zeno's causal account of apprehension, but not in isolation from the other parts of his tripartition, or from the way that Zeno and his followers conceive of nature as a force unifying the world whole.

Representations of the Real

Zeno's causal account of apprehension is representationalist. That Zeno affirms a type of representationalism is evident from the fundamental importance he assigns to φαντασία (= *visum*, Cic., *Acad.* 2.18, 77 (= *SVF* 1.59, part)).[1] An impression comes to be from an externally induced "impact" (*oblata extrinsecus*, *Acad.* 1.40 (< LS 40B, *SVF* 1.55), cf. *Acad.* 2.48), and it has its cause in the activity of individual "things external" to the soul (τὰ ἐκτὸς ὑποκείμενα, Sextus, *PH* 2.51, 72). External to a given soul, things act on and present themselves to other things in the world, including the soul, such that things occupy real spatial and

---

[1] Cf. Plato, *Tht.* 152b10–c1, where an earlier use of φαντασία is found in Socrates's explication of the doctrine, ascribed to Protagoras, that things are as they "appear" to each person, and that each person "has τὸ κριτήριον [αὐτῶν = of 'all things' (πάντων, 178b3), or the properties of 'all things' that appear through perception] within himself, and when one thinks that they [i.e., things] are the way he is affected by them, one thinks what is true and real for oneself" (178b5–7). These passages evidently persuaded some of Plato's ancient interpreters to think that the main question of the *Theaetetus* is the "criterion" of knowledge *sensu stricto* (Anon., *In Pl. Tht.* 2.11–19, Alcinous, *Did.* 154.8–9).

temporal relations with other things. Zeno's impressionism attributes to these external things *qua* individual bodies the causal efficacy of acting on individual corporeal souls and of generating representations or affections (τὸ δ' ἐκτὸς καὶ τοῦ πάθους ποιητικόν, Sextus, *M.* 7.194) in mortal animals partaking in reason. Zeno's impressionism thereby renders apprehension transactional between the individual bodies that produce impressions and the mortals animals partaking in reason capable of being excited by impressions.[2] The representationalist view of this transaction is motivated by the additional thought that a certain kind of corporeal being—the mortal animal partaking in reason—involved in this causal interaction has the capacity to distinguish the original cause of the externally induced (τὸ ἐκτός) impact from its effect (πάθος). Furthermore, this representationalist view maintains that actual states of affairs involving the causal impact of bodies are fundamentally accessible to mortal beings endowed with the capacities of representing, assessing, assenting, or withholding assent to the representations deriving from the bodies that present themselves to these beings.

Cleanthes takes Zeno to say that the soul "is perceptive because the part of it which is led from beings and the beings that obtain (ἀπὸ τῶν ὄντων καὶ ὑπαρχόντων) through the sense-organs is capable of being imprinted and of receiving their imprints. For these capabilities are peculiar to the soul" (Arius Didymus *apud* Euseb., *Praep. ev.* 15.20.2–3 (< *SVF* 1.141)).[3] The soul has the capability of representing a state of affairs involving some being that obtains in such a way that the inherent nature of the external thing, which precedes and is independent of the representation, is not altered or modified in the representation of it. Now for the soul in possession of reason the impression is formed with semantic or propositional content, that is, with some claim that a particular representation makes, a claim that requires assessment prior to giving or withholding rational assent. For the early Stoics, the part of the soul led by the reality of external things is the *hēgemonikon*, the governing part of the soul partaking in reason, giving rise to impressions, assents, perceptions, and impulses (Aëtius, 4.21.1–4 (*SVF* 2.836, part (= LS 53H)). Hence, the rational soul has access to some individual body as it really obtains in a causal network by means of a set of psychological conditions, or representational capabilities, making it possible for the governing part of the rational soul to form veridical

---

[2] Lachterman, *Ethics of Geometry*, 99.
[3] This passage is omitted from both volumes of LS, but it is translated (differently than above) and discussed by Matthew Colvin, "Heraclitus and Material Flux in Stoic Psychology," *Oxford Studies in Ancient Philosophy* 28 (2005): 257–61.

impressions about the real spatiotemporal beings in the world, and to assent to certain impressions as veridical.

In order to take representations as representative of "beings and the beings that obtain"—that is, for impressions to be taken to correspond to real spatiotemporal bodies, which have intrinsic and relational properties and present themselves as such to the mortal animal in a causal situation—the human animal must be able to assess and reflect on her own representational states. That reflection, in stride, must then identify the conditions of the intentional relation to the external bodies in order to resolve the matter of whether the representations under reflection ought to be taken as veridical. Now such representational capabilities imply for Zeno that the content of a generated representation is such that it can serve as a basis of objective knowledge.[4] Bernard Williams expresses the main idea governing what it means for representations to be objective with the succinct expression that "knowledge is of what is there *anyway*."[5] The expression captures a number of realist premises sustaining the doctrine of Stoic apprehension and setting the conditions for apprehensive success or failure. On Zeno's variety of metaphysical realism, human animals process the information that impacts the rational soul from outside, and thus are considered the special kind of mortal animal capable of representing the real (intrinsic and extrinsic or relational) properties of present bodies through the power of perception— assuming, that is, (1) individual bodies are able to move in space and time and bring with them independent of any representational capacity or access on the part of a given mortal animal the semantic content of subsisting sayables; and (2) that such spatially positioned bodies possess, independent of any given mortal animal's capacity to access reality, intrinsic properties and the relational properties bodies have to other bodies or things; and (3) furthermore, that bodies are able to produce the kind of impression that warrants rational assent to how things are *anyway*. In fewer words, the tenets of metaphysical realism underpinning the causal conception of Stoic apprehension can be abridged as follows: if a human has true representations, then the animal has experiences

---

[4] In making "apprehension" (κατάληψις) the basis of "knowledge" (ἐπιστήμη), Zeno distinguished apprehension or apprehensive knowing from knowledge proper, the special kind of dispositional knowing characteristic of the sage. The latter is more fully dispositional in the sense that the one who knows is genuinely a sage if he or she knows a system of mutually supporting apprehensions and cannot be shaken by argument in that knowledge (Stob., *Ecl.* 2.73.16–74.3 (= LS 41H)). This state of knowing involves knowing that one is unshakably disposed to apprehensive knowing. Instructive comments on the distinction between apprehensive (or "cognitional") knowing and "dispositional" knowing in relation to modern epistemology can be found in Brouwer, *Stoic Sage*, 32–3.

[5] Williams, *Descartes*, 48.

caused by real things external to it.⁶ The causal conception is, therefore, premised on the judgment that if apprehension is objective, then it is an apprehension of a real state of affairs involving at the very least an individual body that manifests itself as it really is *anyway*.⁷

On this representationalist view, the purported animals of apprehension capable of giving or withholding assent must also be capable of taking up a representation as a distinct representation of a purported state of affairs ("as if of" some spatiotemporal body that obtains) prior to assessing the veridicality of the propositional content expressed by the representation. Each and every impression (spurious or veridical) possesses *representational purport* in virtue of which it is taken up as being "as if of" some thing that is the case.⁸ For instance, in order for the representations of dreaming states to be determined as spurious internal images that fail to grasp real states of affairs obtaining independently of dreaming states, those representations must first be taken up as distinct representations of thus-and-such. A reflective analysis of the *representational purport* of impressions is required in order for the propositional content of the representation to be taken as true or false. Access to what obtains is unavoidably mediated by purported representations the analysis of which reveals the conditions under which some representations are successful and others spurious. Since this representationalist view holds that bodies outside the *hēgemonikon* function as the primary metaphysical correlate generating representations, *representational success* depends at a minimum on the nature of the individual bodies that present themselves.

---

⁶ Ibid., 43. For analysis of Plotinus's similar attack on the Stoic's causal model, see Gabriel, "Zum Außenweltproblem," 35–42. The causal model entails what is often designated, in the terminology of epistemology, the externalist view of Stoic apprehension. For a mitigated defense of Stoic externalism with an internalistic supplement, see Annas, "Stoic Epistemology," 194–202; Casey Perin, "Stoic Epistemology and the Limits of Externalism," *Ancient Philosophy* 25, no. 2 (2005): 389–99; Tamer Nawar, "The Stoic Account of Apprehension," *Philosopher's Imprint* 14, no. 29 (2014): 3–6, 11–15.

⁷ As Long and Sedley clarify (LS 1, 251), Zeno adds a condition to his account of the apprehensive impression in response to Arcesilaus, stipulating "that only real things as they really are can produce the clarity and distinctness characteristic of cognitive [apprehensive] impressions." Cf. Tobias Reinhardt, "Cicero and Augustine on Grasping the True," in *Philosophie in Rom—Römische Philosophie?: Kultur-, literatur- und philosophiegeschichtliche Perspektiven*, Beiträge zur Altertumskunde vol. 358, ed. Gernot Michael Müller and Fosca Marinani Zini (Berlin: De Gruyter, 2017), 310. For Reinhardt, Cicero's translation of φαντασία as *visum* reflects Zeno's realist view of perception. As stipulated in Chapter 1, if sayables subsist independent of any rational agent having an impression (*M.* 9.211 (= *SVF* 2.341, LS 55B)), then consideration of Zeno's realist view of perception ought to examine such semantic contents. See also Mauro Bonazzi, *Il Platonismo* (Turin: Einaudi, 2015), 48.

⁸ Robert Brandom, *Making It Explicit: Reasoning, Representing, and Discursive Commitment* (Cambridge, MA: Harvard University Press, 1994), 72–4, esp. 73: "[. . .] representational purport is what is *expressed* by a representing, for instance a sign design, rather than what is *represented* by it if it is successful." Brandom uses the locution "as if of" to describe the purport of a sign design (rather than what is represented by the sign design).

This causal model of representation ought to be an effective resource for an argumentative strategy equipped to defend the model against any interlocutor challenging its coherence or legitimacy. That is to say, defenders of the Stoic model ought to be able to establish that a sufficiently large set of impressions for human beings represent the way bodies are *anyway*. The challenge for representationalism is routinely specified and rationally reconstructed in modern doxographies of Hellenistic philosophy in terms of an "epistemological debate," which concerns the question of the criterion of truth.[9] To alter the mode of rational reconstruction by focusing instead on the ontology of representationalism, the question of the criterion of truth for early canonical Stoicism can be reformulated in the following way: how is it that human animals are able to guarantee that a sufficiently large set of representations are veridical, given that, *ex hypothesi*, such animals are constitutionally unable to bypass their (mediated) representations and assess their representations in view of some unmediated access to bodies in the world? Since the causal model precludes an unmediated or non-representational access to individual beings, a special subset of representations will have to function as the intentional states grounding an animal's access to what is there *anyway*. Now the propositional content embedded in each and every impression can be questioned, and so on those occasions when a Stoic defends a proposition as true against an interlocutor who might dispute its veracity, the Stoic defender would presumably resort to the fundamentals of his dialectical training, that is, to a method of defending in question and answer a given impression or claim as true. An integral feature of the science of dialectic is the defense of such claims as claims that represent what is really true. Given that some purported representations are often found to be false, in the sense that they do not come from what actually obtains, the challenge is therefore to identify the conditions according to which impressions successfully represent what actually obtains independent of any given mortal animal's representation.

In fact, Zeno himself provides an account of the apprehensive impression that specifies the conditions according to which a human can be certain that a representation grasps "the individual indication" (*propriam* [*quandam haberent*] *declarationem earum rerum*, Cicero, *Acad.* 1.41 (< LS 40B, SVF 1.55, cf. 1.60, part, 1.61)) identifying a given body and differentiating it from other

---

[9] Striker, "Κριτήριον τῆς ἀληθείας," in *Essays on Hellenistic Epistemology*, 22: "The epistemological debate between the Greek philosophical schools of the third and second centuries BCE—the Skeptics on the one hand and the Stoics and Epicureans on the other—can be described without undue simplification as a dispute over the question of the criterion of truth."

intrinsically individualized bodies. These conditions stipulate the terms of Zeno's instruction for the cultivation of infallible assent, that is, the norm that a human being striving to perfect one's rationality ought to assent only to apprehensive impressions. As epistemological centrists tend to emphasize, Zeno's account draws in part on the discussion of knowledge in Plato's *Theaetetus*. His account employs terminology used in the discussion of the alleged criterion of perceptual knowing, especially the terminology of "stamping" in the wax tablet analogy.[10] Again, Zeno maintains, in stipulating the conditions of the apprehensive impression, that human beings experience and frequently give assent to a special kind of perceptual impression capable of representing some individual body as it really presents itself in the world. Assent to a true representation entails that the representation is that which could not come from what fails to present itself in space and time.[11] Zeno grants that human experience involves the formation of false or spurious impressions, but the important point to emphasize is that some perceptual impressions, according to Zeno, represent the relevant properties of bodies marking each as an individual body that it is *anyway*. Zeno joins the notion of a perceptual criterion to a realist ontology, what moderns might prefer to call a rather "luxuriant ontology," thereby abandoning the questionable criterion of Protagorean relativism in *Theaetetus*.[12] On this realist construal of what is there *anyway*, the soul of the mortal animal partaking in reason is causally affected by beings that present themselves as they really are, such that what appears in the soul of the individual animal can function as criterial for true objective judgments about other individual spatiotemporal bodies in themselves. In offering the following definition of the apprehensive impression, Zeno identifies the three conditions under which an impression effectively represents what originally presents itself. An impression is apprehensive if it [1] "comes from what is present or obtains (ἀπὸ ὑπάρχοντος)," and [2] "is stamped and impressed in accordance with that very present or obtaining thing itself (κατ' αὐτὸ τὸ ὑπάρχον ἐναπομεμαγμένη καὶ ἐναπεσφραγισμένη)," and finally [3] "is of such a kind as could not come about from what is not present/does not

---

[10] Anna Maria Ioppolo, "Presentation and Assent: a Physical and Cognitive Problem in Early Stoicism," *Classical Quarterly* 40 (1990): 433–49; Anthony A. Long, "Zeno's Epistemology and Plato's *Theaetetus*," in *From Epicurus to Epictetus* (Oxford: Clarendon Press, 2006), 223–35.

[11] In view of D.L. 7.52, some Stoics evidently claimed that κατάληψις is not strictly perceptual, such that there are cases in which reasonable impressions are formed of non-empirical or non-perceptual matters. Tad Brennan, "Reasonable Impressions in Stoicism," *Phronesis* 41, no. 3 (1996): 323–6, makes the case for non-perceptual apprehensive impressions on the basis of a passage concerning the Stoic Sphaerus (D.L. 7.177). Cf. Nawar, "Apprehension," 7–9.

[12] Brandom, *Making It Explicit*, 71. For Brandom, "ontological self-indulgence" is a comparatively harmless vice, but it can be "symptomatic of a failure to shoulder an explanatory burden."

obtain (ὁποία οὐκ ἂν γένοιτο ἀπὸ μὴ ὑπάρχοντος)."[13] The first two conditions stipulate that [1] apprehensive impressions must be appropriately caused and that [2] such impressions must represent the obtaining body with sufficient accuracy. It is said that Zeno adds condition [3] in response to arguments from indiscernibility raised by Arcesilaus (Cicero, *Acad*. 2.77 (= *SVF* 1.59, part), cf. Sextus, *M*. 7.253). With condition [3], Zeno responds to the polemic of Arcesilaus by explicitly ruling out the counterfactual possibility that an apprehensive impression could have come from what is not spatiotemporally present, or causally networked in space and time. More explicitly than the other conditions, condition [3] designates the metaphysics fundamental to the instruction for the cultivation of infallible knowledge, for with this condition in particular, as I now argue, Zeno appeals to a notion of possibility in the general sense of what could and what could not come to be.

Conditions [1] and [2] repackage the terminology of the wax tablet as used in *Theaetetus*. Plato and Zeno compare the soul to a tablet of wax upon which stampings and impressions are inscribed.[14] For Zeno, however, some individual body comprised of an inherent identity of its own causes the experience and formation of apprehensive impressions. The human animal assents to an impression because a real being, along with its "individual indication," presents itself through the medium of representation as what actually obtains. The veracity of the apprehensive impression derives from what really obtains independent of the mortal animal's rational capabilities. Despite Zeno's commitment to a realist ontology of individual beings, the discussion of perception and appearance in *Theaetetus* is still significant for the Stoic articulation of a distinct notion of κατάληψις. The root word of Zeno's notion is the verb λαμβάνειν, which denotes in Plato's dialogue the psychological activity of "grasping" something true or false. Zeno's innovation is to conceive of a distinct epistemic type of "grasping" that takes hold of what is necessarily true in so far as the impression is taken to have embedded within it real propositional content corresponding to what actually obtains independent of the impression. Notwithstanding Zeno's deviation from the usage of λαμβάνειν in *Theaetetus*, the meaning of "grasp[-ing]"

---

[13] Sextus Empiricus, *M*. 7.248 (< LS 40E): "ἀπὸ ὑπάρχοντος καὶ κατ' αὐτὸ τὸ ὑπάρχον ἐναπομεμαγμένη καὶ ἐναπεσφραγισμένη, ὁποία οὐκ ἂν γένοιτο ἀπὸ μὴ ὑπάρχοντος." Cf. 7.402 (< LS 40H), 426, 11.183, *PH* 2.4, D.L. 7.46 (= LS 40C), 7.50 (< LS 39A). For a similar translation and examination of Zeno's definition, which initiates though does not fully complete the task of specifying the metaphysical aspect of incorporeal beings and the definition as a whole, see Stojanović, "Apprehensive Appearances," 169.
[14] Aristotle (*DA* 2.12, 424a17–26) uses the wax analogy to explain the capacity of the senses to "grasp" (λαμβάνει) the "mark" (σημεῖον) of a certain sensible thing without receiving the matter of that thing.

at 208c–e prefigures one other important aspect of Stoic doctrine. Here Plato's Socrates, moving beyond the examination of Protagorean doctrine, is interested in clarifying for Theaetetus the notion of "true belief with an account":

> If you grasp the distinguishing characteristic that distinguishes one being from other beings (τὴν διαφορὰν ἑκάστου ἂν λαμβάνῃς ᾗ τῶν ἄλλων διαφέρει) . . . you will grasp a *logos* of that being . . . (208d5–7)
>
> And whoever along with correct belief about a given being grasps in addition its distinguishing characteristic (τὴν διαφορὰν) by which it differs from [all] other beings will have become a knower of the being about which he previously believed. (208e3–5)

Socrates describes the activity of epistemic grasping in terms of grasping "some mark" (τι σημεῖον, 208c7) of a given being, such that the "distinguishing characteristic" in virtue of which the self-identical being that "differs from all other beings" (τῶν ἁπάντων διαφέρει, 208c8) delivers the rational basis of true belief. In clarifying Stoic κατάληψις, Cicero's Varro refers explicitly to Zeno's preferred Greek term φαντασία, in order to trace the origin of impressions to a kind of "externally induced impact" (*oblata extrinsecus*). The apprehensive impression is the special type of impression that Zeno trusts because it represents the "individual indications" of the corresponding things themselves that originally cause the apprehensive impression to come into being.

Zeno's condition [3]—"is *of such a kind* that it could not come to be from what is not present/does not obtain"—attaches a supplemental, internalistic claim to the apprehensive impression. Accordingly, apprehensive impressions are of a certain kind, namely, they are the kind of impression that has the distinctive feature of being "clear" (*perspicuitas*) and "evident" (*evidentia*, Cicero, *Acad.* 2.17, 2.45–6).[15] Moreover, for Cicero's Lucullus, it is the case for Zeno that an impression can serve as the criterion of truth if it is taken to possess that distinctive characteristic (*proprium*): the true-tracking feature of an apprehensive impression. Apprehensive impressions bear the individualized *nota* or "mark" (*Acad.* 2.33, 36 (= LS 42F)) of the real beings causing them to arise, and this feature also serves to distinguish them as a kind from non-apprehensive impressions, which convey no such clear or evident mark. The

---

[15] Myles F. Burnyeat, "The Origins of Non-Deductive Inference," in Barnes et al., *Science and Speculation*, 194, argues that talk of clarity and distinctness is internalist. The claim that φ is clear and evident is the claim that φ is clear and evident to some hypothetical "agent" in such a way that the agent infers that φ obtains as true. On a similar basis, Nawar ("Apprehension," 10–16) argues against purely externalistic interpretations of automatic assent. Below I follow Nawar in rendering *evidentia*/ἐνάργεια with the abstract noun "evidentness" (2 n3).

claim is designated internalistic because it requires the human animal to have some awareness of the clarity of the impression relative to the actual obtaining body that caused it.[16] While apprehensive impressions internally represent with accuracy the relevant features of the external body that causes the representation to arise, such impressions are also special for being taken up as clear or evident. For this reason, the internalistic claim of condition [3] supplements the external requirement of condition [1], which stipulates that apprehensive impressions are appropriately caused, and the external requirement of condition [2], which stipulates that such impressions are accurate with respect to the very obtaining body that caused it. Condition [3] reinforces those external conditions, but it also alludes to the internal character of apprehensive impressions for human beings: clarity and evidentness. The apprehensive impression is therefore the means by which the soul of a mortal animal partaking in reason apprehends a perceptible state of affairs regarding some present body, and the content of this special kind of representation is taken to express a proposition p that represents clearly and evidently some perceptible state of affairs about a real body B that is spatiotemporally present. Mortal animals with reason can guarantee that a representation is veridical if and only if the impression comes from, or is appropriately caused by, the external body that is present *and* there is the kind of internal relation between the animal and the impression in which the animal entertains the impression as clear and evident. The representation is veridical if the impression provides the animal with a certain kind of rational basis for believing that p obtains, a basis which the animal appreciates as the rational ground for the belief that p obtains. In addition, for an impression to be an apprehensive impression, the impression must also be the kind of impression that the animal recognizes as the rational basis for eliminating other possibilities. So, for example, if a mortal animal partaking in reason has the impression that the individual before it is Nina, that impression cannot be apprehensive if it is possible for all the animal knows on the basis of that impression that that individual is *not* Nina. The rational basis for truly believing that the present body is Nina is supplied by the apprehensive impression of Nina, and that is because the impression has provided a reason for believing that the present animal is Nina, the kind of incontrovertible reason that leaves the animal with no grounds

---

[16] In a passage distinguishing earlier and later Stoics on the issue of impressions, Sextus reports that the apprehensive impression commands assent in being "clear" or "evident" (ἐναργής, M. 7.257, 403) and "striking" (πληκτική, M. 7.257, 7.403). Without mention of older or later Stoics, Sextus elsewhere reports that the Stoics in general thought of the apprehensive impression as "intense" (ἔντονος, M. 7.408), "distinct," or "imprinted" (ἔκτυπος, M. 7.171, cf. D.L. 7.46 (= LS 40C) for the denial of ascribing ἔκτυπος and τρανής ("clarity") to non-apprehensive impressions).

for doubting that here stands Nina. As we shall see, Zeno and his followers are inclined to deny, with the help of an appeal to the clarity and evidentness of apprehensive impressions, the possibility that a clear and evident impression could have come from what is not present.

It is likely that Zeno's successors elaborated on his original terminology, and did so in ways that intentionally or unintentionally preserve the influence of the discussion in *Theaetetus* of "true belief with an account." In sources that refer to the Stoa generally, new terminology is used to clarify the notion of the "individual indication," such that now each individual body is qualitatively unique and individualized in virtue of possessing its own "peculiar quality" (ἰδία ποιότης, Stobaeus, *Ecl.* 1.177.21–179.17 (= LS 28D)). One passage from Sextus Empiricus, speaking of the Stoa generally, identifies the decisive role of "peculiar qualities" for the successful grasping of things as they really are:

> Not to mention its being stamped and impressed, so that all the peculiarities of the things that appear are skillfully stamped on (πάντα τεχνικῶς τὰ ἰδιώματα τῶν φανταστῶν ἀναμάττηται). For just as carvers tackle all the parts of things they are completing, and in the same way as seals on signet rings always stamp all their markings exactly on the wax, so too those who arrive at apprehension of the underlying things ought to focus on all their peculiarities.... For the Stoics say that the person who has the apprehensive impression skillfully gets in touch with the objective difference in the things (τῇ ὑπούσῃ τῶν πραγμάτων διαφορᾷ) since this kind of impression has a certain peculiarity, compared with other appearances, like what horned snakes have compared with other snakes. (Sextus, *M.* 7.250–2 (< LS 40E, SVF 2.65, part))[17]

Suppose for a moment that one could confirm that this is a later refinement of Zeno's canonical formulation of apprehension; as such, the analogue between the stamping of seals from signet rings and the empirical stamping of impressions from things is still at work in both formulations, preserving the realism of the causal model in Zeno's impressionism.[18] In the causal model of Stoic apprehension generally, the core claim remains intact: bodies convey through the medium of

---

[17] Casey Perin, "Academic Arguments for the Indiscernibility Thesis," *Pacific Philosophical Quarterly* 86, no. 4 (2005): 496, 514 n13, observes that the apprehensive impression need not grasp "all the properties" of an object, but rather that collection of properties or peculiar qualities such that a given object is the *only object in the world* that possesses that collection. On such appeals to the world, cf. n61 below.

[18] Chrysippus moves away from conceiving the impression in relation to an imprinting on the soul (Sextus, *M.* 7.228–36). Nevertheless, his account retains the causal model of "impressor" and "impression" (φανταστόν/φαντασία). Cf. Aëtius, 4.12.1–5 (= SVF 2.54, part, LS 39B) for Chrysippus' formulation of "impression," linking the etymology of both terms in the causal model with the effects of "light" (φῶς, or ἀπὸ τοῦ φωτός).

perception the relevant indication, or underlying "objective difference," of the real individual body that is spatiotemporally present for some human animal. Zenonian impressionism must, in its early or later formulations, rely on a realist ontology of individual bodies in order to articulate and defend the notion of the apprehensive impression.

The instruction that humans ought to cultivate the disposition of infallible assent sanctions the voluntary giving of assent only to apprehensive impressions. As a specific instruction, it makes use of an ontology of individual bodies in which bodies often present themselves as they really are in a particular place and at a particular time. The posit of this instruction involves, therefore, an "absolute conception" of reality, a conception of the real posited not only as being there *anyway*, namely, independent of the representations of any mortal animal, but a reality to which all representations are related and analyzed for epistemic success or failure.[19] The basic metaphysical assumption of Stoic impressionism is that human animals find themselves at some place and time in a causal relation with real individual bodies that already have their own properties and dispositions. A notion of individual bodies is already at work conceptually in the initial drawing of the boundary between the external body (cause) and the impression/representation (effect). Furthermore, given that each and every numerically distinct body differs—in what might be an improved account of Stoic impressionism—from every other with respect to at least one intrinsic property, the updated causal account also depends on a conception of the totality of individual beings (corporeal and incorporeal), in the same way that Zeno's earlier formulation depends on a conception of the totality of individual beings. As noted above, Zeno's impressionism presupposes that each and every causal body has its own "individual indication" to present in the transaction with the souls of mortal animals partaking in reason. By revising the account such that it affirms that any given body has its own peculiar qualities, rendering it distinguishable from every other causal body, the causal account of κατάληψις maintains its commitment to a realism of absolute difference. That is, in the transactional model of impressionism, bodies are conceived as bearing some real relation with other corporeal and incorporeal beings, thereby setting up the overall ontological conditions of epistemic success for κατάληψις. The realism of absolute difference is committed to the view that a thing or being is not identical with any other actual or possible thing, but intrinsically identical with itself

---

[19] Williams, *Descartes*, 196: "the 'absolute conception' of reality—a conception of reality as it is independently of our thought, and to which all representations of reality are related."

alone, independent of its appearance to any given mortal agent. The realism of absolute difference for early canonical Stoicism is defined by the premise that "no [corporeal] thing is identical with something else" (Cicero, *Acad*. 2.85, 2.56). So for any body *x*, for any body *y*, if *x* is numerically distinct from *y*, then there is some collection of properties *p* such that *x* is *p* and *y* is not *p*. Given that *x* is a body and identical with itself alone, it must also be distinct in kind from every other incorporeal thing, for properties are themselves bodies and incorporeal things do not possess physical properties. Zeno's account of κατάληψις and what appears to be its improved formulation require a certain ontological context for the alleged infallibility of apprehension to be possible for human animals.

Indiscernible Beings

At this point, it is appropriate to clarify the task of this study as the task of specifying *de re* how Arcesilaus's indiscernibility arguments function to challenge the ontological context(s) of apprehension. Let me continue to suppose that the early Stoic commitment to absolute difference is later refined by the specification of peculiar qualities.[20] It makes no difference to the *de re* interpretation *de traditione* offered here whether that specification originated with Zeno's causal model or with one of his early canonical followers. Either way, the arguments issued by Arcesilaus would function to challenge the implied ontological context of Zeno's earlier specification, in which bodies causally present their own "individual indications." The task of this philosophical historiography is not to identify the origin and evolution of the Stoic commitment to metaphysical uniqueness, or to defend the supposition that the terminology expressing commitment to metaphysical uniqueness was originally added to Zeno's realist

[20] I recommend, on this question, the cautious statement of Frede, "Stoic Epistemology," 300: "It is difficult to say, though, to what extent the more elaborate theory attributed in our sources to the Stoics in general can be traced back to Zeno himself." According to David Sedley, "The Stoic Criterion of Identity," *Phronesis* 27 (1982): 263-4, the early Stoic view of external objects is subject to a uniqueness thesis, that is, the thesis that each and every external object is an individual object because "every individual object is qualitatively unique." In his reconstruction of the Stoic response to the Academic criticism of this thesis—a reconstruction that ventures beyond direct evidence for peculiar qualities (D.L. 7.58 (= LS 33M), Stob., *Ecl.* 1.177.21–1.179.17 (= LS 28D), Plutarch, *Comm. not.* 1077c (< LS 28O), Philo, *De immut. mundo* 48 2.397 (< LS 28P))—Sedley speculates that "it was not until Chrysippus appeared on the scene that a full scale defence of infallible perception was launched." A later full-scale defense mounted by Chrysippus does not mean, however, that the uniqueness thesis originated with him. As Sedley states, Chrysippus "defended a position, which may or may not have originated with him, that there is never any need to misidentify an external object, *because every individual object is qualitatively unique*." One implication of this reconstruction is that infallible perception likely came under attack by an Academic prior to Chrysippus defending the position.

account by Chrysippus himself, or some other follower of Zeno. The task is rather to defend the view that Arcesilaus's indiscernibility arguments are just as effective at undermining the ontological context of peculiar qualities as they are at undermining articulations of Zenonian impressionism without the explicit language of peculiar qualities.

The opening move of indiscernibility arguments is the provisional acceptance of Zeno's ideal of cultivating infallible assent (Cicero, *Acad.* 2.77). By provisional acceptance, I mean accepting or conceding a proposition or claim as a basis for further argument. The arguments provisionally accept that the first two external conditions of Zeno's account of the apprehensive impression are often satisfied. Moreover, for the sake of critically testing the accepted ideal and its dependence on both conditions, Arcesilaus's arguments introduce cases of indiscernible beings. Arguments from indiscernible beings accept [1] that there are impressions coming from what obtains, [2] that often enough impressions are stamped and impressed in accordance with the very substantial being that obtains, and finally that mortal animals partaking in reason ought to assent only to those impressions that come from what obtains, stamped and impressed in accordance with the substantial being that obtains. To reiterate this sequence of the argument, it is assumed that there are true impressions in the restricted sense that conditions [1] and [2] stipulate. But to accept the veridicality of some impressions in the Stoic sense, the arguments must also accept the metaphysical premises involved in the first two conditions of the causal account, namely, that external bodies are causally efficacious in stamping and impressing themselves on the souls of mortal animals partaking in reason.[21] For impressions to be true in this sense, the impression must represent the very body that obtains and causes the stamping and impressing. Lest one forgets: it is alleged that Zeno himself assigned bodies their own identifying marks, so that a true impression would have to represent at minimum "the individual indication" (Cicero, *Acad.* 1.40–1 (= *SVF* 1.55, 1.61, 60, part, LS 40B)) that determines the identity of the causal body obtaining relative to a human animal in some causal scenario. Take, for instance, the individual being named Oedipus. The quality of being Oedipus may be either a single quality O-ness or an identifying collection of common qualities marking the individual Oedipus. In compliance with the veridicality of impressions accepted in the opening moves of the argument, Arcesilaus tacitly accepts the causal premise

---

[21] Thorsrud, "Socratic Skepticism," 205, claims that Arcesilaus's provisional agreement with Zeno's view that the wise person will have no mere opinions extends to the "whole package of Stoic epistemology and ethics." On my view, the package is whole because it implicates the structure of Stoic metaphysics.

that impressions come from individual beings like Oedipus, which might obtain in a spatiotemporal network, and the premise that impressions are often caused in the appropriate way for correctly representing what obtains relative to the actual substantial body. Finally, it is said that Arcesilaus accepts as seemingly true Zeno's claim that it is possible for a human being not to opine, and that it is even necessary to avoid opining for the achievement of wisdom (Cicero, *Acad.* 2.77, cf. 2.66). Independent of considering how Arcesilaus himself conceived of these stratagems and of his own commitments to the provisionally accepted premises, the effect of granting these concessions before the actual introduction of indiscernible beings is to force Zeno, or some other Stoic follower, to improve and revise condition [2]. If it turns out that the Stoic cannot adequately respond to arguments from indiscernible beings, then the ideal of the sage as one who does not opine but assents to a system of apprehensive impressions would be just another opinion. Zeno's account of the sage would therefore epitomize, according to his own requirements, the foolishness of a non-sage making assertions and issuing opinions about the requirements of possible sagehood. In other words, his view of the sage would turn out to be nothing other than an instance of the error the purported sage is supposed to avoid, rendering the articulation of this account of sagehood a shameful assertion of foolishness. In this light, the Stoic would be making false assertions by believing in what Zeno considers to be a possibility for human beings. If, on the other hand, condition [2] is successfully defended or revised, it would eliminate the possibility of a non-apprehensive impression coming to be and representing its content in the way in which an apprehensive impression of that external thing actually represents it, and the dependency of the Stoic sage on the apprehensive impression would be upheld.

Recent scholars agree with the claim that Arcesilaus's arguments prompt Zeno to clarify his defense of the apprehensive impression by adding condition [3]. What is more, there is the credible view that these arguments are the source of the Academic conclusion that condition [3] can never be satisfied or successfully defended.[22] Again, it is important to stress that the provisional concessions of conditions [1] and [2] include provisional concessions to the metaphysical views embedded within the causal model, views giving content or substance to conditions [1] and [2]. This inclusion is obscured by the selective analysis of epistemological centrism in the historiography of this dispute, as the content of Stoic physics is typically excluded by centrists favoring the humanistic focus of epistemological specification. In other words, Arcesilaus's anti-Stoic arguments

---

[22] E.g., Brittain, "Introduction," xxi.

provisionally concede conditions [1] and [2], but epistemological centrists almost invariably present Zeno's defense of the apprehensive impression by concealing the implied metaphysical reference to bodies and incorporeal beings.[23] Margherita Isnardi Parente shares an important insight neglected by the *de re* specifications *de traditione* which make "Stoic epistemology," or the "Stoic account of apprehension," the central organizing theme of humanistic reconstruction. Isnardi Parente states: "Non possiamo comprendere appieno questa posizione gnoseologica se non teniamo conto dell'impostazione *fisica zenoniana* [italics added]; . . . fisica e logica, nella filosofia ellenistica, si implicano strettissimamente, e la fisica è condizione prima della teoria del conoscere" ("We cannot fully understand this gnoseological position if we do not take into account *Zenonian physics* [. . .]; physics and logic, in Hellenistic philosophy, are strictly implicated, and physics is the primary condition of the theory of knowing").[24] Apply this observation of implication to the alternative *de re* interpretation *de traditione* presented here. The application yields the following insight: historiographers do not accurately specify, or rationally reconstruct, what Stoic epistemology *really* entails if they fail to specify the structure of Zeno's ontology of apprehension. With the help of this insight, the deficiency of epistemological centrism emerges more clearly. To reiterate the alternative metaphysical specification, Arcesilaus's arguments accept *a limine* the metaphysical background of the first two conditions, stipulated by Zeno's causal model: [1] that apprehensive impressions come ἀπὸ ὑπάρχοντος, that is, from causally efficacious bodies that really obtain in relation to a human being in a particular spatiotemporal configuration, and [2] that apprehensive impressions come from such bodies obtaining in a particular spatiotemporal configuration with their own individual indications stamped and impressed on the receptive body of the mortal animal partaking in reason. As a result, Arcesilaus provisionally concedes that some impressions coming from bodies that obtain in space and time are often *true*. Now, indiscernibility arguments

---

[23] On the epistemology of the apprehensive impression in a standard summary of Arcesilaus's counter-arguments, see Brittain, "Arcesilaus," § 3, suitably entitled "Criticism of Stoic Epistemology." The first premise that Arcesilaus provisionally grants is adumbrated in a way that conceals any reference to the metaphysical conception of individual bodies. The adumbrated premise reads: 1. "some impressions are true (a Stoic view)." See also Castagnoli, "Hellenistic Academy," 191–2, for the epistemological formulation "some impressions are false (not all impressions are true)." To assume the Stoic premise that "some impressions are true," or that "not all impressions are true," one must also assume that some impressions derive from the causal power of individual bodies, for the Stoic view "some impressions are true" entails that *some of the impressions that come from individual bodies that obtain are true* about the bodies and the incorporeal beings in the causal network in which bodies and incorporeals obtain.

[24] Margherita Isnardi Parente, *Introduzione a lo stoicismo ellenistico* (Rome: Editori Laterza, 1993), 12.

undermine condition [3] by challenging an assumption concerning the way that bodies supposedly present themselves, namely, the way that bodies with individual indications make apprehensive impressions possible. In sum, the preliminary concessions concerning external conditions [1] and [2] make it possible for Arcesilaus to argue that *true* impressions can be representationally indistinguishable from false impressions and that, to use the terms of Sextus, "no true impression is found to be such that it could not become false" (οὐδεμία τοιαύτη ἀληθὴς φαντασία εὑρίσκεται οἵα οὐκ ἂν γένοιτο ψευδής, *M.* 7.154).

These concessions initiate a *reductio ad absurdum* argument against the causal model. *Reductio ad absurdum* arguments typically start by granting the premises under examination and then proceed until they come to an absurd or impossible conclusion, thereby showing the initial premises to be problematic, if not false. The argument to absurdity in this case grants a number of metaphysical premises built into the causal account, and proceeds to connect those premises to absurd conclusions. In order to explicate the reasoning that reduces Stoic metaphysics to its own absurd conclusions, thus associating the absurdities with the overall incoherence of the causal model of Stoic apprehension, one must reconstruct the arguments from indiscernible beings and from dreaming states, hallucinations, and fits of madness (*Acad.* 2.54–8, 2.84–6).

Arguments from indiscernible beings (twins, pairs of eggs, grains of sand, etc.) and from the states of dreams, hallucinations, and madness are what Arcesilaus's (Stoic) opponents depicted as weapons that he deployed "in his effort to conceal the clearest things in darkness" (*conatus est clarissimis rebus tenebras obducere, Acad.* 2.16 (= LS 68C)).[25] Proponents of epistemological centrism construe this accusation on the part of his opponents as the accusation that his polemical arguments were deployed to carry out an epistemological offensive against the apprehensive impression, such that for Zeno and canonical Stoa "the clearest things"—the "things" or "objects" often left unspecified as causal *bodies* with individual indications in the standard reconstructions of epistemological centrism—now seem inaccessible to epistemic subjects, and that is because, again, the epistemic possibility of the apprehensive impression is

---

[25] Cf. Sextus, *M.* 7.402–8 (< LS 40H). Perin, "Academic Arguments," 507–8, argues that Sextus's interpretation of the Academic appeal to dreams and madness is misleading, to the "extent that it presents the Academic appeal to the false impressions entertained in dreams and madness as intended to establish only that certain false impressions are indiscernible with respect to the features of clearness and vivacity from any true perceptual impression of ordinary waking experience." For Perin, the appeal to dreams and madness is meant to establish the more general conclusion that the false impressions entertained in dreams and madness are "indiscernible with respect to the way in which they *represent their objects from some actual or possible true perceptual impressions*" (italics added).

construed as the focal point of the dispute.[26] In epistemological reconstructions, arguments from indiscernible beings and psychic states seem to have a certain metaphysical neutrality with respect to Zeno's causal model. By neutrality, I mean that Arcesilaus's arguments do not purport to challenge the content and systematicity of Zeno's metaphysical views as those views support and substantiate his impressionism.

With the introduction of indiscernible beings, the arguments against condition [3] oppose Zeno's attempt to eliminate the possibility that apprehensive impressions are of such a kind that they *could come* from what does not obtain. Arguments from indiscernible beings aim to establish that it is possible to receive an impression from what does not obtain with exactly the same representational content as a true impression that comes from a body that actually obtains. In pursuit of this aim, the arguments conceding the metaphysical background of the causal model focus on attacking Zeno's attempt to eliminate the possibility that apprehensive impressions could come from what does not obtain. Arcesilaus submits a counterfactual possibility with the introduction of indiscernible beings: that for any numerically distinct body or substantial being *B*, there could have been at least one other numerically distinct body or substantial being *B** that is indiscernible from *B* and capable of causing an impression with the same representational content as a true impression coming from substantial being *B*. The argument from indiscernible beings is most commonly taken to be an argument for the epistemological thesis that it is not possible—relative to what a given epistemic subject knows on a given occasion—to assent to apprehensive impressions, given the conditions that Zeno requires for apprehensive impressions to originate. This thesis is often designated

---

[26] E.g., Brittain, "Arcesilaus," § 3 ("Criticism of Stoic Epistemology"): vague reference to generic or nonspecific "objects" of grasping is entirely detached from the specification of the doctrines of early Stoic physics. For an account that recognizes the ontological significance of Arcesilaus' attack on Stoic apprehension, see Olof Gigon, "Zur Geschichte der sogenannten Neuen Akademie," *Museum Helveticum* 1 (1944): 51–3. The problem with Gigon's ontological reconstruction is that it ascribes to Arcesilaus an esoteric ontology of intelligible beings, from which he allegedly countered the Stoic metaphysics of bodies. The esoteric interpretation has been decisively refuted, most thoroughly, by Carlos Lévy, "Scepticisme et dogmatisme dans l'Académie: l'ésotérisme d'Arcésilas," *Revue des Études latines* 56 (1978): 335–48. Bonazzi, "Plutarch," 286–7, 291, offers a different perspective on Arcesilaus's relation to ontological dualism, arguing that for Plutarch, Arcesilaus's criticism of Stoic philosophy "implies a conception of reality" that is compatible with that of "explicit dualists" such as Parmenides and Plato. Bonazzi claims that Arcesilaus's metaphysical skepticism "argues for dualism," as it paves the way for a different dualistic account of reality. Here Bonazzi ventures into speculative *de dicto* ascription. Ascribing to Arcesilaus himself the belief in a "general structure of reality" that is dualistic is impossible to verify from our secondary sources. On my reading, Arcesilaus's criticism of Stoic philosophy does not imply a metaphysical conception of reality (monist or dualist) apart from the absurdly monistic one it derives from Stoic metaphysics, which is to say, merely, that his criticism shows that Stoic monism is problematic, if not false.

the thesis of ἀκαταληψία ("inapprehensibility"), which is frequently specified in the context of epistemological centrism as the epistemological specification [ES] that (ES1) "no knowledge is possible."[27] In a more recent study, the thesis of ἀκαταληψία is rendered equivalent to the specified proposition that (ES2) "no impression is cognitive [apprehensive]."[28] Earlier studies favor slightly different propositions for the specification of this thesis as it emerges in Stoic-Academic debates. Again, whereas recent centrists prefer to conceptualize ἀκαταληψία with a purely epistemological specification that (ES1) "no knowledge is possible," others prefer to specify the meaning of the thesis with the more ambiguous specification that "nothing is, or can be, known."[29] All three specifications usually take the negation of the alpha privative (α-) in ἀ-καταληψία to signify the negation or denial of Stoic apprehension. In other words, Arcesilaus's arguments against apprehensive impressions entail the negation of the power of apprehension, that is, the power of giving assent to apprehensive impressions. Again, Schofield makes the simplicity of this negation clear, simplifying the more ambiguous proposition(s) that "nothing is [or can be] known" or "nothing is known for certain" with what he takes to be the more "precise" formulation: that "there is no such thing as cognition [apprehension]."[30] Likewise, Ioppolo maintains "that Arcesilaus infers ἀκαταληψία [i.e., 'nothing can be known'] from his demonstration of the non-existence of the Stoic criterion," which is to say, the criterion of the apprehensive impression.[31] With the epistemic power of

[27] Gisela Striker, "On the Difference between the Pyrrhonists and the Academics," in *Essays on Hellenistic Epistemology*, 139. This formulation is consistent with Reid's epistemological view that "they [Arcesilaus and Carneades] never tried to show that *things in themselves* were incognizable, *but* that human faculties do not avail to give information about them." James S. Reid, ed., *The Academica of Cicero* (London, 1874), 147.

[28] Castagnoli, "Hellenistic Academy," 192. For another variety of this kind of epistemological specification, see Orazio Cappello, *The School of Doubt: Skepticism, History and Politics in Cicero's Academica* (Leiden: Brill, 2019), 1. Cappello specifies ἀκαταληψία in terms of impressions: the propositional content of ἀκαταληψία is specified as the "unknowability of all perceptual and conceptual objects (impressions, or *visa*)."

[29] Striker alternates between the proposition that (ES1) "no knowledge is possible" and the proposition that "nothing can be known." For the latter, see Gisela Striker, "Sceptical Strategies," in *Essays on Hellenistic Epistemology*, 92, 96. The proposition that "nothing is, or can be, known" is favored by Frede, "Two Kinds of Assent," 255; Henry Maconi, "*Nova Non Philosophandi Philosophia*: A review of Anna Maria Ioppolo, *Opinione e scienza*," *Oxford Studies in Ancient Philosophy* 6 (1988): 246; Richard Bett, "Carneades' *Pithanon*: A Reappraisal of Its Role and Status," *Oxford Studies in Ancient Philosophy* 7 (1989): 62; James Allen, "Carneadean Argument in Cicero's Academic Books," in Inwood et al., *Assent and Argument*, 220; Burnyeat, "Antipater," 292; Charles Brittain, *Philo of Larissa: The Last of the Academic Sceptics* (Oxford: Oxford University Press, 2001), 90; Brittain, "Introduction," xxii–xxiii; Brittain, "Arcesilaus," § 2; Perin, "Arcesilaus," 315–16, 328–9; Ioppolo, "Arcesilaus," 40.

[30] Similar to the specification of Schofield, there is the simplification endorsed by Harald Thorsrud, "Carneades," in Machuca et al., *Skepticism*, 52: "the Academic denial of κατάληψις (i.e., ἀκαταληψία)." See also Whitney Schwab, "Skeptical Defenses Against the Inaction Objection," in *The Routledge Handbook of Hellenistic Philosophy*, ed. Kelly Arenson (London: Routledge, 2020), 185, identifies "the thesis of *akatalēpsia*" with the "non-existence of *katalēpsis*."

[31] Ioppolo, "Arcesilaus," 41.

apprehension under the threat of negation, the defense of Zeno's epistemology would presumably find itself under pressure to counter the negative conclusion that "no knowledge is possible" by defending the possibility of apprehension and the power of epistemic subjects to give assent to apprehensive impressions.

Epistemological specifications (ES1–2) of ἀκαταληψία are concerned principally with the notion of epistemic possibility. The notion of possibility associated with these *de re* specifications is *epistemic* in virtue of their joint appeal to an idea of possibility that depends on implicit reference to a purported epistemic subject, and whether the impressions of such a subject can ever be, on any given occasion, apprehensive.[32] Even the more ambiguous proposition that "nothing is, or can be, known" is usually taken to follow from the negation of some purported subject's impressions *qua* apprehensive impressions. This proposition is more ambiguous because it could be specified without reference to the impressions of a purported epistemic subject. That is, it could be taken as a statement about the knowability of things independent of any purported epistemic subject; but scholars typically reduce the ambiguity of the proposition— "nothing is, or can be, known"—to one of the epistemological specifications (ES1 or ES2) that depend more precisely on the notion of epistemic possibility. To illustrate this dependence *in actu*, consider the following hypothetical:

> Suppose, for example, that a man were to meet Socrates, who was well-known to him, on the street and have the impression that this man is Socrates. How can he rule out in this situation that he is merely dreaming or that, unbeknownst to him, Socrates has a twin who looks deceptively similar to him? In these hypothetical circumstances, his impression would be exactly the same: hence, he cannot tell from *the impression alone* whether he is *really* dealing with Socrates, rather than his twin or a figure in a dream (italics added).[33]

---

[32] Williams, *Descartes*, 38–9, introduces the notion of "epistemic" possibility in the following way: "The idea that I might, on a given occasion, be mistaken involves the notion of what is often called *epistemic possibility*, a possibility relative to what one knows. The thought 'I might be mistaken' is, in such contexts, the thought 'for all I know, I am mistaken' . . . This is also how we should take the formulation which uses explicitly the notion of possibility: 'it is possible I am mistaken.'" Appropriating this notion, Perin, "Academic Arguments," 499–505, contrasts epistemic possibility with the notion of *counterfactual possibility*, identifying the latter correctly as the relevant notion of possibility in Arcesilaus's critical examination. Counterfactual possibility does not primarily involve or depend on an agent's epistemic position. Instead, counterfactual possibility involves the notion of what one may call *metaphysical possibility*, a possibility relative to the way that any two beings could have been or appeared.

[33] Striker, "Pyrrhonists and the Academics," 139–40; for similar analyses, in the same volume, see "The Problem of the Criterion," 159–60; Sedley, "Stoic Criterion of Identity," 263; Lévy, *Les philosophies hellénistiques*, 189–90; Schofield, "Academic Epistemology," 342–3; Simon Shogry, "Creating a Mind Fit for Truth: The Role of Expertise in the Stoic Account of the Kataleptic Impression," *Ancient Philosophy* 38, no. 2 (2018): 369–80; Vezzoli, *Arcesilao*, 103–4.

The scenario situates "Socrates" in what is on the canonical Stoic view a certain causal network of bodily interaction, and the truth-conditions of the impression depend entirely in this interpretation on the epistemic position of the subject who entertains the epistemic possibility of an impression coming from Socrates on the street. Under the regime of epistemological centrism, the ambiguous term "nothing" in "nothing is, or can be, known" is used grammatically as the subject term to denote the sum total of what a purported subject knows, or can know. In proposition ES2, the denial that "no impression is apprehensive" involves the negative qualification of epistemic possibility, for without the apprehensive impression the implication is that no knowledge is possible for epistemic subjects endowed with the power of giving or withholding assent to impressions. The indiscernibility argument is supposedly meant to demonstrate that in general epistemic subjects are unable to rule out from their *representations alone* the epistemic possibility that for any given occasion any given epistemic subject might be mistaken. The burden for the Stoic position is thus placed on the epistemic capacity of the subject with respect to their impressions, for the argument would first and foremost call into question the subjective capacity of assenting to impressions purportedly providing access to what *really* is the case.

In epistemological reconstructions, the primary function of the counterfactual is to question either *our* access to what is the case or the epistemic access of some generic human subject. In addition to abstracting from the Stoic specificity of the human animal, epistemological reconstructions dismiss without justification the relevance of Zeno's metaphysical views of causation in the formulation of the three conditions of the apprehensive impression. The metaphysical question of whether the world, and the bodies and incorporeals in the world, may or may not be structured in the way that Zeno and his followers asserted is cast outside the scope of interpretation, clearing conceptual space for the humanistic target of analysis: the epistemic success of human representations on any given occasion. That is to say, the reconstructions of epistemological centrism tend to construe the attack as if it principally contested whether the given human subject is in a position to guarantee, from impressions or representations alone, the epistemic possibility that the impression represents some real state of affairs (in whatever way such real states are conceptualized). With an attack on the notion of epistemic possibility, Arcesilaus supposedly generalizes from a particular occasion in which the human subject confronts an indiscernible being (say, Socrates or his twin) to the thesis that on any given occasion in which a subject receives impressions that subject could be mistaken. But if the arguments from indiscernible beings turn only on the notion of epistemic possibility, then why wouldn't the Stoic simply disarm the force of such arguments by conceding that in some very unusual situations when an impression seems to come from a perceptually indiscernible substantial body, there may not be for the mortal animal any corresponding apprehensive impressions that merit assent? In view of such situations, Zeno or any other Stoic might appropriately advise the suspension of assent, that is, whenever an animal has reason to infer, from the apparent absence of the relevant individual indicator coming from what obtains, that the identity of the body in the causal network appears indiscernible. In fact, this is consistent with the Stoic directive that human animals ought to assent only to apprehensive impressions that come from what actually obtains and what is appropriately caused by the very body that presents itself. One potential response that seems open to Zeno and his followers is to deny that there are any such indiscernible beings, despite the regularity or irregularity of appearances to the contrary, thereby maintaining that no individual body is actually identical with some other being or body.[34] In any case, indiscernibility arguments would then oppose the epistemic possibility of Stoic apprehension while leaving unchallenged the metaphysical premise of real individual bodies that the epistemic possibility of apprehension depends upon for the generation of true and false impressions.

There is textual support for thinking that indiscernibility arguments generalize from pairs of indiscernible beings in a way that differs from the humanistic accounts of prevailing epistemological reconstruction. On the present view defended here, generalization from indiscernibles functions to motivate the strikingly simple idea that for any given individual body endowed with causal power it is possible—independent of any critical reference to the epistemic position of a subject actually receiving an impression—for there to have been another numerically distinct body with causal power indiscernible from the former. In other words, arguments from identical twins show that for any actual body, even if there is in *actuality* no other being that is both numerically distinct and indiscernible from it, it is at least *possible* for there to have been another numerically distinct being indiscernible from the former. An effective way to motivate an argument for the conclusion that this is a genuine possibility for any given actual body is to begin with an appeal to beings that appear perceptually

---

[34] Frede, "Stoic Epistemology," 310, states that the Stoic response to Arcesilaus's argument is based on the *assumption* that "there are no indiscernibles." Frede claims that the "assumption is not *ad hoc*, but supported by Stoic physics and metaphysics." The claim begs the following question: What in turn supports the truth of Stoic physics and metaphysics?

indiscernible from one another (identical twins, snakes, eggs, etc.). Just as for such pairs of perceptually indiscernible bodies, it is possible that for any actual body with its individual indications, there could have been some other body perceptually indiscernible from it that actually obtains for a mortal animal with a true impression. For example, reconsider the example of Socrates present on the street: suppose that Socrates does not actually have a twin, and that some other mortal animal knows that this is a true proposition about Socrates, and that the soul of the one in such a causal interaction with Socrates on the street is stamped and impressed in accordance with the very Socrates obtaining on the street. And suppose, finally, that the subject forms a true impression of the one and only actual Socrates. Casey Perin successfully argues from this example that, even with these concessions granted, Arcesilaus could maintain that the following counterfactual conditional (CC) still remains a genuine possibility:

> [CC] *If* Socrates *had* a twin, i.e., *if* there *were* someone who is perceptually indiscernible from Socrates, and *if* as a result of looking at Socrates' twin I *had formed* the *false* impression that this person is Socrates, my false impression *would have* represented the person before me (= Socrates' twin) *as* Socrates in just the same way my true impression represents the person now before me (= Socrates) *as* Socrates.[35]

So never mind that Socrates, whom the animal has met on the street and knows well, does not *actually* have a twin brother. And never mind that the animal apprehends or knows that Socrates does not have a twin—on the assumption that there are straightforward ways of finding out that this proposition is true about Socrates. The point of the argument from indiscernibility is that it is nonetheless *possible* for Socrates to have had a twin who is perceptually indiscernible from Socrates himself, and it makes no difference whether that twin had ever actually appeared to any given subject or animal. It was noted above that Arcesilaus accepted the metaphysical background of causal conditions [1] and [2]. Now, though, it seems that Arcesilaus introduced a variation into the metaphysical background that challenges the subsequent addition of condition [3]. Consider the variation this way: whereas Arcesilaus conceded, provisionally, that there are true impressions that come from individual bodies obtaining in a causal network, he then introduced the variant counterfactual possibility that for any

---

[35] Casey Perin, "Descartes and the Legacy of Ancient Skepticism," in *A Companion to Descartes*, ed. Janet Broughton and John Carriero (Oxford: Blackwell Publishing, 2008), 58; for a different, but equally useful, example of the counterfactual conditional, see Perin, "Academic Arguments," 505.

individual body that actually presents itself, there could have appeared some other body indiscernible from it. What follows from this metaphysical variation for the causal model? On Perin's construal, the upshot of the CC is a simplistic epistemological thesis pertaining solely to impressions, namely, that "no true impression of O [formalistically, O = any perceptible object] is a cognitive impression."[36] In conformity with the modern doxographical conventions of epistemological centrism, Perin inserts a reference to a generic, formalistic "perceptible object" O that abstracts from specifying the necessary metaphysical attributes of the "object," which would give conceptual content to the causal model of Stoic apprehension. Given the usage of this abstract notation O, it is no surprise to find that Perin's reconstruction conceals the metaphysical aspect of ἀκαταληψία ("inapprehensibility") as specified in this study, the thesis that individual bodies themselves (not a generic "perceptible object") are inapprehensible, as the negative thesis that follows from the use of such CC against Zeno's causal model. In the following alternative reconstruction, I aim to explain how the introduction of CC is one of the first moves in an argument for a negative metaphysical thesis, which is an absurd thesis for Stoic epistemology and the overall coherence of the causal model.

The most extensive account of an indiscernibility argument (Cicero, *Acad.* 2.84–5 (< LS 40J)) supports the view that Arcesilaus and his Academic followers deploy anti-Stoic arguments by granting the metaphysical premise that there are in actuality individual bodies and that such bodies actually generate true impressions of what obtains.[37] Scholars are nearly unanimous in affirming that the critical strategy of later Academic arguments—those reportedly "retained by Lacydes and strengthened by Carneades" (*Acad.* 2.16 (= LS 68C))—continue the polemic of provisional concession while focusing the anti-Stoic attack on condition [3].[38] Cicero himself seems to continue this polemic with an appeal to a single case of indiscernible pairs, the identical twins Servilius and Quintus. From that single case, Cicero deduces the following conclusion:

---

[36] Perin, "Descartes," 59.
[37] At *Acad.* 2.84–5, Cicero replies to the metaphysical principle stated by Lucullus (*Acad.* 2.50, 54–8), which holds that nothing is identical with some other individual thing.
[38] Gourinat, "L'épistémologie stoïcienne," 136, is a notable exception. Gourinat infers from Cicero's recapitulation of Arcesilaus's challenge to condition [3] at *Acad.* 2.77–8 that Arcesilaus provoked Zeno's revisions with arguments that appealed only to instances of hallucination. However, the passage in question provides no grounds for such an inference. According to Sextus (*M.* 7.154 (< F 87 Vezzoli)), Arcesilaus used an assortment of arguments; but detailed discussion of his indiscernibility arguments are not found in Sextus.

You [as an adherent of Stoicism] deny that there is no such indiscernible likeness in the nature of things (*negas tantam similitudinem in rerum natura esse*) . . . Let it be that there is not, it [namely, the indiscernible likeness] could certainly appear to be so, and then it will mislead sensation (*ne sit sane: videri certe potest; fallet igitur sensum*). And so if a single case of indiscernible likeness could mislead, that one case could make all things doubtful.[39]

The standard English translation of *videri certe potest* ("there could be one [a single case of indiscernible likeness] between our impressions") specifies the content of *videri* with reference to "our impressions," even though the Latin phrase refers to the indiscernibility of *things* without any explicit mention of "impressions" being generated by such things for a subject. Importing the supposition that some hypothetical subject is the bearer of impressions, the standard translation has the passage read as if the indiscernibility of the likeness is the generated effect in some subject for whom the impressions actually appear indiscernible.[40] However, Cicero's use of the present infinitive *videri* does not require the technical Stoic terminology of impression, since the infinitive can convey in Cicero the less technical sense of "to appear" or "to seem."[41] Nevertheless, one might insist that *videri* does imply in this context a generic epistemic subject: namely, by inferring that in this context "it could appear so" means that "it could appear to any human subject to be so." This insistence labors under two difficulties: (1) as suggested, it is plain that the Latin *videri certe potest* makes no explicit reference to impressions or a human subject, and the addition of an implied subject is not required to make sense of the conditional. Also, (2) recall that the argument proceeds with an initial concession to a claim which makes no reference to a subject or to impressions, that is, the metaphysical claim that there is in actuality no "indiscernible likeness in the nature of things," and then the argument moves to juxtapose this metaphysical claim about actual things with the counterfactual possibility of a single case in which an indiscernible likeness

---

[39] Cicero, *Acad.* 2.84: *negas tantam similitudinem in rerum natura esse; pugnas omnino, sed cum adversario facili. ne sit sane: videri certe potest; fallet igitur sensum. et si una fefellerit similitudo, dubia omnia reddiderit.*

[40] Brittain, *Cicero*, 49. On this non-technical use of *videri* and its many nuances, see James S. Reid, ed., *M. Tulli Ciceronis, Academica* (London, 1885), 205 n17, and Reinhardt, "To See and to Be Seen," 69–72, and 78–90, who rightly criticizes the tendency to translate "all occurrences of variations of *quod videtur* or *visum* by using the English noun 'impression.'" Unfortunately, Reinhardt disregards the variant usage of *videri* at *Acad.* 2.84, thus failing to observe that Brittain's standard English translation of 2.84—the translation Reinhardt uses—is an instance of the homogenizing tendency he otherwise criticizes. For a different reading of *videri certe potest* at 2.84, which refers to the "appearing" (erscheinen) of "the things themselves" (die Dinge selber), a reading that abstains from importing a reference to impressions, cf. Rudolf Hirzel, *Untersuchungen zu Cicero's philosophischen Schriften*, t. 3 (Leipzig, 1883), 328.

[41] Cicero, *Acad.* 2.81, 122.

"in the nature of things" could appear. In other words, the actuality/possibility contrast is drawn with respect to the nature of things, which is to say that one is dealing here with a metaphysical contrast between the nature of things as they actually are, on the one hand, and the way that the nature of things could appear in one single case, on the other. It is not the possibility of the appearance of indiscernible likeness to some subject that misleads the subject's faculty of sensation; rather, it is the possibility of indiscernible likeness itself appearing between two things which will in turn mislead the faculty of sensation. It is only after the metaphysical contrast is drawn that the Latin refers to the effect that the possibility of the latter will have on the faculty of sensation. Consider the more accurate translation favored by Carlos Lévy, which signals the "problème ontologique" that Cicero alludes to here with the Latin *videri certe potest*: "il peut du moins sembler qu'il y en ait" ("it may seem at least that there is").[42] With this translation, the indiscernible likeness is not assigned to impressions, at least not yet. The likeness is one between two beings that *could* appear similar to one another. The likeness in this rendering does not make reference to, or depend on, sensation and some hypothetical subject for whom there is some apparent similarity between impressions, but rather it is the possibility of the likeness itself appearing in the nature of things that will mislead sensation. Cicero's hypothetical possibility has to do with a numerically distinct being that could itself appear with an indiscernible likeness to some other individual being. Admittedly, Cicero goes on to invoke the faculty of sensation, and the effect that this possible metaphysical likeness will have on the faculty of sensation, but this comes only after introducing the possibility of some thing appearing indiscernible from some other thing. On the basis of the counterfactual possibility taking place independent of considering some subject's actual sensation of the likeness, Cicero will only then infer the conclusion that if such likeness *in the nature of things* were to appear, it will then mislead sensation.

The concessive subjunctive *ne sit sane* signals that Cicero concedes the metaphysical view that "that there is no indiscernible likeness in the nature of things." The concession corresponds in one sense to the example of indiscernibility Cicero uses just a few lines prior to the passage cited above. In that example, Cicero grants the epistemic position of a hypothetical agent, for he speaks of an instance in which "the man you are looking at actually is the man you think you are looking at" (*Acad*. 2.84). The next step is crucial for the argument from

---

[42] Carlos Lévy, *Cicero Academicus. Recherches sur les Académiques et sur la philosophie cicéronienne* (Rome: École Française de Rome, 1992), 235. Lévy here follows the translation of Michel Ruch, *Cicéron. Academica posteriora. Liber primus* (Paris: Presses Universitaires de France, 1970).

counterfactual possibility. If, as Cicero says, it is possible for Quintus to appear as Servilius, then why is it not possible for some individual being who is not Cotta to appear to be Cotta—even if one grants that Cotta has in actuality no identical twin? The possibility of some individual being who is not Cotta appearing as Cotta does not depend on this being ever appearing to an epistemic subject, or on generating in a subject some impression or representation; there is mention of a subject for the appearance of Cotta himself, but only to concede that there are instances in which some subject has in view the actual individual the subject is perceiving. The example resembles the way that Arcesilaus's arguments provisionally concede conditions [1] and [2]: that there are some impressions that come from individual bodies that obtain, and that some impressions of those bodies are true in the sense that some impressions grasp the individual indications of the individual body in question.

Evidently, Arcesilaus and his Academic successors argue from a single case in which two beings appear indiscernible from one another (with an example of identical twins), for it seems to be an effective way to motivate a more general argument that starts with any actual individual body and contends counterfactually that it is nonetheless possible for a numerically distinct body to have appeared with an indiscernible likeness to that actual body. The possibility here is one in which any given being could lack a distinct set of individual indications, or inherent properties, supposedly marking it as the body (*Acad.* 2.50, 2.54–8) that it is *anyway*, because of its indiscernible likeness to some other being. Invoking a different notion of possibility, the argument establishes that even if a Stoic were to supplement the metaphysics of individual bodies with the view that individual bodies in actuality adhere to the metaphysical principle of substantial uniqueness, the causal model of Stoic apprehension cannot eliminate the possibility that for any actual body there could have appeared a numerically distinct being indiscernible from it. The peculiarly qualified body has intrinsic properties that make it what it actually is, and yet given the three conditions that the Stoic instruction for giving and withholding assent now requires, the presentation of actual individual bodies cannot rule out the possibility that any single body could have been indiscernible from some other body. The argument from twins and indiscernible beings shows that no true impression satisfies the counterfactual requirement of condition [3]; furthermore, it shows that for any individual body x that generates a true impression ϕ, there is an alternative causal genealogy that ϕ *could have had* which would not result in any objective difference in the way in which ϕ represents body x. To simplify the conclusion of the argument as it reappropriates Stoic terminology, the conclusion specifies that the bodies of the causal model of Stoic apprehension will be inapprehensible.

It is my contention that the thesis of ἀκαταληψία ("inapprehensibility") denotes the disposition of the individual bodies posited in the causal model, including the bodies conceptualized by Zeno and the intrinsically unique bodies that supposedly generate the impressions worthy of assent. At this point, it is important to emphasize that the specification of the metaphysical thesis of ἀκαταληψία does not endorse the claim that inapprehensibility is an intrinsic property (peculiar or common) of each and every body that obtains or might obtain. The specified content of the metaphysics of "inapprehensibility" is that bodies in the Stoic model are *relatively disposed* to having, in virtue of their lack of relation to animals with the power of giving and withholding assent.[43] By relatively disposed, I am referring in this context to a relational status that some being or beings are disposed to having in virtue of their relation or lack of relation to some other class of beings. In this context, the individual beings deemed inapprehensible are disposed to having a relative disposition that is negative because their inapprehensibility holds for them in virtue of their lack of relation to some special class of beings designated in the Stoic ontology of apprehension. This relative disposition is not only negative, it is also pure in the sense that it consists in the having of a relation to more than one individual being.[44] Take again the example used in the Introduction: the disposition of being a lover of Zeno, the Stoic founder. On my view, being such a lover involves a relative disposition that is impure, for being a lover in this way consists in being disposed to having a relation to one individual being alone, namely Zeno of Citium. By contrast, a relative disposition that is pure designates the status of some individual being or beings that consists in the having of a certain relation to some class of beings. Given the overall structure of Zeno's ontology, the relevant class of beings in relation to which a given individual body is inapprehensible is the subclass of bodies involving human beings, that is, mortal animals partaking in reason allegedly disposed with the power of giving and withholding assent to the impressions that often come from real bodies as they are *anyway*.

---

[43] On pure relational properties and the view that such "properties *are* and are in the Universe," see Moore, *Some Main Problems*, 323–5. For the classification of properties according to three basic types, see Khamara, "Indiscernibles," 144–6, esp. 146: "properties fall into one or other of three basic types: (i) intrinsic, and hence pure (for all intrinsic properties are pure); (ii) relational but pure; and (iii) relational and impure."

[44] Khamara, "Indiscernibles," 145.

Reconstructing ἀκαταληψία and ἐποχὴ περὶ πάντων

To bring this part of the metaphysical reconstruction to the next phase, allow me a brief overview of the provisional acceptances initiating anti-Stoic arguments from indiscernibility. First, let it seem true that a given individual body does not *actually* have an indiscernible other. Additionally, let it be that humans often have a true impression of the individual body, or intrinsically unique body. The upshot of indiscernibility arguments against the causal account of apprehension is that it is nonetheless *possible* for that individual body to have had a numerically distinct indiscernible other. Defenders of Zeno's canonical impressionism are left with the task of responding to the absurd consequence that individual bodies, or better yet intrinsically unique bodies, often obtain and generate true impressions, and yet in doing so those very bodies are disposed to produce the kind of true impression that represents the obtaining body in actuality as discernibly distinct *and* inapprehensible. Given condition [3] of the causal model of apprehension, the following challenge seems intractable for the defense of Zenonian impressionism: for how can an actual individual body ever be able to produce the kind of true impression that is sufficient to eliminate the counterfactual possibility that the true impression could also have had an alternative causal genealogy?

With an appeal to states of mind such as dreams, hallucinations, and fits of madness the polemical target enlarges to integrate a criticism of the internalistic claim of condition [3]. The internalistic claim of condition [3] is vulnerable to arguments from indiscernibility owing to its dependence on a realist ontology of individual bodies. In what is perhaps an improved reiteration of that realist ontology, the internalistic claim presupposes a reality of absolute difference, according to which each individual body that obtains differs from every other actual or possible body with respect to at least one intrinsic property or collection of properties, such that a human is aware of a clear and distinct impression tracking an actual body that obtains in some causal network. While indiscernibility arguments from dreams, hallucinations, and fits of madness make reference to a subject or mortal animal with reason, the arguments do not challenge the epistemic position of the animal who claims to know, in entertaining an impression that the man on the street is actually Socrates present on the street or that he or she is actually awake and sane in doing so. These arguments demonstrate that it is possible to entertain an impression arising from a causal genealogy (e.g., dreaming of meeting Socrates in the *agora*) that deviates from the genealogy coming from the actual individual being that obtains in the real causal network, presenting in this alternative fashion an impression that nonetheless represents its content in a way that is indiscernible with respect to the way in which it represents its content from some true impression of Socrates actually on the street. The argument is that it is at least possible for there to be some representation coming from what is not spatiotemporally present, entertained in dreaming, a hallucination, or fit of madness that is no less clear and distinct than any true representation. To emphasize this point using a different set of terms: for any supposedly true impression, it is at least possible to entertain in a dream, hallucination, or fit of madness an impression coming from what does not obtain that is indiscernible with respect to the way in which it represents its content from a supposedly true impression of what actually obtains. Because of this potential indiscernibility, experiences of dreaming and madness show that the clarity and distinctness of actual true impressions do not necessarily track with success the reality of individual bodies as they manifest independent of representation. Again, the burden of the argument falls on Zeno and canonical Stoics to eliminate the possibility that in dreaming or hallucinating the representational content of any supposedly true impression could be duplicated in an impression that comes from what does not obtain, as it may in the experience of dreaming. Arguments from dreams and madness do not directly challenge the claim of an epistemic subject to know, in entertaining an impression, that he or she is not at that moment actually dreaming or insane. The arguments merely aim to show that it is possible, even if a given animal is in a position to know that he or she is not at the moment dreaming or mad in entertaining a true impression of an external body, for clear and distinct impressions to come from what does not obtain. This possibility undermines the true-tracking feature of clear and distinct impressions, for it is no longer conceivably the case that clear and distinct impressions come only from actual individual bodies that obtain external to the mortal animal.

There is, in this counterfactual scenario, a problem for Zeno's instruction for the cultivation of infallible assent, and for those intending to cultivate such infallibility by adhering to the terms of the instruction. Consider it this way: given that no impression seems sufficient to eliminate the possibility of some impression being such that it represents what does not obtain in the same way in which a true impression represents what actually obtains, it follows that condition [3] of the apprehensive impression cannot be satisfied. Hence, Zeno has failed to secure the project of cultivating and perfecting the giving of assent to the so-called apprehensive impressions of what obtains. That is, without condition [3], it follows that there is no true impression that is of such a kind that it could not be false (οὐκ ἂν γένοιτο ψευδής, Sextus, M. 7.154 (< F 87 Vezzoli, LS 41C)); moreover, given the absence of apprehensive impressions, "neither will apprehension come to be" (οὐδὲ κατάληψις γενήσεται). The negative thesis that "no impression is apprehensive," which is simplistically specified by some proponents of epistemological centrism as the thesis of ἀκαταληψία, is not the transitional premise for deducing the corollary thesis, namely, the sage's ἐποχὴ περὶ πάντων. Proponents of the framework of epistemology frequently ignore the negative proposition that "all things are inapprehensible," and the function of this proposition as one of two transitional premises in the argument for suspension. Take, for instance, one proponent of epistemological centrism who asserts that Arcesilaus deduces from the argument (and the provisional concession to the Stoic instruction for infallible assent) that "no impression is apprehensive" the following epistemological specification: that the sage "will suspend judgment about any impression p."[45] Scholars who tend to privilege a humanistic focus in epistemological specification often reduce ἀκαταληψία to the simplistic thesis that "there is no apprehension," or that "no impression is apprehensive," taking such specifications of ἀκαταληψία to further entail the conclusion that "no knowledge is possible."[46] In such epistemological reconstructions, the arguments

---

[45] Castagnoli, "Hellenistic Academy," 192, formalizes the steps in the argument leading to the epistemological specification of ἐποχὴ περὶ πάντων. For a similar epistemological specification of suspension, see Perin, "Descartes," 59: "therefore, for any object O, no true impression of O is a cognitive [apprehensive] impression. If that is so, then there are no cognitive [apprehensive] impressions. That conclusion in conjunction with the Stoic maxim for assent compels the Stoic to withhold her assent from *every impression* and to suspend judgment about *everything*" (italics added). Perin, "Academic Arguments," 505, identifies the negative conclusion of Academic arguments in the following way: "so no true impression is a cognitive impression. And *that* conclusion in conjunction with Stoic norms for assent compels the Stoic to suspend judgment about everything." Perin, "Arcesilaus," 313, neutralizes the ontological significance of "everything" by interpreting "everything" in terms of an interpretive dilemma for which there is, in his view, no third option: that is, either "everything" means "all philosophical matters" (what Perin designates the dialectical interpretation) or it means that "one ought not to believe anything [philosophical matters or non-philosophical matters] at all" (what Perin designates the dogmatic interpretation). Again, for a specification of ἀκαταληψία nearly identical with those of Castagnoli ("no impression is cognitive") and Perin ("there are no cognitive impressions"), see Striker, "Sceptical Strategies," 96 (cf. n29 above). Notice the commonality: Castagnoli, Striker, and Perin eliminate from the specification of ἀκαταληψία any reference to the Stoic causal conception of bodies.

[46] In conformity with this humanistic focus, Perin, "Arcesilaus," 315–16, interprets ἀκαταληψία ("noncognizability" or "NK" in Perin's notation) in terms of the epistemic claim that "in no case does believing something satisfy" the conditions of knowledge. "NK" or "noncognizability" is then identified with the proposition "that nothing can be known." Here Perin follows the specification of Burnyeat, "Antipater," 292, and Brittain, "Arcesilaus," § 2, for whom the notion of ἀκαταληψία is "roughly equivalent" to the thesis that "nothing can be known." Cf. Brittain, *Philo*, 90, esp. 4 n7. The epistemological construal of the proposition "nothing can be known" fails to specify that it is first and foremost (though not exclusively) Stoic bodies in the causal model which are inapprehensible, and that such bodies are inapprehensible in relation to the subclass of living bodies with the power of assent to the true impressions of the actual bodies that obtain external to them. In comparing Socrates and Arcesilaus with respect to the thesis of ἀκαταληψία, Charles Brittain and John Palmer, "The New Academy's Appeals to the Presocratics," *Phronesis* 46, no. 1 (2001): 42, acknowledge the

of Arcesilaus are simplified into arguments polemicizing against "Zeno's core epistemological doctrine" of the apprehensive impression, to show how the collapse of that doctrine "cornered the Stoics into the unpalatable (and perhaps absurd) conclusion that their ideal wise person (σοφός, *sapiens*) would have to suspend judgment about everything."[47] The term "everything" is explicated in the language of "any impression *p*," or in the language that restricts the universality involved in the suspension to the universality of assent or belief— such that ἐποχὴ περὶ πάντων is specified as the recommendation to suspend *all* assent or *all* judgment/belief, even to suspend assent or judgment *all the time*. One scholar, for example, specifies the transition from ἀκαταληψία to ἐποχὴ περὶ πάντων in the anti-Stoic arguments originally developed by Arcesilaus as follows: "if there are in fact no apprehensive impressions, the wise thing to do is to suspend judgment *all the time*" (emphasis mine).[48] This reconstruction of the transition cites Sextus *M*. 7.150–7 (< F 87 Vezzoli, LS 41C) as the sole textual basis for this epistemological specification of ἐποχὴ περὶ πάντων, which it then clarifies with the proposition that "the sage will *always* suspend judgement." However, the cited passage does not support this way of specifying the content of ἐποχὴ περὶ πάντων:

> (156) since all things are inapprehensible (πάντων ὄντων ἀκαταλήπτων) on account of the unreality of the Stoic criterion, if the wise person assents, the wise person will opine. For since no thing or being is apprehensible (μηδενὸς γὰρ ὄντος καταληπτοῦ), if the wise person assents to something (συγκατατίθεταί τινι), he will assent to the inapprehensible, but assent to the inapprehensible is opinion. (157) So that if the wise person is among those who assent, the wise person will be among those who opine. But the wise person is not among those who opine (for according to them this goes with folly and is a cause of errors); therefore the wise person is not among those who assent. But if this is so, he will have to decline assent about all things (περὶ πάντων αὐτὸν δεήσει ἀσυγκαταθετεῖν). Declining assent is nothing other than to suspend, it will

---

metaphysical aspect of ἀκαταληψία with the propositions that "things themselves are non-cognitive" and that "all things are non-cognitive" (48). But again even this metaphysical construal is abstract. One should further specify that things *qua* Stoic bodies and incorporeals are "non-cognitive" in relation to the animals that receive true impressions and have the power of assent in the causal model of apprehension. Christopher Shields, "Socrates among the Sceptics," in *The Socratic Movement*, ed. Paul Vander Waerdt (Ithaca, NY: Cornell University Press, 1994), 346, slides between the simplistic epistemological proposition "that nothing is discerned or reliably ascertained (*incognita*)" and the more ontologically charged "Everything is undiscerned," without further specifying the content of "everything" according to Stoic ontology. For similar accounts recognizing the ontological dimension of ἀκαταληψία, see Ioppolo, *La testimonianza*, 35–6, Thorsrud, "Socratic Skepticism," 207–8. See Introduction, n21, for additional references.

[47] Castagnoli, "Hellenistic Academy," 192–3.
[48] Sharples, *Stoics, Epicureans and Sceptics*, 27.

follow that the wise person suspends [assent] about all things (περὶ πάντων ὁ σοφός [ἀσυγκαταθετεῖν]).[49]

It should be fairly obvious that the meaning of ἐποχὴ περὶ πάντων in Sextus is not that the wise person will *always* suspend judgment, but rather that the wise person should suspend assent "about all things."[50] The passage in Sextus indicates that ἐποχή involves "declining assent" (ἀσυγκαταθετεῖν), and that the wise person suspends or declines assent περὶ πάντων ("about everything" or "all things"). The περὶ preceding the genitive πάντων conveys the sense not of the temporal adverb *always*, but more precisely the sense of "about" or "on account of," which is to say, on account of all things being inapprehensible, the wise person will have to suspend assent about all things. The universality involved in ἐποχὴ περὶ πάντων follows from, or is conceptually linked to, the universal claim that all things are, or will be, "inapprehensible" (ἀκατάληπτα, 7.155; ἀκαταλήπτων, 7.156). The transition from this qualification of things to suspension is often concealed in epistemological readings of *M.* 7.150-7. For instance, citing the passage *M.* 7.155-7, Brittain claims that "universal *epochē*" is equivalent to the proposition that "one should suspend assent universally," which is then immediately reduced to the recommendation that one should "form no beliefs."[51] Brittain is not entirely wrong in specifying "universal *epochē*" in this way; the problem, however, is that this particular formulation relies mainly on Cicero, not Sextus, and it ignores the content of the passage from Sextus that

---

[49] (156) πάντων ὄντων ἀκαταλήπτων διὰ τὴν ἀνυπαρξίαν τοῦ Στωικοῦ κριτηρίου, εἰ συγκαταθήσεται ὁ σοφός, δοξάσει ὁ σοφός· μηδενὸς γὰρ ὄντος καταληπτοῦ εἰ συγκατατίθεταί τινι, τῷ ἀκαταλήπτῳ συγκαταθήσεται, ἡ δὲ τῷ ἀκαταλήπτῳ συγκατάθεσις δόξα (157) ἐστίν. ὥστε εἰ τῶν συγκατατιθεμένων ἐστὶν ὁ σοφός, τῶν δοξαστικῶν ἔσται ὁ σοφός. οὐχὶ δέ γε τῶν δοξαστικῶν ἐστιν ὁ σοφός (τοῦτο γὰρ ἀφροσύνης ἦν κατ' αὐτούς, καὶ τῶν ἁμαρτημάτων αἴτιον)· οὐκ ἄρα τῶν συγκατατιθεμένων ἐστὶν ὁ σοφός. εἰ δὲ τοῦτο, περὶ πάντων αὐτὸν δεήσει ἀσυγκαταθετεῖν. τὸ δὲ ἀσυγκαταθετεῖν οὐδὲν ἕτερόν ἐστιν ἢ τὸ (158) ἐπέχειν· ἐφέξει ἄρα περὶ πάντων ὁ σοφός (Sextus, *M.* 7.156-8). Here I follow Richard Bett's translation of Sextus Empiricus, *Against the Logicians* (Cambridge: Cambridge University Press, 2005), 33-4, with one potentially significant modification worth noting. Bett prefers to render the plural πάντων ὄντων ἀκαταλήπτων as the singular "everything is inapprehensible" (and the plural περὶ πάντων as "about everything").

[50] Sextus, *PH* 1.232: περὶ πάντων ἐπέχει. Cf. Plutarch, *Adv. Col.* 1120c, οἱ περὶ πάντων ἐπέχοντες,1122a, τὴν δὲ περὶ πάντων ἐποχήν; Euseb., *Praep. ev.* 14.4.15 (cf. 14.7.15), περὶ ἁπάντων ἐπέχειν δεῖν; Augustine, *Cont. Acad.* 2.6.14, *nulli rei esse adsentiendum*. Translating περὶ ἁπάντων ἐπέχειν in *Praep. ev.*, Allen ("Carneadean Argument," 224) and Hankinson (*Sceptics*, 170) prefer the translation "suspend judgment about all matters"). There is some textual support for the adverbial "always" in the qualification of suspension, but not in the passage from Sextus (*M.* 7.150-7). At *Acad.* 2.67 (cf. 1.45), Cicero writes (again, following the standard translation of Brittain): "if the wise person ever assents to anything, he will sometimes hold an opinion; but he will never hold an opinion (*numquam autem opinabitur*); so he will not assent to anything (*nulli igitur rei adsentietur*)."

[51] Brittain, "Arcesilaus," § 2. Likewise, Gerson, *Ancient Epistemology*, 119: for the "conclusion that is supposed to follow" from the Academic argument against the apprehensive impression "is that all judgment should be suspended."

is cited in support, according to which the recommendation that one should suspend assent about all things is based on the thesis that things are (or will be) inapprehensible. Again, textual support for the epistemological specification of ἐποχὴ περὶ πάντων as the recommendation to suspend *all* assent can be found in Cicero (*omnium adsensionum retentio*, *Acad.* 2.78; *sapientem adsensus omnes cohibiturum*, 2.68). However, as I argue below, this specification reproduces a tendency in Cicero that obscures the distinction between object and impression insofar as it connects the universality of ἐποχὴ περὶ πάντων to impressions, belief in or assent to impressions, thereby losing sight of the reference in Sextus to things or beings (not impressions). To be more precise, what is lost in Brittain's rendering of "universal *epochē*" is recognition of the difference between the proposition in Sextus that in opining the wise person would "assent to something" (συγκατατίθεταί τινι, 7.156), which is to say, some inapprehensible thing, and the proposition (preferred by Brittain) that in opining the wise person would "assent to non-cognitive impressions."[52] Notice that Sextus does not explicitly state that all "impressions" (φαντασίαι) are inapprehensible, but rather that *all beings* are inapprehensible (πάντων ὄντων ἀκαταλήπτων, *M.* 7.155). And so on the basis of beings or things being inapprehensible, Sextus reports that Arcesilaus derived the absurd conclusion for the Stoic idealization of the sage: that is, that the sage will suspend judgment περὶ πάντων [= ὄντων ἀκαταλήπτων], which is to say, "concerning all beings" (*M.* 7.157). The beings about which the sage suspends are not impressions (e.g., "any impression *p*" or "every impression"), but the things or objects *qua* spatiotemporal bodies regularly causing true and false impressions to arise, for again it was provisionally accepted that some impressions come from what obtains, stamped, and impressed in accordance with the very being itself that obtains independently of representation. The suspension of assent about all things entails that the mortal animal with the power of assent seeking to comply with the instruction of infallible assent suspends judgment about the beings that generate true impressions. But if one is inclined to collapse the distinction between impression and object in favor of connecting assent to impressions, then one might easily misread the phrase συγκατατίθεταί τινι ("assenting to something") at 7.156 as assenting to some ("non-cataleptic") impression, as Brittain tends to do—rather than understand the phrase more

---

[52] Defending a standard summary of the Academic argument against Stoic epistemology, Brittain, "Arcesilaus," §3, specifies one of the premises in the argument as the claim that it is irrational "to assent to non-cognitive impressions (as the Stoic held)."

literally as assenting to some inapprehensible thing (which presents itself to a mortal animal partaking in reason by way of a "non-cataleptic" impression).[53]

Epistemological reconstructions of the argument for ἐποχὴ περὶ πάντων are partial and misguided. When citing and reconstructing the passage from Sextus (*M.* 7.155-6), they bypass not only the content of the metaphysical thesis of ἀκαταληψία—namely, the thesis concerning the relative disposition of individual bodies—as it appears in a key ancient source, but they also neglect to specify the metaphysical absurdity at the conclusion of the argument: given the causal power of bodies to produce some true impressions in mortal animals partaking in reason as those bodies actually obtain *anyway*, impressions that seem insufficient to eliminate the possibility of some other impression being such that it represents what does not obtain in the same way in which a true impression represents the body actually obtaining, all beings (i.e., bodies or properties, and the incorporeals) that accompany obtaining bodies are, or will be, "inapprehensible" (πάντ' ἔσται ἀκατάληπτα, Sextus, *M.* 7.155 (< F 87 Vezzoli, LS 41C)). Just as Arcesilaus grants that there are true impressions in the course of questioning whether true impressions of what obtains are apprehensive, he also grants that there are individual bodies in the course of questioning whether such bodies are apprehensible. As a result, the second absurdity that Zeno and the Stoics seem stranded with is not, or not simply, that generic objects are somehow epistemically inaccessible to humans without the availability of apprehensive impressions. Instead, the following is the correct *de re* specification: Having provisionally conceded the causal genealogy of true impressions, and that such impressions come from bodies that are intrinsically unique, indiscernibility arguments establish that the beings that actually act so as to imprint themselves on the bodies of mortal animals partaking in reason do so in such a way that each and every being of this kind presents itself as disposed to being inapprehensible. The suspension of assent about everything does not follow from the conflict between the instruction for infallible assent and the conclusion that no impression is apprehensive, but from an agreement between the terms of the instruction and the absurd conclusion that all beings in the ontology of Stoic apprehension are disposed to having the relative disposition of being inapprehensible. If the proposition that Arcesilaus concedes is that true impressions represent the very bodies that obtain, then

---

[53] Elsewhere, in the direction of an alternative reading of 7.156, which drops explicit reference to impressions, Brittain ("Introduction," xlii) maintains the "distinction between a 'cataleptic' [*kataleptikē*] impression—i.e., one that provides apprehension of something—and an 'apprehensible' [*kataleptos*] object or state of affairs—i.e., the thing we have an apprehension of."

the conclusion of ἀκαταληψία must pertain to individual things as they actually present themselves to mortal animals with the rational power of assent. The selectivity of epistemological specifications of ἀκαταληψία and περὶ πάντων is unnecessarily selective as it leaves the beings involved in the Stoic account of apprehension unspecified. Simplifying the universality of ἐποχὴ περὶ πάντων in Sextus underestimates the extent of the systemic absurdity that follows from Arcesilaus's anti-Stoic arguments for ἀκαταληψία. The simplification of ἐποχὴ περὶ πάντων to the universal suspension of assent eliminates from the notion of ἐποχὴ περὶ πάντων the metaphysical implication that each and every "thing" implied by the reference to the genitive plural πάντων is inapprehensible. That is to say, the simplification conceals the clear implication that πάντων in ἐποχὴ περὶ πάντων at 7.157 further clarifies the πάντων in πάντων ὄντων ἀκαταλήπτων at 7.156, which identifies all beings (on the Stoic account) as inapprehensible beings. The main problem, to restate the criticism, with this simplification of ἐποχὴ περὶ πάντων is that it associates the universality of suspension only with impressions and the human faculty of assent or belief. In this way, epistemological specifications of ἀκαταληψία become the pretext for eliminating the metaphysical significance of ἐποχὴ περὶ πάντων and for diminishing the absurdity that the Academics deduce from the epistemological and metaphysical commitments of Stoic philosophy. Having excluded the consideration of the relative disposition of objects from specification, the objects supposedly grounding the epistemic possibility of giving or withholding assent in the Stoic account of apprehension, the simplification of ἐποχὴ περὶ πάντων paves the way for falsely attributing a kind of metaphysical neutrality to the Academy's criticism of Stoic epistemology.

Moreover, specifications of ἀκαταληψία as "nothing can be known" (*Acad.* 2.15) or "nothing can be apprehended" (*percipi nihil potest*, *Acad.* 2.59, cf. *Acad.* 1.45 (< LS 68A)) are ambiguous in the sense that they can be understood simplistically as negative claims concerning the rational capacities of certain animals, or as more complex claims entailing a negative relation between the purported objects of knowledge and the animals in whom true impressions are supposedly formed. Such specifications of ἀκαταληψία tend to obscure its semantic affiliation with ἀκατάληπτα/[πάντων ὄντων] ἀκαταλήπτων ("inapprehensibles," *M.* 7.155–6), a Greek term qualifying in this context the beings that Zeno assumes appropriately cause metaphysically substantive apprehension. The same can be said of the two epistemological specifications of ἀκαταληψία (e.g., that "no impression is apprehensive," or that "there is no apprehension"), which stem, I now argue, from a conceptual confusion originating with Cicero and his Latin translation of the terms involved in the

Greek arguments. In specifying the meaning of ἀκαταληψία, the negations involved in these epistemological specifications omit any explicit reference to the negation associated directly with the purported "objects" that, on the Stoic view, generate impressions. This omission justifies designating these standard specifications purely epistemological specifications, for they are concerned principally with the epistemic powers of apprehension and assent. The more important point, however, is that the omission of any explicit reference to the beings of Stoic apprehension creates a significant conceptual deficiency in epistemological specifications of ἀκαταληψία.

Identifying this conceptual deficiency, this study presents an alternative specification of the meaning of ἀκαταληψία. Again, the alternative maintains that ἀκαταληψία denotes, in addition to the simple epistemic negation of apprehension, the relative disposition of the "objects" implicated in the Stoic account of apprehension, the bodies external to the animals purportedly capable of giving and withholding assent to impressions. Hence, I designate this alternative the metaphysical specification of the meaning of ἀκαταληψία. The specification is metaphysical in virtue of the explicit thematization of the notion of an extrinsic or relational property to conceptualize the relative disposition of the purported "objects" of Stoic apprehension; this thematization specifies the philosophical meaning of ἀ-καταληψία—in particular, the alpha privative (ἀ-) prefixed to the Greek term καταληπτός—with explicit reference to Stoic metaphysics. Similar to other feminine substantives ending in -ία (e.g., ἀθανασία ("immortality") from ἀθάνατος, "immortal"), the abstract noun ἀκαταληψία is derived from the adjective stem ἀκατάληπτος where the τ becomes σ- before -ία.[54] The passive adjective ἀκατάληπτος modifies the objects or class of objects relative to the purported animals of Stoic apprehension. The Greek term ἀκατάληπτος thus refers to an object or thing that has the property of being "inapprehensible" in virtue of its relation, or, more precisely, its lack of relation, to some other thing or class of things, that is, mortal animals partaking in reason who lack apprehensive impressions. By contrast, the feminine substantive ἀκαταληψία, like other abstract nouns in Greek, refers to the kind of negative relational property itself as an abstract noun.

As Brittain observes, Cicero is responsible for "obscuring the distinction in the original Greek arguments between the active adjective 'catalept*ic*' (καταληπτική) and the passive adjective 'apprehens*ible*' (καταληπτός)."[55] In a

---

[54] Herbert Weir Smyth, *Greek Grammar*, rev. Gordon M. Messing (Cambridge, MA: Harvard University Press, 1956), 231 (§ 840).
[55] Brittain, "Introduction," xxxix–xlii.

note to a passage (*Acad.* 2.40) in which indiscernibility arguments are explicated, Brittain alerts readers of his translation that Cicero's usage of *quod percipi posse*, and the English term used to translate the Latin phrase, can mislead (English and Latin) readers. In the note, it is said that Cicero applies the Latin phrase *quod percipi posse* (at *Acad.* 2.40-1, Brittain's "apprehensible") to impressions, not to the objects, or what I prefer to specify less generically in this context as bodies capable of producing impressions.[56] Unlike the Greek passive adjective καταληπτός, the Latin phrase can refer either to the epistemic impression about an object or to the object itself (*qua* καταληπτός/ἀ-κατάληπτος). In other words, it would appear that in Latin both objects and impressions can be "apprehensible"/ "inapprehensible." However, in the *Academica*, or, more exactly, in the Latin of Cicero's *Academica*, the main difficulty is that Cicero does not seem to recognize, according to Brittain (citing *Acad.* 2.18, 2.77, 2.112-13 as textual support), the importance of the conceptual distinction between object and impression, for he "systemically applies" the periphrasis *quod percipi posse* to impressions.[57]

The Greek passive adjectives καταληπτός/ἀ-κατάληπτος ("what can or cannot be apprehended") are distinct in meaning from the active adjective καταληπτική ("what is able to apprehend"). The latter denotes fitness for a certain psychic activity, similar to the way that other adjectives with -τικό or -ικό added to the verbal adjective ending τό- convey a certain capable fitness for an activity.[58] In one passage, Cicero's rendering of ἀκατάληπτον seems to preserve the passivity of the Greek adjective with the Latin passive infinitive *conprehendi*, identifying ἀκατάληπτον with the negation that "nothing could be apprehended" (*negaret quicquam esse quod conprehendi posset*, *Acad.* 2.18). At *Acad.* 2.15, Lucullus attributes a similar denial to Arcesilaus, comparing him unfavorably to seditious Roman politicians who enlist famous figures of the past with apparent populist

---

[56] Brittain, *Cicero*, 26 n54. Presumably, to register an ambiguity in Cicero's Latin, Brittain, ("Introduction," xli) has *quod percipi posse* in his table of interchangeable Greek, Latin and English phrases correspond, on one hand, to the Greek καταληπτική φαντασία (which Brittain renders in the table of terms/phrases "apprehensible impression"), and, on the other, to the Greek term καταληπτόν, which he notes pertains to "objects" or is "of objects" and translates in the table as "apprehensible." The double usage of *quod percipi posse* (as "apprehensible impression" and/or "apprehensible object") demonstrates Cicero's tendency to collapse reference to external objects into reference to impressions in his discussion of Stoic epistemology. Brittain's translation of καταληπτική φαντασία as "apprehensible impression" is at odds with the distinction he draws between the active καταληπτική and the passive καταληπτόν. A similar conflation is made, in an earlier study, by the translation of the passive ἀκατάληπτα in Sextus (*PH* 1.235) with the active "non-cataleptic" (Brittain, *Philo*, 4 n7) instead of "inapprehensibles."

[57] Yet, at 2.76, Cicero uses the phrase *quod percipi posse* without applying it to perceptual impressions in his brief reference to the Cyrenaics: *qui negant esse quicquam quod percipi possit extrinsecus* ("that nothing external is apprehensible"). Cf. the more ambiguous uses of *quicquam* at *Acad.* 2.15 and 2.18. See Chapter 2, n59 below.

[58] Smyth, *Greek Grammar*, 237 (§ 858).

leanings in an effort to destroy the stability of the Republic. From this perspective, Arcesilaus was as destructive of systematic philosophy as troublesome politicians were for the Roman Republic: appealing to past philosophers to destroy the stability of Stoicism by denying "that anything could be known or cognized" (*negavissent quicquam sciri aut percipi posse*). The denial contradicts the Stoic view that "something can be apprehended and perceived" (*esse aliquid quod conprehendi et percipi posset, Acad.* 2.17). In these lines, observe the ambiguity in Cicero's Latin noted earlier, and its potential effect on interpreting the Latin pronouns *aliquid* ("something") and *quicquam* ("anything"). Here the Latin term *aliquid* ("something") denotes, as Reid observes, "the external object [καταληπτόν] which causes the κατάληψις in the mind of the person who perceives it." Yet, as Reid warns, "object and perception were often by the ancient philosophers carelessly confused."[59] Evidently mindful of such a warning, Brittain observes that Cicero often elides the distinction between object and perception, including the passive and active forms of the Greek adjectives. For example, Cicero translates the active adjective of καταληπτική (*Acad.* 1.41) with the passive Latin *comprehendibile*, "that which is apprehensible." More charitably than Reid, Brittain conjectures that Cicero may have been confused in eliding the distinction between object and perception, or he may have collapsed the distinction for reasons we have yet to consider. That is to say, Cicero may have "thought it was a negligible terminological simplification: his readers would understand that the question under debate is not whether *we* have reliable access to *our* own thoughts or impressions, but rather whether *our* impressions provide *us* with reliable access to the *world*" (italics added).[60] One wonders, in considering the more charitable alternative: what does the term "the world" refer to in this context? Should readers take it to signify that Cicero may have been referring to the Stoic notion of "the world," the finite totality that is itself a body comprised of other bodies? Or perhaps Cicero may have been making some kind of intuitive reference to mind-independent objects or things, such as the world more generically, where the Stoic notion of world is not necessarily the focal concept. But then is the focal concept *our* notion of the world, or the world that *we* inhabit? It's unclear. The content of the notion is not specified according to the Stoic conception of the world as a living animal, hence the lack

---

[59] Reid, *Ciceronis, Academica*, 193 n11, and 152 n7. On Cicero's use of the Greek term καταληπτόν, "this should mean, strictly, the *object* which causes the impression; the impression itself should be κατάληψις not καταληπτόν; but, as we shall see in *Lucullus* [*Academica 2*], words denoting the object and words denoting the impression are readily interchanged."

[60] See Brittain, "Introduction," xlii. Criticisms aside, this is an informative discussion of the distinction between the passive (καταληπτός/ἀκατάληπτος) and active adjectives (καταληπτική).

of clarity.⁶¹ As noted in Chapter 1, modern and contemporary epistemologists in the tradition of Locke and Ferrier, that is to say, in the tradition of separating methodologically *our access to what there is* from *what there is*, commonly invoke "the world" to refer to what is there *anyway*. Such theorists often use the term "the world" to summarily identify ontological correlates, which *our* rational efforts strive to access. The epistemological project is inclined to grant methodological priority to questions concerning *our access to what there is*, often adhering to the ideal that with the correct foundational epistemology rational subjects (such as *ourselves*) can gain access to "the world," or some part of it. Again, this project typically skips over the question concerning the conceptual posit of "the world," thereby skipping over the fact that the concept of "the world" is the conceptual product of presuppositions and judgments that can be contested, like any other judgment. As a result, the project of epistemology fails to question its own ontological presuppositions concerning the nature of "the world" that it posits. The same failure applies to the historiographical approach informing Brittain's charitable conjecture. The world is posited as potentially explanatory of Cicero's authorial point of view, but one is not informed of what the world is, or how it can be accessed by anyone supposedly questioning *our* epistemic access to it.

Given that the epistemological reconstruction of the question under debate between Stoics and Academics imports the methodological distinction between "the world" and our access to it, thereby focusing the question on the latter, the debate is presented as if Stoic views of an ontological correlate lie outside the scope of the Academy's humanistic questioning—whether one takes that correlate to be "the world" as a finite totality in the Stoic sense, or the totality of bodies and incorporeals that the Stoics posited as constituents forming the structure of the world. That is, the epistemological "question under debate" conceals the higher-order question concerning the ontological correlates (world, individual bodies, individual incorporeals) that Zeno and the Stoics contend make impressions possible. From the perspective of the alternative framework of the ontology of knowledge, the question that Zeno and canonical Stoics encounter in Arcesilaus's arguments is not the humanistic issue of whether *we* apprehend the world, or whatever it is that lies beyond the veil of representations, but rather the higher-order question of whether the individual beings in the world that Zeno affirms with the causal model of apprehension

---

⁶¹ Generic use of the notion of "the world" is reproduced in a more recent discussion of Stoic impressionism by Schwab, "Skeptical Defenses," 184–5: "An impression is a mental state that represents *the world* to its possessor."

are such that they can produce apprehension in mortal animals partaking in reason. In the framework of epistemology favored by modern doxographers, the question concerning the nature and structure of the ontological correlates in Stoicism is "skipped over," as the focal question is thought to concern whether impressions grant epistemic access to "the world." The distinction between the epistemological question and the higher-order ontological question corresponds to the relevant distinction that Cicero (intentionally or unintentionally) elides: that is, the distinction between the humanistic question of whether impressions provide mortal animals partaking in reason with reliable access to the world (assuming that *we* are such animals), on the one hand, and the question of whether the individual bodies and incorporeals structuring the world in early Stoic philosophy are themselves apprehensible, on the other.

There is, in my view, a second reason for understanding Cicero's terminological simplification as the starting point of later confusions. The application of the periphrasis *quod percipi posse* to impressions, connecting thereby the meaning of "apprehensible"/"inapprehensible" to impressions, reduces the notion of possibility to the epistemic possibility of apprehending impressions and fosters a similar kind of simplification in the favored epistemological formulations of ἀκαταληψία in contemporary English. The simplification that I am identifying is the one that simplifies a two-sided negation involved in ἀ-καταληψία to the single epistemic denial of the apprehensive impression, or what is roughly the same, the epistemic negation of the Stoic power of apprehension. The simplification of epistemological ἀκαταληψία obscures the second negation, the one involved in qualifying the things internal to the Stoic account of apprehension ἀκατάληπτα ("inapprehensibles"). The association of the meaning of the passive adjective ἀκατάληπτος with impressions, and not with the external things causing the (true) impressions, is the first step taken in the direction of eliminating the metaphysical aspect of Stoic bodies *qua* "inapprehensible" from the specification of ἀκαταληψία, and the most decisive conceptual maneuver of reconstructing the thesis of ἀκαταληψία with the simple epistemic denials found in epistemological centrism, namely, that there is no apprehension, or that there are no cognitive impressions.

To locate the Greek term ἀκαταληψία in Cicero, scholars typically cite *Acad.* 1.44–5, where Cicero the character responds to Varro with an account of what motivates on his view the debate between Arcesilaus and Zeno.[62]

---

[62] Bett, "Carneades' *Pithanon*," 62, cites Cicero at *Acad.* 1.45 as evidence for the specification of inapprehensibility as "nothing can be known," which he construes epistemologically as Arcesilaus's response to the "thesis of the cognitive impression." See also Brittain, "Arcesilaus," § 2; Burnyeat,

These scholars adduce a portion of Arcesilaus's reasoning as reconstructed by Cicero at *Acad.* 1.44–5 to corroborate standard epistemological specifications of ἀκαταληψία mentioned above, which again usually reduce the content of the claims that "nothing can be cognized" or that "nothing is, or can be, known" to the formulation that "there are no apprehensive impressions." Cicero gives his understanding of that reasoning by saying that Arcesilaus thought that with "all things hiding themselves in darkness, nothing could be discerned or understood" (*sic omnia latere censebat in occulto: neque esse quicquam quod cerni aut intellegi posset*).[63] Cicero's reconstruction of Arcesilaus's reasoning is the subject of lengthier discussion in the concluding chapter, but for now observe how Cicero reconstructs the reason for "why Arcesilaus denied that any thing could be known" (*itaque Arcesilas negabat esse quicquam quod sciri posset*, *Acad.* 1.45). The denial in the latter clause can be read as if it simply qualifies in a completely negative way the fitness or capacity of discerning or knowing (*scire*). Or more fully, the denial seems to disqualify the fitness of human capacities for discerning (*cerno*) and understanding (*intellego*) anything whatsoever. For review, recall that the negation or privation in the standard English simplification of ἀ-καταληψία is primarily if not exclusively taken to negate the faculties of epistemic subjects, and on this reading Cicero seems to suggest that Arcesilaus affirmed that the mind or intellect is weak and the senses limited. The problem with using Cicero's reconstruction as evidence for simplistic specifications of the content of ἀκαταληψία is twofold. First, while Cicero explicitly refers to the passive adjective ἀκατάληπτος in *Academica* 2 (*Lucullus*), nowhere in the two recovered books of the *Academica* does he use, or refer to, the Greek feminine substantive noun ἀκαταληψία ("inapprehensibility"), the noun formed from the passive adjective ἀκατάληπτο-ς. Yet, Cicero the author was evidently aware of the Greek feminine substantive noun ἀκαταληψία, for he uses the Greek noun in a letter to Atticus (*Ad Att.* 13.19.3). In the letter, Cicero mentions a second edition of his four Academic books, and informs Atticus that in this edition the character Varro articulates the arguments of Antiochus "*contra* ἀκαταληψίαν" ("against inapprehensibility"). In the *Academica*, Varro's speech (*Acad.* 1.15–42) presents Antiochus's view of the history of philosophy, but again the noun ἀκαταληψία is not explicitly used by Varro or targeted in response to Varro. For present purposes, it is worth asking: Why do scholars cite this passage when discussing and specifying the Greek term ἀκαταληψία? Very schematically, I

"Antipater," 292; Perin, "Arcesilaus," 315–16; Castagnoli, "Hellenistic Academy," 209–10; Schofield, "Academic Epistemology," 328.
[63] Cf. Lévy, "La Nouvelle Académie," 146.

want to suggest two motivations. The attraction of this passage is partly due to the association of Arcesilaus with Socrates's confession of ignorance, and his relation to those Presocratics (Democritus, Anaxagoras, Empedocles, *inter al.*) who say that "nothing could be cognized, apprehended, or known" (*nihil cognosci nihil percipi nihil sciri posse*) because of the limitation of the senses and the weakness of intellect. In this context, pessimistic views on the faculties of the mind imply the denial of the fitness of the mind or senses for apprehension and knowledge, and thus they seem to justify attributing to Arcesilaus and his successors in the Hellenistic Academy a form of "epistemological pessimism."[64] Therefore, the denial of Stoic apprehension would disqualify the epistemic fitness of perceptual impressions for human "discerning" (*cerno*) or "understanding" (*intellego*).

In response to Varro, Cicero abstracts almost entirely from Arcesilaus's opposition to Stoic philosophy, which is to say, that Cicero abstracts almost entirely from the content of Stoic epistemology and the Stoic ontology of κατάληψις. And yet, the passage from *Acad.* 1.44–5 seems to suit epistemological centrism rather well, in the sense that Cicero himself passes over a precise specification of the nature of the things (*qua* Stoic bodies) that allegedly hide themselves in darkness. Proponents of the framework of epistemology are attracted to this passage in part because of this abstraction, for it seems to support the transfer of negativity in the alpha privative in ἀ-καταληψία away from the bodies or things themselves as they function in Stoic physics, as the negativity is fully absorbed by denying the faculties of rational subjects and each and every impression *qua* apprehensive. Still, it is not clear how the denial of knowability in this passage relates to the conceptual content of the anti-Stoic thesis of ἀκαταληψία, which negates the causal conception of κατάληψις. This is the second problem with taking Cicero's response to Varro as evidence for the epistemological reduction of ἀκαταληψία as "nothing can be known" to the simplistic negation of apprehensive impressions. The epistemological transfer, which the passage seems to support, distorts the metaphysical negativity of ἀκαταληψία as it results from Arcesilaus's attack on the ontology of Stoic apprehension, namely, the thesis that the bodies causally responsible for generating true impressions in space and time are relatively disposed such that they cannot generate apprehensive impressions for any mortal animal partaking in reason. Specifying the debilitation of the faculties of the mind and senses in isolation from the nature of the individual things presupposed in the Stoic account of apprehension obscures the negative relational property belonging to those bodies, according to the reconstruction of

[64] Brittain, "Middle Platonists," 297.

Arcesilaus's polemical arguments defended here. The abstract noun ἀκαταληψία is expressive of a particular quality belonging to some thing or class of things. In this case, the passive quality of the abstract noun is expressive of the pure relative disposition of a body *qua* ἀκατάληπτον. The philosophical specification of ἀκαταληψία does seem to imply a certain lack of fitness or incapacity on the part of the mortal animal partaking in reason as conceived by the Stoics, but such a lack also implies a lack in relation to the individual bodies supposedly obtaining and producing impressions worthy of assent.

Cicero's Latin does tend to obscure the distinction between a Stoic mental faculty and the object of that faculty, and yet there are traces of his recognition that Arcesilaus questioned not only the faculty of apprehension, but also the knowability of things themselves, invoking the "obscurity of things themselves" (*earum rerum obscuritate*, *Acad.* 1.44). From the perspective of Cicero's Lucullus, it can be said that Arcesilaus argued to the conclusion that "all things will be unclear" (*omnia fore incerta*, *Acad.* 2.32). Lucullus does not ascribe this argument to Arcesilaus himself, but the implication is that certain Academics in debate with the Stoa would "blame nature" (*accusa naturam*) for concealing the truth in the abyss, thereby rendering *all things* unclear, not simply impressions.[65] Notice that Stoic "nature" is blamed from the Academic point of view not because it imposes limits on *our* mental faculties; nature is blamed because it is held responsible for making all things "obscure." Elsewhere, Cicero testifies to Arcesilaus's affinity for the negative pronouncements concerning knowledge and truth issued by Presocratic philosophers (2.14), pronouncements with metaphysical as well as epistemological connotations in the sense that they convey judgments about beings or things (and the limitations of mental faculties). In other words, the statements recovered from the Presocratics in Cicero and associated with Arcesilaus and the Academy convey pessimistic judgments about the limitations of mental faculties (perception or thought), but also about things in general. Accordingly, "all things are shrouded in darkness" (*omnia tenebris circumfusa esse*, 1.44).

Recent scholars stress that the Stoic response to indiscernibility arguments would be incoherent without the metaphysical view of unique individual bodies. Echoing Michael Frede, David N. Sedley states that the coherence of the Stoic response depends on the causal network of bodily interaction, according to which

---

[65] Plausibly, here the unnamed is (or at least includes) Arcesilaus, and for the reasons that Ioppolo, as well as Brittain and Palmer ("New Academy's Appeals," 54–7), contend. Anna Maria Ioppolo, *Opinione e scienza: il dibattito tra Stoici e Academici nel III e nel II secolo a.C.* (Naples: Bibliopolis, 1986), 69–70.

numerically distinct and perceptually discernible bodies are capable of generating representations yielding the individualized qualities of a given external body as it really presents itself.[66] Casey Perin, in a humanistic vein, claims that the Stoic response to arguments from indiscernibility "reveals something important about the conditions under which the Stoics think we should assent to an impression." The Stoic response shows, according to Perin, that the metaphysical view of a unified totality of individual things "guarantees that there is a perceptible difference" between apparent indiscernibles.[67] According to Harald Thorsrud, the Stoic response to indiscernibility "relies on the principle of the identity of indiscernibles along with the notion that all distinct entities are at least in principle discernible."[68] With such observations, Frede and company allude to the idea that the structural ontology of individual bodies and incorporeals secures the epistemic possibility of Stoic apprehension. It is worth posing a series of additional questions about Stoic metaphysics in relation to Arcesilaus's indiscernibility arguments, questions advancing beyond the conventional framing of Hellenistic epistemology. What "guarantees" that the Stoic ontology of individual bodies is true? In other words, does the metaphysical view of individual bodies guarantee that there is a perceptible difference in the bodies themselves such that unique bodies can legitimately function as the ground of infallible apprehension? It seems that for the defense of Zeno's impressionism, an effective response to Academic attack must involve the following thought: the metaphysical view of individual bodies is true because apprehensive impressions confirm the relevant facts about the ways that bodies present themselves, and the incorporeal beings of space, time, and sayables as they actually obtain independent of representing animals. That is, the relevant information one needs for the apprehension of some part of the world's structure to be justifiable as a real part derives from a causal network of bodies with semantic content positioned at some place and time, where each body is qualitatively different from every other body or incorporeal thing. The structural ontology of individual bodies and incorporeal beings comprises an "absolute conception" of reality to the extent that bodies independent of apprehension ground the totality of beings, including the incorporeality of space, time, and sayables. Such bodies and their grounding relation to these incorporeal beings precede the rational effort of mortal animals to assess their representations. In this

---

[66] David N. Sedley, "Hellenistic Physics and Metaphysics," in Algra et al., *Cambridge History*, 404. See also Sedley, "Stoic Criterion of Identity," 266 (and LS 1, 174): the Stoic "response to the Indistinguishability Thesis is incoherent unless the metaphysical theory is introduced to back it up."
[67] Perin, "Stoic Epistemology," 397.
[68] Thorsrud, "Arcesilaus and Carneades," 65.

way, the structure of reality is *ipso facto* posited as an ontological context made up primarily (though not exclusively) of a unified totality of causally efficacious bodies capable of generating true impressions awaiting rational assessment and possible assent.

But there is a problem with this response. The problem is rooted in a judgment, or decision, governing the causal conception of Stoic apprehension, and it is first exposed by arguments from indiscernibility. The judgment posits that all relevant information about the totality of beings and the structural relations among different kinds of being—what Heidegger identifies as "the totality of relevance" (*Bewandtnisganzheit, Sein und Zeit,* § 18, 86)—can only come from real individual bodies obtaining at some place and time, the only kind of being capable of generating impressions worthy of assent. The realist ontology of absolute difference comprising the causal conception lays out the totality of relevant conditions supposedly determining the success or failure for apprehension. But it remains unclear why the structural conditions of this realist ontology should be taken as the relevant ontological conditions, for the justification of these conditions as the relevant metaphysical conditions by means of empirical induction would involve an overt form of circular reasoning. After all, how could Zeno or any other Stoic demonstrate that all bodies are individually distinct by means of the causal conception without having already presupposed the independent reality of such bodies? For the causal conception of apprehension seems to depend on the *a priori* judgment that there *are* bodies external to the ruling part of the soul with intrinsic and extrinsic properties of their own, and it is in virtue of such real properties that each and every body is conceived as cognitively discernible from every other being, whether bodily or incorporeal. Moreover, if a Stoic were to insist that this realist ontology is itself a theoretical consequence of causal effects from the activity of bodies as they really present themselves, then they would need to acknowledge the possibility that this realist ontology, as an effect distinguishable from its underlying causes, could be spurious or come from what is not present, like every other representation posited in the causal conception. In other words, the argumentative task for Zeno and the Stoics would then be to defend, according to the causal conception, the conditions of the realist ontology as a set of true representations that come from bodies themselves. In making this argument, the Stoic defense would be unable to avoid appealing to *what there is*—individual bodies and incorporeals—without presupposing unmediated access to bodies and incorporeals themselves as the relevant ontological conditions of external bodies independent of apprehension. These conditions might be plausible, but they are not self-evident nor are they infallibly secure. The articulation of such conditions controverts the premise of Zeno's representationalist view of apprehension, which stipulates that successful apprehension comes from the bodies that obtain and does so in accordance with the way those present things actually are. If the articulation of such conditions cannot be justified by means of the causal model without generating this circle of reasoning, then there is nothing to prevent indiscernibility arguments from undermining the ontology of Stoic apprehension.

Given the causal model's dependence on a judgment about the structure of the world as a whole, it is incapable of eliminating the possibility that the world of beings could have been structured in ways that diverge from the purported realism of individual beings. As Brunschwig reasons, "the Stoic image of the world, even in its details, derives from this strong intuition [of a 'unified totality of bodies'], which precedes all proofs..."[69] The attack on early Stoic philosophy initiated by Arcesilaus shows, according to the rational reconstruction defended in this chapter, that the corporeal and incorporeal beings of Stoic apprehension could have been structured in ways that fundamentally differ from the way that Zeno and canonical Stoics tacitly judged in defending the account of apprehension. One should agree with Brunschwig that the structure of Stoic ontology "depends not on empirical considerations but rather on conceptual decisions," but one should also insist that Arcesilaus's arguments contested those very decisions.

---

[69] Brunschwig, "Stoicism," in Brunschwig and Lloyd, *Greek Thought*, 988.

3

Total Inaction and the Impossibility of Stoic Ethics

One ancient source indicates that Arcesilaus posed problems for "parts" of the Stoic tripartition other than just the logical (i.e., other than what recent historiographers reconstruct as the epistemological part). Zeno's successor Cleanthes reportedly said the following about his older contemporary: "Even if he [Arcesilaus] eliminates appropriate action in argument (λόγῳ), he affirms it at any rate in his actions (τοῖς ἔργοις, D.L. 7.171, F 112 Vezzoli)." This report suggests that in his actions Arcesilaus conducted himself in a manner that was taken by a follower of Zeno to be consistent with the latter's account of imperfect or non-virtuous appropriate action.[1] But if Arcesilaus eliminated by means of argument the canonical doctrine of appropriate action, how could he have affirmed appropriate action in his actions? To clarify this unlikely coupling of theoretical elimination and practical affirmation, it will be necessary to begin with a brief review of what Arcesilaus reportedly said about regulating actions.

Sextus Empiricus reports that Arcesilaus invoked the notion of the "reasonable" (τὸ εὔλογον, Sextus, *M.* 7.158 (< F 87 Vezzoli, LS 69B)) to explain the regulation of actions generally. The sequence of the argument is relevant to specifying the content of this notion. Sextus informs readers that after contesting the causal account of the apprehensive impression, Arcesilaus proceeded to invoke the outlines of a view concerning how one may act rightly without the regulative criterion of apprehensive impressions.

---

[1] Upon the death of Arcesilaus, Lacydes of Cyrene becomes head of the Academy. Sources indicate that Lacydes maintained the arguments of Arcesilaus against the Stoa (Cicero, *Acad.* 2.16, Philodemus, *Acad. hist.* col. 21.36–42). In another source, Lacydes is presented as accepting a version of Cleanthes's charge: "What we say about these things in our lectures is one thing, Lacydes said, and how we live another" (Numen. *apud* Euseb., *Praep. ev.* 14.7.9). For discussion of the conflicting reports on Lacydes in Cicero and Philodemus, see Carlos Lévy, "Les petits Académiciens: Lacyde, Charmadas, Métrodore de Stratonice," in Bonazzi et al., *L'eredità platonica*, 53–60.

Arcesilaus says that, suspending [assent] about all things, one will regulate choice and avoidance and actions generally by the reasonable; and by proceeding in accordance with this criterion of the reasonable (τῷ εὐλόγῳ), one will act rightly. For happiness comes about through insight, and insight lies in right actions (ἐν τοῖς κατορθώμασιν), and the right action is that which, when done, has a reasonable justification (ἀπολογίαν, M. 7.158 [trans. modified from Bett, ed., *Against the Logicians*, 34]).[2]

Arcesilaus suggests, immediately following an argument for the metaphysical thesis of inapprehensibility, that one will nevertheless adopt a criterion of action, the εὔλογον ("the reasonable"). Conceptually, this alternative criterion abandons any auxiliary commitment to assent, or the ontology of apprehensible bodies, and thus it seems perfectly consistent with the suspension of assent about all inapprehensible things. Arcesilaus appropriates concepts used in Zenonian ethics, such as εὔλογον, ἀπολογία, κατόρθωμα, but in doing so reduces the latter ("right action") to the Stoic notion of appropriate action that is assigned to the non-virtuous. Appropriating in this way, Arcesilaus introduces the possibility of acting rightly by severing "insight" and "happiness" from the Stoic assumption that there is such a thing as a unified world structurally comprised of knowable principles and parts.

Yet, at *PH* 1.232–4, Sextus seems to partially assimilate Arcesilaus to the Pyrrhonists. That is to say, Arcesilaus "is not found making assertions about the reality or non-reality of anything, nor does he prefer one thing to another by way of credibility or incredibility, but suspends [assent] about all things" (ἀλλὰ περὶ πάντων ἐπέχει, 1.232, trans. modified from LS 68I). However, Sextus also represents Arcesilaus as saying or perhaps affirming that "suspension of assent is the end," and that "particular suspensions of judgment are goods and particular assents are bads." Here Sextus introduces a possible deviation from the Pyrrhonian way of speaking, that is, a manner of speaking about what is apparent without affirming the reality or non-reality of anything. For "some say," so Sextus reports, that Arcesilaus affirms "with reference to nature" (ὡς πρὸς τὴν φύσιν, 1.233).[3]

---

[2] ὅτι ὁ περὶ πάντων ἐπέχων κανονιεῖ τὰς αἱρέσεις καὶ φυγὰς καὶ κοινῶς τὰς πράξεις τῷ εὐλόγῳ, κατὰ τοῦτό τε προερχόμενος τὸ κριτήριον κατορθώσει· τὴν μὲν γὰρ εὐδαιμονίαν, περιγίνεσθαι διὰ τῆς φρονήσεως, τὴν δὲ φρόνησιν κεῖσθαι ἐν τοῖς κατορθώμασιν, τὸ δὲ κατόρθωμα εἶναι ὅπερ πραχθὲν εὔλογον ἔχει ἀπολογίαν. ὁ προσέχων οὖν τῷ εὐλόγῳ κατορθώσει καὶ εὐδαιμονήσει. Following Ioppolo, *La testimonianza*, 110–3, and Mutschmann's reading of ὁ περὶ πάντων ἐπέχων here, not οὐ περὶ πάντων ἐπέχων. Cf. Bett, ed., *Against the Logicians*, 34 n71.

[3] Ioppolo, "Arcesilaus," 40, 42–3. As Ioppolo argues, given the problematic nature of the testimony here at *PH* 1.232–4, this passage is hardly a basis upon which to confirm that the ascribed expression

From the viewpoint of Zeno and early Stoic orthodoxy, the appropriated notion of right action and the explicit association of goodness with particular suspensions of assent are untenable ethical views, compelling explicit objection. Both ideas depart from the assumptions of realism governing the overall structure of early Stoic metaphysics. Recall that Zenonian impressionism is committed to the apprehensive impression as that which provides the criterion of truth about the real spatiotemporal bodies obtaining independent of any representation. What is more, on the orthodox Stoic view, without this special sort of impression, there is simply no transactional mechanism available to mobilize the psychological transformation of the mortal animal's *hēgemonikon* into the sage's perfect rationality. Apprehensive impressions are necessary for proficiency in Zenonian logic (including its subparts, rhetoric and dialectic), just as mastery of the subparts is necessary for ethical progress.

The Ontology of Stoic Virtue

The Stoics respond to Arcesilaus's arguments against the causal account of apprehension with an objection, what is commonly called the "inaction" objection (ἀπραξία/*omnem actionem tollit e vita*).⁴ In formulating this objection, Arcesilaus's opponents recognize that the metaphysical theses of ἀκαταληψία and ἐποχὴ περὶ πάντων convey destructive ethical implications. Evidently, the Stoics object by announcing that such arguments against Zenonian impressionism would destroy the possibility of action (Plutarch, *Adv. Col.* 1122a–e (< LS 69A, F 75 Vezzoli), Cicero, *Acad.* 2.31–2), as well as the joint possibility of virtue and happiness (Sextus, *M.* 7.158 (< F 87 Vezzoli, LS 69B), cf. Cicero, *Acad.* 2.23–5, 31, 39). To reiterate, it seems then that in formulating this objection the Stoics were aware that, by arguing to the thesis that bodies are ἀκατάληπτα and to the conclusion that one should suspend assent about bodies and things more generally, Arcesilaus was ipso facto destroying the connection and mutually dependent possibilities of acting virtuously (ethics) and knowing the world *qua* natural living whole (physics).⁵ If real spatiotemporal bodies are inapprehensible, and if there are no apprehensive impressions granting

---

ὡς πρὸς τὴν φύσιν ("in reference to nature") refers to Arcesilaus's tendency to speak affirmatively about the "ontological" nature of things, including what is really good or bad.

⁴ For the Greek term referring to "inaction," or the "lack of action," see Plutarch, *Adv. Col.* 1122a. Cf. Cicero, *Acad.* 2.39, for a similar expression in Latin.

⁵ In addition to Cleanthes's critical remark cited above, consider the rebuke of Arcesilaus by Colotes (320–268 BCE), a pupil of Epicurus and contemporary of Arcesilaus, which is reported by Plutarch

epistemic possibility to bodies as they really are, then the right course of action is to suspend assent about each and every actual body generating true impressions. One might infer from this objection that the dispute between Arcesilaus and Stoic orthodoxy has less to do with epistemology than it does with the so-called "basic connection between epistemological theory and ethics."[6] However, given the importance of the Stoic doctrine of the natural body as causally efficacious, it is important to see how the "connection" itself connects to an even more basic condition. The framework of the ontology of Stoic apprehension demonstrates that indiscernibility arguments *really* challenge the metaphysical basis of this connection (i.e., the epistemological-ethical), and thereby reveal the inseparability of this connection from the underlying conditions prescribed by Stoic physics.[7] To fully explicate the conceptual content of the "basic connection" as it functions in Stoic philosophy, one should specify the content of the causal account of Stoic apprehension, as argued above, in the terms of Stoic physics.[8] Against the selective framework of epistemology and its abstract posit of epistemic subjects and generic *objects* in isolation from the content of Stoic physics, the specifications of *de re* interpretation *de traditione* defended in the previous chapter reconstruct Arcesilaus's opposition to early Stoic philosophy as an opposition that challenges the ontological conditions of apprehension. But now, looking ahead, it will be argued more explicitly that the ontological conditions of corporeal and incorporeal beings are the very same ontological conditions purportedly making the ideal of Stoic virtue a realizable aim for mortal animals partaking in reason.

Henceforth, the framework of the ontology of knowledge serves a dual purpose. The ontology of Stoic apprehension functions as the interpretive framework of the ontology of Stoic virtue. The ontological conditions for Stoic apprehension

---

Comm. not. 1059b–c (= F 72 Vezzoli, LS 40G)): Arcesilaus "initiated the violence and offense (ὕβρεως καὶ παρανομίας) against habituation (συνήθειαν)."

[6] Spinelli, "Ancient Stoicism," 40.
[7] For M. Frede's reference to Stoic physics in relation to the epistemological and ethical connection, see Chapter 1, n42.
[8] Discussing Stoic moral psychology, Tad Brennan issues useful cautionary remarks for contemporary readers. He addresses the ancient interface between ethics and psychology, or "the ancient mixing axiom of moral psychology." Before turning to the historiographical task of specifying the conceptual content of Stoic moral psychology, Brennan is upfront about adopting a contemporary understanding of the fields of inquiry: "Psychology is clearly a descriptive field, and ethics is the normative field *par excellence*; the one tells us how the human mind *does* function, the other tells us how human agents *ought* to act." Brennan informs readers that the ancients held a different understanding of the fields of inquiry: "Because they all embrace some type of naturalism in their ethical foundations, ancient theories tend to begin their ethical theorizing along with their psychology, not prior to it." Unfortunately, no such prefatory remark is issued with regard to the naturalistic interface of epistemology and ethics in the section of the paper examining "the background in epistemology and ethics." Tad Brennan, "Stoic Moral Psychology," in Inwood, *Companion to the Stoics*, 257–65.

stipulate that the souls of mortal animals partaking in reason undertake certain transformative practices for knowledge and virtue *qua* epistemic dispositions to be possible. The stable and enduring disposition of perfect rationality entails that the philosopher trains not only in conducting oneself appropriately in almost any situation, but that along with training in deeds the aspiring sage must train in the disciplines of logic and physics.[9] Cicero and Sextus present Arcesilaus's polemic with Stoic philosophy as a critical investigation of the Stoic idealization of the sage (Cicero, *Acad.* 2.115, 2.75–7, Sextus, *M.* 7.155–7 (< F 87 Vezzoli)). Two of Cicero's main characters ostensibly agree about the topic of their adversarial dialogue: for example, Cicero's Lucullus (*Acad.* 2.57) and Cicero's representation of himself as Cicero (*Acad.* 2.66, 2.115). It is agreed that the entire debate between the Academics and Stoics revolves around the subject of the sage (*sapiens*), which obviously pertains to the possibility of virtue. In Sextus's presentation, the so-called basic connection between apprehension (epistemology) and virtue (ethics) is more implicit than explicit; readers are told that after Arcesilaus's attack on impressionism and the Stoic criterion associated with the causal mechanism of individual bodies, "it was necessary to investigate" the question of the conduct of life as well, which Sextus says "is not of a nature to be accounted for without a criterion" (*M.* 7.158).

Logic, as a partial whole comprised of its own subparts, is essentially endowed by the Stoics with the task of securing a method of reasoning that guards against the giving of assent to impressions coming from what is not present, or from what is present but not in accordance with the present body as it really is. The task is also meant to secure the dispositional knowing required by the ideal of Stoic virtue. For further insight into Zeno's idealization of the sage, one may look to the association of τέχνη ("expertise") with φύσις ("nature"). In Olympiodorus's *Commentary on the Gorgias* (*In. Pl. Gorg.* 12.1, *SVF* 1.73, LS 42A), readers find the following account of expertise: "Zeno says that expertise is a system of apprehensions unified by being exercised together (σύστημα ἐκ καταλήψεων συγγεγυμνασμένων) in the interests of some goal from among those that are advantageous in life."[10] In Cicero, it is reported that Zeno identifies

---

[9] On the physical dimension of Stoic virtue as a "force," see Thomas Bénatouïl, "Force, fermeté, froid: la dimension physique de la vertu stoïcienne," in *Philosophie Antique* 5 (2005): 7–13.

[10] For discussion of this definition, see F. E. Sparshott, "Zeno on Art: Anatomy of a Definition," in *The Stoics*, ed. John M. Rist (Berkeley: University of California Press, 1978), 284–90; John Sellars, *The Art of Living: The Stoics on the Nature and Function of Philosophy*, 2nd ed. (London: Bloomsbury, 2003), 69. Chrysippus clarifies Zeno's definition by adding ἐμπειρίᾳ ("in experience") after the term καταλήψεων (David, *Prol. philos.* 44.5 Busse). For useful comments on this addition, see Jaap Mansfeld, "*Techne*: A New Fragment of Chrysippus," *Greek, Roman, and Byzantine Studies* 24 (1983): 58–60, 63–5.

nature with "designing fire" (*ignem artificiosum*/[ἡ φύσις ἐστι] πῦρ τεχνικὸν), granting nature the agency of expertise as designing fire proceeds "to bringing things into being in a certain way" (Cicero, *De nat. deor.* 2.57 (= *SVF* 1.171), D.L. 7.156 (= *SVF* 2.776)), for it supposedly "cares and plans ahead for what serves the advantages and purposes of all [things in nature]." In other reports of the Stoic doctrine, designing fire is identified with the intelligence of god: "The Stoics make clear that god is thinking, a designing fire proceeding methodically towards the generation of the world" (Aëtius, 1.7.33 (= *SVF* 2.1027, LS 46A)). The expertise of fire thinks insofar as it plans ahead, brings order, and cares for things, but as is learned from additional testimony (cited below), the methodical procedure of this providential care does not depend upon or make rational use of impressions or a system of apprehensions. More simply stated, the sage depends upon and makes use of impressions, but the expertise of nature itself (i.e., the intelligence of god) incurs no such dependency.

It seems that Chrysippus is responsible for making explicit the distinction between the sage's expertise and the expertise of nature *qua* designing fire.[11] The sage's expertise, or what may otherwise be designated the special type of "fitting expertise" (ἄσκησιν ἐπιτηδείου τέχνης, Aëtius, 1 proem. 2 (= *SVF* 2.35, LS 26A), ἐπιτηδείαν δὲ τέχνην τὴν σοφίαν, Ps. Galen, *Hist. Phil.* 5, 602.19 (Diels), cf. Cicero's reference to *aptus* at *Acad.* 2.31), which characterizes the exercise of wisdom, depends upon the availability of the apprehensive impression and a unified system of apprehensive impressions received in experience generally.[12] The expertise of the sage is therefore the result of experienced training in the exercise of discriminating true from false impressions, and the corresponding practice of giving assent only to those (apprehensive) impressions coming from what is present and accurately representing what is present. Furthermore, on the basis of training and exercise in every sphere of life, the sage comes to know nature *qua* designing fire, and the knowledge of designing fire allows the sage to comprehend her expertise in life as the expertise of "fitting" oneself as an individual mortal animal partaking in reason into the providential nature of the whole. In sum, the sage comprehends what it means for the reason of an individual soul to partake in the reason of the world.

---

[11] Chrysippus amends Cleanthes's definition of τέχνη by adding μετὰ φαντασιῶν ("with impressions") (Olympiodorus, *In Pl. Gorg.* 2.2) or μετὰ φαντασίας (David, *Prol. philos.* 43.30–44.5 Busse). The clarification would also improve on another formulation of τέχνη ascribed to Zeno: τέχνη ἐστὶν ἕξις ὁδοποιητική (*SVF* 1.72). Cf. Mansfeld, "Techne," 57, 60–5; Brouwer, *Stoic Sage*, 47.

[12] Brouwer, *Stoic Sage*, 44–9.

For the individual aspiring to the Stoic ideal of wisdom, training in the discipline of giving assent to impressions promises to yield beneficial consequences in the sphere of action, where one makes decisions or choices about what to do in particular circumstances. Without training in logic, the mortal animal aspiring to virtue would be deprived of the means of discovering the higher expertise of nature *qua* designing fire. The possibility of living in agreement with the order and structure of nature as a whole depends upon the system of apprehensions delivered and secured by means of giving assent to apprehensive impressions. The specifications yielded thus far from the framework of the ontology of Stoic apprehension reveal that the ontological conditions for the possibility of apprehension serve as the very same conditions for the possibility of wisdom. On the supposition that the ideal of Stoic virtue is a "disposition in agreement" (διάθεσιν εἶναι ὁμολογουμένην, D.L. 7.89), the exercise of cultivating the disposition of virtue requires proficiency in the practice of unifying apprehensions into a system, which helps bring the mortal animal partaking in reason into a self-conscious harmony with the supreme rationality of the world as a structured whole.

Although training in logic is necessary, it is certainly not sufficient to realize the Grand End of living in accordance with the supreme rationality of the world. Zeno is the first philosopher of antiquity to compose a technical treatise to stipulate a number of ethical precepts for the regular performance of so-called appropriate actions. In the treatise "On Appropriate Action" (Περὶ τοῦ καθήκοντος, D.L. 7.4), Zeno is said to have catalogued a comprehensive range of "precepts" for mortal animals partaking in reason on how to act in a comprehensive range of roles and situations. Seneca records (*Ep.* 83.9) one set of precepts that Zeno generalized in syllogistic form to deduce an appropriate action: "No one entrusts a secret to a drunk. But one will entrust it to the good man. Therefore, the good man does not get drunk." An "appropriate action," according to Zeno, is "that which when done admits of a good or reasonable justification" (εὔλογον [. . .] ἀπολογισμόν, D.L. 7.107, *SVF* 1.230), even if that justification does not come from the one committing the act (*SVF* 3.394). "Appropriate action" may refer to the non-virtuous actions of mortal animals directed instinctively, and without reason, at the preservation of their natural constitution, or it may refer to the actions of mortal animals who select what is appropriate to do, according to reason. In fact, the Stoic notion of "appropriate actions" (τὰ καθήκοντα/*officia*) is conceptually inclusive such that it can embrace the actions of plants (D.L. 7.107), mortal animals in general, as well as the actions of the ideal sage (Cicero, *De fin.* 3.59). For the mortal animal partaking in reason imperfectly, or non-virtuously, appropriate action is nevertheless the kind of action that is variably responsive to rational consideration, the sort of responsive rationality that is dependent on the use of apprehensive impressions. At this level, the difference between the appropriate action of the non-virtuous mortal animal with reason and the appropriate action of the sage consists in the relative stability of the disposition from which the mortal animal acts. The unstable disposition of the non-virtuous is prone to making moral mistakes in particular situations, frequently erring in giving assent to evaluative impressions that are non-apprehensive. Thus, the perfect disposition of the sage seems to be "based on knowledge about *moral objects*, i.e., on a set of assents to apprehensive moral/evaluative impressions about moral particulars" (italics added).[13] Virtuous action is the sort of appropriate action exercised on the basis of a true and stable set of apprehensions about nature, or some part of it, and the naturalness of the good. Perfectly appropriate actions are deemed equivalent to the "right actions" (κατορθώματα, Stob., *Ecl.* 5.906.18–907.5) characteristic of the sage, and the performance of such actions presupposes a stable and unshakeable disposition, a soul in perfect conformity with the governing principle of nature (Cicero, *De fin.* 3.20–1). Hence, the Zenonian sense of "reasonable justification" (εὔλογος ἀπολογία/*probabilis ratio*, Stob., *Ecl.* 2.85, Cicero, *De fin.* 3.58) applies to the deeds of the sage in the strict sense that only the sage is able to realize and express the "good justification" of such deeds. Good justification is therefore informed by a set of assents to impressions coming from what some might specify as *moral objects*, or specified metaphysically, on a system of apprehensive impressions originating from the experience of individual bodies obtaining in a causal network. In this study, I denominate the early Stoic notions of justification and the reasonable, as well as the corresponding rank of imperfect/perfect appropriate action, the tenets of a Grand End theory of action.[14] The Grand End theory of action, in its Stoic guise, holds that the reasonability of mortal animals partaking in reason (in both its perfect and imperfect exercises) is a homologous part of a grand, supreme, and more comprehensive rational order functioning as the basis of what is appropriate and good for mortal animals capable of partaking in the rationality of this grand order of things.

The broad and inclusive sense of "appropriate action" is conceptually linked to the Stoic notion of the "impulsive impression." The Stoics say that "what moves impulse is nothing other than an impulsive impression of what is immediately

---

[13] Pavle Stojanović, "Moral Apprehensive Impressions," in *Epictetus: His Continuing Influence and Contemporary Relevance*, ed. Dane R. Gordon and David B. Suits (Rochester: RIT Press, 2014), 184.
[14] Cf. Sarah Broadie, *Ethics with Aristotle* (Oxford: Oxford University Press, 1991), 198–202.

appropriate" (Stob., *Ecl.* 2.86.17–18 (= *SVF* 3.169, LS 53Q(1)), cf. LS 2, 318 (LS 53Q 2–3)).[15] Impulse is considered a necessary and sufficient condition for action: when a mortal animal has an impulse to do something, it is said that the animal does it then and there (Cicero, *Off.* 1.132 (= LS 53J)). Mortal animals partaking in reason supposedly receive impressions deriving from real bodies; stimulated by impressions of those bodies in a given causal network, the motions of aversion or attraction, or impulses, spring into formation. Impulsive impressions are likely to involve the instinctual response that it is appropriate "then and there" to do *K*—supposing *K* to be some potential action that is appropriate to pursue. Impulses are for mortal animals direct responses to the apparent content of an impression, but in the case of mortal animals partaking in reason, or in the case of mortal animals partaking in the gradual emergence of the governing faculty of reason, the faculty of reason implies a developmental capacity to mediate the deliverances of instinctual response and transform impulses into a form that is more appropriate to the kind of mortal animal endowed with the power of becoming aware of itself as a mortal animal partaking in reason. Reason, as the governing power of the soul, grants the mortal animal with the capacity to reflect and evaluate whether this or that action is, here and now, appropriate and worth pursuing for a mortal animal partaking in reason.

The transformation of impulse by certain mortal animals seems to imply that there is a specific sort of apprehensive impression, perhaps more precisely specified as apprehensive impressions of *moral objects* or true representations of *moral states of affairs*.[16] In addition, it is worth considering whether there is such a species of "moral apprehensive impressions," a special sort of the apprehensive impression containing moral predicates, such as "prudence" or "courage," in the event some individual body obtains in a particular causal situation at some mortal animal partaking in reason. If one is inclined to make such a specification, then perhaps it follows that for the perfection of appropriate action the most important kind of impression is the species of morally evaluative apprehensive impressions. Furthermore, a species division within the genus of apprehensive impression

---

[15] τὸ δὲ κινοῦν τὴν ὁρμὴν οὐδὲν ἕτερον εἶναι λέγουσιν ἀλλ' ἢ φαντασίαν ὁρμητικὴν τοῦ καθήκοντος αὐτόθεν (Stob., *Ecl.* 2.86.17). Translation of αὐτόθεν in this context is controversial. Consider, for instance, the alternative translation in Inwood, *Ethics and Human Action*, 224: "They say that what stimulates impulse is nothing but a hormetic presentation of what is obviously [or immediately; the sense of *authoten* [*sic*: *autothen*] is uncertain] appropriate." For a rendering of αὐτόθεν ascribing a first-person perspective to the indexical element of αὐτόθεν, see Stojanović, "Moral Apprehensive Impressions," in Gordon et al., *Epictetus*, 180–1.

[16] Stojanović, "Moral Apprehensive Impressions," 169–73, uses the distinction between "morally neutral" states of affairs ("descriptive") and moral states of affairs ("evaluative") to divide the apprehensive impression into two species: purely descriptive, or "morally neutral," apprehensive impressions, on the one hand, and descriptive/evaluative apprehensive impressions, on the other.

could help to recover and defend the *de re* specifications of epistemological centrism as more viable reconstructions of Arcesilaus's epistemological dispute with the causal account of apprehension. What I mean is the following: from the perspective of epistemological centrism, the challenge that Arcesilaus poses for the causal account could be defined as primarily epistemological in the specific sense that his arguments target the species of the so-called evaluatively neutral apprehensive impression, which is to say, the species of apprehensive impression that is purely descriptive, hence nonevaluative. This species of the apprehensive impression would be non-prescriptive in the sense that it describes what really obtains, but does not identify what to pursue or avoid, select or not select, in the sphere of ordinary action. On the basis of this application, proponents of epistemological centrism might then be in a better position to defend themselves against the metaphysical specifications of the previous chapter, to establish a new and improved version of the epistemological *de re* specification that Arcesilaus (and perhaps the Hellenistic Academy, more generally) focuses the polemic primarily on the species of morally neutral apprehensive impressions— the specific sort of impression essentially involving cases of discriminating between extremely similar, but distinct, nonmoral *objects*. Accordingly, the epistemological debate between Arcesilaus and the Stoa, to take one example from recent literature pursuing a similar line of reconstruction, is thus concerned with the possibility of "an impression that presents something as an apple that is actually an artificial apple," and not about whether it is good to eat this or that fruit.[17]

There seems to be some indication that the early Stoa conceived of apprehensive impressions as inclusive of predicates that are descriptive and morally neutral (e.g., x is an artificial apple), as well as predicates that are both descriptive and evaluative (e.g., x's beauty is good). Zeno thought of prudence as knowledge of what is good, bad, or neither good nor bad (D.L. 7.92, cf. Plutarch, *Virt. mor.* 441a (= *SVF* 1.201), Stob., *Ecl.* 2.59.4–7), and since knowledge is thought to involve secure and unshakeable κατάληψις, the correct identification of someone being prudent in a given scenario must be informed by a set of assents to evaluative apprehensive impressions. Because particular acts of prudence are considered corporeal (Stob., *Ecl.* 2.64.20–2), and the dispositions of an individual soul

---

[17] Vogt claims: "the debate between Sceptics and Stoics is about an impression that presents something as an apple that is actually an artificial apple—it is not about the sage's assent to the hormetic impression 'I should eat this.'" Katja Maria Vogt, *Law, Reason and the Cosmic City: Political Philosophy in the Early Stoa* (Oxford: Oxford University Press, 2008), 173 n31. For a brief summary of the dispute that adopts the "morally neutral" species of apprehensive impressions as focal to the polemic, see Stojanović, "Moral Apprehensive Impressions," 166–8.

stimulating those actions are also corporeal, the moral property of a rational body "being courageous," or "being prudent," should obtain (ὑπάρχειν) in such a way that the apprehensible body bearing that moral property generates apprehensive impressions that are descriptive and evaluative. This entails that the paradigmatic form of the apprehensive impression "*s* is *P*"—taking *s* as an individual apprehensible body and *P* as a predicate corresponding to some property possessed by the body causing the impression—must also embrace a species of that paradigmatic form: the propositional structure of the moral apprehensive impression "*s* is *mP*"—taking *s* as an individual apprehensible body and *mP* as a moral predicate corresponding to some moral property possessed by the body causing the impression. Moreover, there are additional indications that the morally apprehensive impressions have an important function in later Stoic thought, at least for those Stoics apparently engaged in clarifying and improving upon the original doctrine of apprehensive impressions. Plutarch reports that Chrysippus says "that goods and bads are perceptible" (*St. rep.* 1042e–f (= LS 60R, *SVF* 3.85), cf. 1038c) and that it is possible "to perceive foolishness, cowardice, and many other vices, but also instances of right action, such as insight, courage and the remaining virtues." The text confirms, at least for this Stoic, that individual actions are perceptible in an evaluative way. Whether Zeno himself thought that the evaluative predicates of apprehensible bodies are perceptible is more difficult to establish. In fact, the difficulty extends to the following set of questions: does Zeno himself differentiate the perceptual impressions grasping evaluative predicates of apprehensible bodies from the perceptual impressions grasping nonmoral predicates of apprehensible bodies? If apprehensive impressions can be perceptual and more or less evaluative, what does this mean for impulsive impressions? Can impulsive impressions be apprehensive? One place to begin here is with the standard scholarly view denying that impulsive impressions can be apprehensive.[18] Arguments in support of this denial are informative of how scholars typically specify the ethical import of the apprehensive impression as a genus or kind. One factor seemingly in support of the denial is the evident contrast in causal origin between correct applications of the moral predicate to what is prudent in particular actions which already obtain and correct applications of what is immediately prudent for one to do then and there. The latter involves a first-person perspective on what should be done in the immediate future, which is to say, the application involves a perspective on some

---

[18] However, Stojanović, "Moral Apprehensive Impressions," 176–9, argues persuasively against the claim advanced by Striker, "Sceptical Strategies," 70–2; Brennan, "Reasonable Impressions," 324 (and more recently Tad Brennan, *The Stoic Life: Emotions, Duties, and Fate* (Oxford: Oxford University Press, 2005), 76), that is, the claim that impressions *cannot* be both evaluative and perceptual.

future action, an action that has yet to obtain. By contrast, the former involves the presence of both the mortal animal partaking in reason and the properties of the action being perceived. The evaluative perception of the action need not lead the perceiver to do anything—other than simply assent to the proposition that so and so is being moderate, or acting appropriately in the situation. For instance, the perceiving animal may rationally apply the moral predicate of prudence or moderation to particular actions in assenting to the moral apprehensive impression that it is prudent for the agent to go on the embassy, or that it is appropriate for the bird to flee the snare. In such cases, the impressions appear to be non-impulsive, for they are not of the type to motivate then and there the movement or action of the animal's first-person perspective. Moreover, impulsive impressions of mortal animals partaking in reason apparently fail to satisfy at least one of the three conditions for an impression to be apprehensive: that is, the first causal requirement, or externalist condition, stipulated by the ontology of apprehension. Consider the mortal animal who assents to the impulsive impression that it is appropriate for her to eat, thus initiating an impulse toward the predicate "to eat." If the result of this action means *inter al.* that the animal takes on the property of eating, in other words, if as a result of eating, the property of eating "obtains," the logical implication is that the appropriate action indicated by the impulsive impression did not actually obtain before the animal started eating. Chrysippus clarifies the logic of this implication by saying that

> only the present obtains (ὑπάρχειν); the past and the future subsist (ὑφεστάναι) but obtain in no way (ὑπάρχειν δὲ οὐδαμῶς), just as only predicates which are [actual] properties are said to obtain (ὑπάρχειν), for instance, walking around obtains at me (ὑπάρχει μοι) when I am walking around, but it does not obtain (οὐχ ὑπάρχει) when I am lying down or sitting. (Stob., *Ecl.* 1.106.20–3 (< LS 51B, part, *SVF* 2.509))[19]

Before the mortal animal gives assent to the impulsive impression that it is appropriate for the animal to eat then and there, the property of eating is not spatiotemporally present, nor does it "obtain at the animal" as an actual particular property that could contribute to causing the impression that it is appropriate for the animal to pursue eating here and now. For this reason, it seems that the impulsive impression is the sort of impression that cannot be caused in the way that descriptive and evaluative apprehensive impressions need to be caused.[20]

---

[19] The translation adopted here is that of Bailey, "Structure of Stoic Metaphysics," 265.
[20] For a novel attempt at rationally reconstructing how evaluative impressions might meet the three conditions stipulated in the original account of the apprehensive impression, see Stojanović, "Moral Apprehensive Impressions," 184–91.

This kind of reasoning would seem to support the view that impulsive impressions differ in kind from apprehensive impressions. One potential difficulty with characterizing impulsive impressions as essentially non-apprehensive is that it seems to render impulsive impressions relatively insignificant to the task of differentiating perfect right actions from the appropriate actions of the non-virtuous. One might wonder: How should one understand the function of non-apprehensive impulsive impressions for the sage and the non-virtuous? One approach to this issue might invoke the species division of the apprehensive impression outlined above: with one species classifying the evaluatively neutral or nonmorally descriptive apprehensive impression, and the other classifying the morally evaluative apprehensive impression. It is worth recalling that Zeno holds a view of action maintaining that it is reasonable in certain situations for mortal animals partaking in reason to act so as to improve one's health, or to enhance one's material prosperity. According to Diogenes Laertius (D.L. 7.108–9 (= LS 59E)), the Stoics teach and believe that honoring parents or spending time with friends in many contexts is the appropriate action to select. Such reasonable actions are not considered good in the strict sense. The non-virtuous sense of the "reasonable" (εὔλογος) is inclusive of actions that for the most part conform to general precepts (*praecepta*, Cicero, *Off.* 1.6, Seneca, *Ep.* 94–5, esp. 94.33–7), namely, propositions which Zeno presumably formalized in his treatise *On Appropriate Action*, to instruct mortal animals partaking in reason at varying levels of moral training on how to discern what is appropriate to do then and there. Consistency in the practice of correctly applying these *praecepta* in the relevant situation is meant to inculcate, or begin the process of inculcating, the disposition of discernment that the non-virtuous agent requires for developing the correct evaluative stance in each context of action and for completing the transformation to virtue (Seneca, *Ep.* 94.18–19).[21] Thus one approach to the distinction between perfect right actions and the appropriate actions of the non-virtuous begins with the observation that Zeno evidently deemed it worthwhile to articulate moral propositions using morally evaluative apprehensive impressions. For example, from a set of impressions correctly evaluating and identifying the drunken behavior of certain animals in certain situations as inappropriate behavior, the Stoic could formulate a general

---

[21] Brad Inwood, "Rules and Reasoning in Stoic Ethics," in *Topics in Stoic Philosophy*, ed. Katerina Ierodiakonou (Oxford: Clarendon Press, 1999), 98–110, reconstructs a compelling argument for the Stoic advocacy of "a situationally fluid, heuristic process of choice, framed (but not determined) by a general normative context."

moral precept that wine-drinking is usually inappropriate for certain animals in certain situations sufficiently similar to the situations in which the morally evaluative apprehensive impressions obtained. Although impulsive impressions are considered non-apprehensive, they can be deduced in certain situations with the help of, and in coordination with, the propositions prescribing the actions that are appropriate, propositions based on the evaluative apprehensions of appropriate or inappropriate actions performed by other mortal animals partaking in reason. Again, this might be the correct way to explain how the sage's expert actions differ from the imperfect actions of a morally inferior mortal animal otherwise partaking in reason. The key to the explanation is narrowly restricted to the species of moral apprehensive impressions coming from the efficient causality of spatiotemporal bodies with moral properties. The coordination of moral propositions and evaluative apprehensive impressions of apprehensible bodies that really obtain makes it possible for mortal animals to choose a course of action and begin cultivating an evaluative stance with regard to actions deemed appropriate to pursue or select there and then.

This explanation of the distinction labors under the following difficulty. With a limited focus on the morally evaluative species of apprehensive impressions, the explanatory account of what distinguishes virtuous action from the ordinary actions of mortal animals partaking in reason relies almost exclusively upon moral apprehensive impressions. The neat separation of moral apprehensive impressions from purely descriptive apprehensive impressions is an artifact of a theoretical perspective bifurcating the totality of beings into two distinct realms: the realm of descriptive facts relative to what occurs by nature, and the realm of ethics or morality, what philosophers more recently refer to as the realm of value or freedom. This conceptual division of labor might however sustain current doxographical attempts to specify the doctrines of Stoic "epistemology" in metaphysically neutral terms. The metaphysical neutrality usually associated with the reconstructions of Stoic epistemology permits the *de re* historiographer to isolate the task of reconstructing the Stoic theory of *our access to what there is*: the domain of investigation separated methodologically from the metaphysical conditions involved in the providential and value-laden features of Stoic physics.[22] In other words, the classificatory division of purely descriptive and morally evaluative apprehensive impressions would seem to allow particular *de re* interpretations to refine and hold on to the metaphysical neutrality of

---

[22] For critical discussion of a modern historiographical perspective similar to the one outlined here, see Gábor Betegh, "Cosmological Ethics in the *Timaeus* and Early Stoicism," *Oxford Studies in Ancient Philosophy* 24 (2003): 273–4.

epistemological reconstruction in the historiography of Stoic-Academic debate. I explore this possibility in the next section.

The Abyss of Stoic Nature

The division of the apprehensive impression into two separate species depends on a conceptual distinction between the problem-area of morality (values), on one hand, and the problem-area of establishing descriptive facts, on the other hand. Perhaps the most traditional mode of analyzing the latter in isolation from the former is to investigate the proposal that a purported hypothetical subject S knows p if and only if (i) p is true, (ii) S believes that p, (iii) and S is justified in her belief that p. That is to say, modern epistemologists tend to rely on three proposed criteria (i–iii) for their investigation and the progressive refinement of scientific methodologies to determine what counts as a justified belief for the methods of empirical science. Again, modern *de re* historiographers laboring under the regime of epistemological centrism frequently reconstruct Stoic epistemological doctrines as though those doctrines primarily purport to explain our epistemic access to some generic object, not the individual bodies specified in Stoic metaphysics. However, armed conceptually with the species division of the apprehensive impressions, the regimented orthodoxy of explicating "Stoic epistemology" now seems positioned theoretically to illuminate how the Stoics conceptualize the apprehension of value-free facts involving a specific kind of object.

It is worth briefly returning to the Stoic sage to clarify the problem with this possible application of epistemological centrism. First, recall that the sage's execution of reasonable action requires perfect agreement with the governing principle of the world. For a mortal animal to acquire and manifest such knowing agreement in the stable disposition to act in certain ways, and continue to preserve and pursue certain actions in accordance with the world itself, the animal must undertake the study of nature. The idealized sage is therefore supposed to understand how the providential structure of the world manifests itself in the disposition of her own body and in the constitutional functioning of living bodies generally. With the world in view as supreme rational caretaker, the sage acts so as to promote the good of the world. Undertaking the study of nature is therefore a core component of cultivating the proper evaluative stance in relation to nature as a whole. Under the influence of epistemological centrism, *de re* interpreters of Stoic epistemology tend to presume a generic view of nature corresponding to a value-free domain of descriptive facts about generic objects. Given Zeno's idea of expertise as a system of apprehensions unified by practice toward some useful end in life, it is fair to issue the following criticism of historiographical reconstructions that presume a generic correspondence to this value-free domain. It would be a distortion of Stoic ethical theory to restrict, or prioritize, the apprehensions relevant to the expertise of wisdom by isolating the morally evaluative species of apprehensive impressions as they function in syllogistic precepts. The expertise of the sage involves the perfection of the power of assent in general, not merely the power over a particular kind of assent relative to *moral objects*, or a specific sort of particular. The sage's knowledge is a form of expertise comprehending the basic structure of the world as a whole and its governing principle, which in turn makes the rationality of the world as a living totality an exemplary model of expertise for mortal animals partaking in reason. In other words, the perfect actions of the sage involve much more than a system of so-called evaluative apprehensions concerning *moral objects*. The experience of the sage is supposed to achieve a higher, more comprehensive system of unification whereby each and every apprehensive impression makes knowledge of individual bodies and incorporeal beings possible. In agreement with the designing fire of the world that "cares and plans ahead" for what serves the advantages and purposes of all things, the sage must take care of the power of giving or withholding assent correctly in each and every situation.

One historiographer resists this line of interpretation, preferring instead a humanistic viewpoint for the reconstruction of Stoic ethics. Accordingly, the world as a whole is considered an "unsuitable foundation" for *human* ethics.[23] Ethical theory begins, it is alleged, from reflection on the human's "final good and how this is to be made determinate in a way which will enable the agent to make sense of her life and correctly order her priorities." The appeal to cosmic nature "does the opposite of what is required; it pulls the agent away from the kind of attachment to her own concerns which is needed for useful reflection on her final end to be possible."[24] The methodology of "ethics proper" is limited

---

[23] Annas, *Morality of Happiness*, 161–2, reconstructs Stoic ethics along these lines. In a later study devoted to Stoic ethics, Annas makes a different, more robust claim: that "foundations do not fit into the Stoic project." See Julia Annas, "Ethics in Stoic Philosophy," *Phronesis* 52, no. 1 (2007): 65–75 (n42), 76–85. In defense of Stoic holism as "foundational" for Stoic ethics, see Marcelo D. Boeri, "Does Cosmic Nature Matter? Some Remarks on the Cosmological Aspects of Stoic Ethics," in *God and Cosmos in Stoicism*, ed. Ricardo Salles (Oxford: Oxford University Press, 2009), 176–94.

[24] Annas, *Morality of Happiness*, 159–66, argues more generally that the Stoic study of ethics has "two levels": the study of ethics "proper," and then later the study of ethical theory and its place in the wider scheme of Stoic philosophy as a whole. Against Annas's argument for this double role, see Brad Inwood, "Review of J. Annas' *The Morality of Happiness*," *Ancient Philosophy* 15, no. 2 (1995):

to the reflection and articulation of an agent's intuitions about human life and the corresponding theoretical concepts and distinctions making sense of those intuitions. Why does reflection on the world lead the human away from proper ethical reflection? The charge of pulling an individual agent away from their own human concerns is motivated in part by the thought that *our* intuitions about *ourselves* should be the focus of reflection and articulation. One might surmise that there is textual support for this humanistic specification of Stoic ethics. It derives from "the classic pedagogical order in which Stoic philosophy was taught, logic–ethics–physics, the last culminating in 'theology' or the study of the role of God and providence in the universe as a whole." According to this presentation of pedagogical ordering (Sextus, *M.* 7.22–3), "ethics proper" apparently precedes physics, and only with the study of physics does the study of the principles of nature as a whole clarify the role of the universe or world. On this view, the methodology of "ethics proper" forgoes the articulation and clarification of theoretical concepts and premises in the formation of dialectical precepts, which vaguely appeal to the concepts of nature and the world. To support the ascription of "ethics proper," and its methodology to Stoicism, one might further contextualize Chrysippus's remarks on the order of expounding philosophical doctrines (Plutarch, *St. rep.* 1035c).[25] That is to say, in taking up Chrysippus's view that "there is no other or more familiar way of approaching the account of good and bad, or the virtues or happiness, than from common nature and from the organization of the world," one should simply assign this view to his physical writings. Only after going through the classic pedagogical ordering of philosophy would the human agent then supposedly backtrack and clarify the rudimentary concepts of ethical theory from the point of view of disciplinary holism and the structural organization of the world.

There is, however, another attested expository order of Stoic pedagogy. Diogenes Laertius reports that Zeno "put logic first, physics second, and ethics third" (D.L. 7.40). This alternative ordering supports, in turn, an alternative specification of Stoic ethics: that is, the specification which holds that premises in ethics proper "need not be restricted to premises about 'ethical' matters, but could well include premises indicating (in the rough and undetailed way that suits dialectical argument) the unity and the rational nature of the whole

---

657–60. In the later study, Annas revokes any explicit designation of "ethics proper." Cf. Annas, "Ethics in Stoic Philosophy," 71.

[25] Jacques Brunschwig, "On a Book-Title by Chrysippus: 'On the Fact that the Ancients Admitted Dialectic along with Demonstrations,'" *Oxford Studies in Ancient Philosophy*, Suppl. vol. (1991): 91–5.

cosmos and its unitary functioning."[26] Consider an example: Zeno's premise that "nothing is better than the world." The proposition functions as a middle premise in two different arguments:

A1
The rational is better than what is not rational.
Nothing is better than the world (οὐδὲν δὲ γε κόσμου κρεῖττόν ἐστιν/*nihil autem mundo melius*).
Therefore, the world is a rational thing. (Sextus, *M.* 9.104, Cicero, *De nat. deor.* 2.21, cf. 3.22)
A2
The intelligent is better than the non-intelligent and the animate [is better] than the inanimate.
But nothing is better than the world.
Therefore, the world is thinking and animate. (Sextus, *M.* 9.104)

The claim that "nothing is better than the world" presupposes two canons of Zeno's metaphysical realism: that there really is a unified thing or body called the world, and that it has a nature of its own. Presumably, Zeno formulated arguments for both in his lost physical works (either in Περὶ φύσεως or Περὶ ὅλου). Whether one grants that Zeno defended these views on the world itself only in his physical works or not, the possibility that Cooper leaves open remains a genuine possibility: namely, the possibility that Zeno in a rough and rudimentary way made use of certain metaphysical views on the world in what Annas calls the area of "ethics proper"—with appeals to the claim that the world as a whole has a nature and to the claim that nothing is better than the world.[27] Moreover, there is no prima facie reason to dismiss the possibility that for Zeno the basic concerns of mortal animals partaking in reason already include intuitions about life that make rough and rudimentary appeals to the structural organization of the world, not as some theoretical concept external to

---

[26] John M. Cooper, "Eudaimonism and the Appeal to Nature in the Morality of Happiness: Comments on Julia Annas, *The Morality of Happiness*," *Philosophy and Phenomenological Research* 55, no. 3 (1995): 597.

[27] Arguments in support of the metaphysical claim that there is a κόσμος and that it is a unified body with a nature of its own are difficult to reconstruct from our Stoic sources. At *De nat. deor.* 2.23–8, Cicero's Balbus argues that vital heat, the sustaining principle of every animate body, pervades the *mundus* and unifies those parts into one organic system. At *M.* 9.78–85 (*SVF* 2.1013), Sextus uses an anonymous source to reconstruct an argument on empirical grounds (1) that the κόσμος is one unified body as opposed to a mere assemblage of distinct component parts, (2) that the κόσμος is not unified by ἕξις alone, but that it also possesses the stronger unity of a "nature" (φύσις), and finally (3) that the "nature" of the κόσμος is rational.

the practice of reflection centrally focused on the human, or "ethics proper," but rather as a theoretical appeal to a living whole vaguely considered active within mortal animals partaking in reason.

Absent the appeal to the notion of nature as a whole, the early Stoa would have been unable to articulate or defend the τέλος of human life, and a fortiori the perfect disposition of the sage as morally superior to the folly of ordinary mortal animals. Zeno's conception of the τέλος for mortal animals partaking in reason (D.L. 7.87–8) is defined in terms of virtue, but also in terms of nature as a whole. Epictetus supplies additional support for considering the necessary link between virtue and nature in Zeno's ethics. According to Epictetus, Zeno's formula for the end of life implicates a view on human nature as well as a claim on "the nature of the world" (*Diss.* 1.20.15–16 (= *SVF* 1.182)). In pursuit of Zeno's ideal of wisdom, the mortal animal partaking in reason must reflect on the following set of questions: "what, then, is god and what is an impression? What is nature in nature of the parts, what is nature in nature of the whole (τί ἐστι φύσις ἡ ἐπὶ μέρους καὶ τί ἐστι φύσις ἡ τῶν ὅλων·)?" Here Epictetus identifies core concepts of Zeno's *metaphysica specialis* (god, nature, the world, wholes and parts), as well as a concept developed and studied in Stoic logic, not the subcategory of apprehensive impressions involving *moral objects*, but more generally "the impression" as such. Each of these assorted concepts is integral to the pursuit of the Stoic end of life, and the rational soul of the mortal animal in pursuit of this end is taught to develop *inter al.* a general understanding of the nature of the world and the role of the impression as such in order to attain the "happiness of a smooth flow of life" (Stob., *Ecl.* 2.77.16–27 (= *SVF* 3.16, LS 63A), cf. D.L. 7.88).

The mortal animal involved in learning how to assent to each and every impression fulfilling the three conditions of the causal model of apprehension implies that the mortal animal in training cares about getting things right in general. That is to say, the mortal animal in training ought to cultivate an abiding interest in knowing each and every apprehensible body as it really obtains, for such bodies make it possible for the mortal animal to form true representations of the world, or some part of the world, as it really is. With the world understood as a unified whole, the sage finds unerring agreement with the world and its many parts to be a disposition or evaluative stance worth pursuing and preserving by means of each and every act of assent over the entire course of life. The disposition of the sage is therefore considered the successful outcome of a rational plan to pursue, by means of the power of giving assent to apprehensive impressions throughout the entirety of life. Nature is allegedly skillful at creating and maintaining animate bodies, which in turn actively supply the metaphysical ground for the power of assent; and on the basis of the rational power of assent, knowledge of nature's providence is possible. Having planned to live according to the providence of nature in every way possible, the idealized sage mobilizes a higher-order impulse to perfect the power of assent in general, along with the more basic impulses to pursue and undertake those actions conforming to so-called evaluative apprehensive impressions. The perfection of appropriate actions entails that such actions, being done ἀπὸ φρονήσεως or "from insight" (Sextus, M. 11.200, cf. Cicero, De fin. 3.3), embody a dispositional knowing that regularly and without deviation gives rise to right action. Although the term κατόρθωμα may not have been Zeno's coinage, Cicero's use of recte factum (Acad. 1.37), the Latin equivalent of κατόρθωμα, in his outline of Zeno's idea of "right action," suggests that the Stoic originator appropriates the Greek term in a novel way.[28] Fundamentally, right actions require the mastery of giving assent to apprehensive impressions about the nature of apprehensible bodies and their apprehensible properties, as they obtain together in experience throughout the course of life.

It is therefore misleading for historiographers to reconstruct an account of the mastery of the sage on morally evaluative, apprehensive impressions alone, or to prioritize the mastery of this sort of apprehensive impression. Such priority seems to suggest that on the Stoic account the animal's rational disposition is somehow less affected by potential errors of giving assent to impressions of the sort purporting to identify whether a particular body is really an apple, or whether a particular plant is really green. Moreover, the knowledge of general propositions concerning the parts of nature as a whole is based on a system of apprehensive impressions unified in practice, and the impressions of such a system range over the descriptive and the evaluative. Taking premises from the apprehensions of the constitution of living bodies, dialectical theorems in Stoic physics express "both what is the case and what ought to be the case."[29] This means that the individual animal qua sage will know, as the end or goal of action, φύσις in the robust or holistic sense, and consistently exercise knowing insight with regard to what ought to be done in specific situations as the kind of action which perfectly agrees with and advances the rational organization of the world. On this view, the animate bodies cultivated by Stoic nature are something other than the "morally neutral" objects of apprehension; bodies causing perception

---

[28] Ioppolo, Opinone e scienza, 131–3. Cf. Maconi, "Nova Non Philosophandi Philosophia," 249 n53.
[29] In agreement with the claim of Anthony A. Long, "The Logical Basis of Stoic Ethics," in Stoic Studies, 147. See Betegh, "Cosmological Ethics," 299–300.

and apprehension are, accordingly, parts of the larger whole that mortal animals strive to live in agreement with, that is, whenever a sage engages in any form of reasoning or reflection about what is really the case. And so when Zeno famously illustrated the difference between the sage and the ordinary fool who just happens to apprehend some thing—comparing an impression to an open palm with fingers straight, assent to the slight curling of the fingers, apprehension to the hand clenched in a fist, and knowledge to the hand clenched in a fist grasped tightly by the other fist (Cicero, *Acad.* 2.145 (= *SVF* 1.66, LS 41A))—he was also illustrating the function of the apprehensive impression *qua* genus for the perfectly virtuous sage. Likewise, the polemical arguments of Arcesilaus evidently target the causal conception of apprehension as such, and that targeted attack is sufficient to provoke the Stoic with the inaction objection.

In fact, the inaction objection represents, as it appears at least in Cicero's *Academica*, the refusal of the Stoics to embark on a defense of their metaphysical views of the world and the benevolent expertise of nature that the Stoic conception of the world depends upon. The conceptual content of Arcesilaus's reply to the inaction objection confirms the inseparable connection between the metaphysical and ethical aspects of Zeno's tripartition. Readers of Cicero are informed, through Lucullus—the character Cicero casts to defend Stoicism against Arcesilaus and his Academic followers—that the Stoics reply to the metaphysical thesis of inapprehensibility by saying that such a thesis "subverts all life from its ground" (*totam vitam evertunt funditus, Acad.* 2.31).[30] Notice how the alleged subversion is not conveyed here in a narrow humanistic sense, namely, that inapprehensibility subverts all *human* action or all *human* life. Rather, it plainly states that such a thesis destroys the ground of all life as such. In fact, Cicero reports that at least one Academic countered the inaction objection by echoing and repurposing Democritus's reported dictum (68B117 DK): "Blame nature for concealing truth in the abyss, as Democritus says" (*Naturam accusa, quae in profundo veritatem, ut ait Democritus, penitus abstruserit,* Cicero, *Acad.* 2.32 (LS 68R), cf. *Acad.* 1.44 (< F 45 Vezzoli)).[31] Cicero's Lucullus admits to having difficulty taking this rash and unsophisticated reply seriously. It is therefore not surprising that Lucullus would then avoid examining the reason this "desperate" Academic holds "nature" accountable for the destruction of all life. Lucullus instead suggests that different Academics would give different

---

[30] For insightful comments on the phrase *totam vitam evertunt* (*Acad.* 2.31) and *eversio* (*Acad.* 2.99), see Reid, *Ciceronis, Academica,* 295 n43.
[31] Cf. the testimony on Democritus in D.L. 9.72: ἐπεῇ δὲ οὐδὲν ἴδμεν· ἐν βυθῷ γὰρ ἡ ἀλήθεια ("Of truth we know nothing, for truth lies in the depths").

responses to the censure that the Stoics expressed in the following conditional: that if Academic counter-arguments are true, "then all things will be non-evident" (*tum omnia fore incerta*, 2.32). The content of this consequent clause is nearly identical in meaning with Greek formulations found in later sources: for instance, from Sextus Empiricus, that "all things (are) inapprehensible" (πάντων [δὲ] ὄντων ἀκαταλήπτων, *M.* 7.155, 156 (< F 87 Vezzoli)), or that "all things are inapprehensible" (ἀκατάληπτα εἶναι πάντα, *PH*. 1.226), or again, this time from Eusebius, that "all things are inapprehensible" (πάντα μὲν εἶναι ἀκατάληπτα, Numen. *apud* Eusebius, *Praep. ev.* 14.7.15 (< F 124 Vezzoli)), along with the conclusion ascribed to Arcesilaus's anti-Stoic arguments: "on account of the total destruction of things" (διὰ τῆς ἀπαξαπάντων ἀναιρέσεως χρημάτων, 14.8.3–4 (= F 126 Vezzoli)).[32] Blaming nature for the inapprehensibility or obscurity of all things is, on the Stoic view, a rash and hopeless way of responding to the inaction objection.

There is, however, another Academic reply to the objection on record, which Lucullus is more willing to examine. In the latter, an unnamed Academic is said to reply by explicitly denying the equivalence between what is ἄδηλον/*incertum* ("non-evident") and what is ἀκατάληπτον ("inapprehensible"). The consideration motivating this Academic response is the refusal to identify the quality of being "inapprehensible" with the quality of being "non-evident" (i.e., "unclear," or "obscure"). Now, it seems from the context that Lucullus understands the negative terms as different Academic qualifications of Stoic *impressions*. Lucullus's remarks do seem to suggest, as one scholar states, that it was "Arcesilaus" who "argued that without the criterial role of the cataleptic impression, each and every impression would be equally 'obscure' (ἄδηλον/*incertum*)."[33] It would follow then that Lucullus is crediting Carneades, or some Academic later than Arcesilaus, with the innovation of qualifying a particular kind of impression as evidently or perspicuously truth-like (hence not "unclear"), while upholding Arcesilaus's arguments against Stoic impressions as non-apprehensive. Lucullus's brief discussion of the alternative Academic responses unfolds in a context that is prefaced as a critical treatment of the arguments of both Arcesilaus

---

[32] In reporting on Philo of Larissa, Sextus uses a different term to express the thesis that "things are inapprehensible" (ἀκατάληπτα εἶναι τὰ πράγματα, Sextus, *PH* 1.235), omitting reference to πάντα ("all things"). One plausible reason to omit the sweeping reference to *all things* is to restrict the qualification of all things that are inapprehensible to *all things as the Stoics conceive of all things*, which Arcesilaus's arguments leave implicit. For a similar use of τὰ πράγματα, see Marcus Aurelius, 5.10.1–2 (trans. Farquharson, 37).
[33] Brittain, *Philo*, 96.

and Carneades (*Acad.* 2.12), so again it seems correct to single out these two Academics and attribute the responses accordingly.

Furthermore, a passage from Eusebius supports (but does not confirm) such attributions, as it indicates how to properly assign the more sophisticated response to Carneades. The passage also demonstrates an alternative way of distinguishing what is ἄδηλον/*incertum* ("non-evident" or "unclear") from what is ἀκατάληπτον ("inapprehensible"), a conceptual distinction between two terms which otherwise maintain their connection with things, namely, as qualifications of things, not impressions per se:

> After these [the immediate followers of Arcesilaus, Lacydes and Evandrus] Carneades inherited the school and established the Third Academy. He employed the manner of argumentation that Arcesilaus had, for he too used to practice dialectical reasoning and demolish all the statements of others. He differed from him only in his argument for suspension of judgment, saying that it is impossible for a human being to suspend judgment about things in general (ὄντα περὶ ἁπάντων), but that there is a difference between what is non-evident (ἀδήλου) and what is inapprehensible (ἀκαταλήπτου), for all things are inapprehensible (πάντα μὲν εἶναι ἀκατάληπτα), but not all things are non-evident (οὐ πάντα δὲ ἄδηλα). (Numen. *apud* Euseb., *Praep. ev.* 14.7.15 (= F 124 Vezzoli))

The Academic reply to inaction that Lucullus considers rash could very well be assigned to Arcesilaus (and perhaps his immediate followers); whereas the more refined response reflects Carneades's innovation as an Academic, maintaining but also modifying, Arcesilaus's polemic. Unlike Lucullus's reconstruction at *Acad.* 2.32, there is no explicit mention here of impressions in distinguishing the "inapprehensible" from the "non-evident." That is to say, in the context of reporting Carneades's distinction between what it means for "all things" (ὄντα περὶ ἁπάντων/πάντα) to be *inapprehensible* and what it means for "all things" (ὄντα περὶ ἁπάντων/πάντα) to be *non-evident*, the notion of impression has no conceptual role in registering the distinction. In consideration of the fact that for the Stoics an impression is a particular kind of corporeal thing, I take it that tacit reference to impressions is entailed by the explicit qualification that "all things are inapprehensible." However, the more important point to emphasize is that the generality of "all things" (πάντα) in the assertion that "all things are inapprehensible" refers explicitly to the things purportedly capable of producing impressions on the Stoic account.

Brittain and Palmer make a convincing case for identifying Arcesilaus as the unnamed Academic in Lucullus's reconstruction who first issues the so-called unsophisticated accusation against nature. However, in the course of defending this identification, analysis of the conceptual content of the accusation mistakenly assumes that the concept "nature" (*natura*/φύσις) in Arcesilaus's reply refers to Democritus's view of nature. Additionally, Brittain and Palmer err by supposing that in making this accusation Arcesilaus found himself on the defensive; in other words, they suppose that "Arcesilaus makes what again appears to be a largely dialectical appeal to Democritus. Arcesilaus finds himself in the position of being unable to judge whether the impressions he has of things are true or false." Because he appears to have "no particular account to give of why he finds himself in the position he does," Arcesilaus presumably deals with his own inability to account for the position he finds himself in by invoking the dictum of Democritus concerning "the real nature of things."

This way of interpreting Arcesilaus's appeal to Democritus blunts the polemical force of the appeal as it serves to undermine the *Stoic* view of nature. Arcesilaus provisionally agrees, to commence the argument against the causal conception of apprehension, that there are true impressions coming from spatiotemporal bodies. Hence, it makes little sense to claim that Arcesilaus found himself in the position of being unable to judge whether an impression is true or false. *Contra* Brittain and Palmer, the appeal to Democritus is not a defensive pivot to the views of an authority. Instead, the appeal continues the offensive against Zeno. In other words, the appeal to Democritus continues and logically extends the argument against the coherence of Stoic metaphysics. In the context of the dispute between Arcesilaus and Stoic philosophy, the accusation against Stoic nature is a manifestation of the subversiveness associated with what *really* follows from Arcesilaus's arguments against the Stoic view of the world as a coherent, rational, living totality. The destructive implication is that Zeno is committed to a view of nature in which nature itself conceals truth, a view that harmonizes with Democritus's dictum that truth lies in the depths of an abyss. Arcesilaus associates the Stoic view of nature with the pessimistic statement of an acclaimed physicist, who occasionally cries out, according to Lucullus, with some irrational view in the manner of someone who is raving (*Acad.* 2.14). Using Democritus in the form of an accusation against the Stoic view of nature, the charge ascribes agency to nature as a force that conceals truth in the abyss. The agency of nature implied by the charge should bring attention to the fact that the arguments of Arcesilaus against the causal conception of apprehension reduce the Stoic view of nature to an absurdity. In whatever mental condition Arcesilaus might have found himself in, he was nonetheless able to continue the attack on canonical

Stoicism for espousing a view of nature which commits their philosophy to the absurd claim that nature conceals truth by making all things inapprehensible. Democritus said that truth lies in the depths of an abyss, and Arcesilaus affiliated this dictum with the Stoic conception of nature as that which is really responsible for the destruction of all life, including the rationality of the living whole. Fragmentary evidence suggests that Democritus is not known for adopting the positive view that nature is the agency that actively conceals, though it seems that he is known *inter al.* for locating truth in the abyss; it is the inaccessibility of the truth relative to mortal animals partaking in reason that serves Arcesilaus's polemics against the Stoa.

Moreover, Sextus's testimony on the innovation of Philo's followers supports the Academic qualification of Stoic things (not impressions) as apprehensible/inapprehensible, which originates with Arcesilaus's metaphysical arguments. That is, the passive adjectives καταληπτόν/ἀκατάληπτον are explicitly predicated of things—not impressions or apprehensive impressions:

> The followers of Philo declare that as far as the Stoic criterion is concerned (i.e., the apprehensive impression), things are inapprehensible (ἀκατάληπτα εἶναι τὰ πράγματα), but that as far as the nature of things themselves (ἐπὶ τῇ φύσει τῶν πραγμάτων αὐτῶν) are concerned, they are apprehensible (καταληπτά). (Sextus, *PH* 1.235 (= LS 68T))

The recurrence of "things" ([τὰ] πράγματα) on both sides of the contrast is emphatic, as Sedley claims: on one side, the anti-Stoic thesis that "things are inapprehensible" (argued, moreover, by Arcesilaus and Carneades); on the other side, the apparently innovative thesis advanced by the followers of Philo that "the nature of things themselves are apprehensible."[34] Sedley is again correct to stress that this is *not* a recurrence of contrasting epistemic statements, but rather a recurrence of contrasting statements concerning "the way the actual putative objects of the knowledge are: it is in virtue of those objects' very own nature that they are knowable."[35] On this metaphysical reading, the actual putative objects possess what Sedley designates an "intrinsic capacity for being known," which is to say, the putative objects are attributed a capacity that they have independent of any purported mortal animal ever "actualizing the capacity." (I'd revise this metaphysical understanding of the capacity by noting that this "capacity for being known" is not intrinsic, but extrinsic in the sense that the capacity depends on its relation to another putative being or class of

---

[34] David N. Sedley, "Antiochus as Historian of Philosophy," in Sedley, *Philosophy of Antiochus*, 86.
[35] Sharples, *Stoics, Epicureans and Sceptics*, 27.

beings, even if no putative animal ever actualizes that capacity.) For present purposes, the more pressing issue is that the juxtaposition of contrasting metaphysical statements upholds the precedent encountered in Sextus's report on Arcesilaus (*M.* 7.150–7), examined in the previous chapter: the precedent of using the passive adjectives (καταληπτά/ἀκατάληπτα) to qualify beings or things, whether it be the external things associated with the Stoic criterial account of the apprehensive impression, or later (perhaps for Carneades and the followers of Philo) "the nature of the things themselves" (i.e., a later Academic conception of "things" independent of the Stoic criterial account of the apprehensive impression, and thus independent of any purported mortal animal partaking in reason as conceived by the Stoics).

In translating *PH* 1.235, in particular the claim ἀκατάληπτα εἶναι τὰ πράγματα ("things are inapprehensible"), Brittain unfortunately conflates the passive adjectives καταληπτά/ἀ-κατάληπτα with the active adjective (καταληπτική) by rendering *things* "non-cataleptic/cataleptic," instead of rendering *things* with the passive "apprehensible/inapprehensible."[36] The pair "non-cataleptic/cataleptic" is the appropriate rendering of what can or cannot actively grasp, whereas the latter pair (καταληπτά/α-κατάληπτα) functions to translate the passive adjectives of what can or cannot be grasped ("apprehensible/inapprehensible"). Brittain correctly translates, it seems to me, καταληπτῇ φαντασίᾳ at *PH* 1.235 as "*cataleptic* impression," but in using "non-cataleptic/cataleptic" to qualify "things" he tends to qualify "impressions" and "things" with the same active adjective, where two different types of Greek adjective are used in the very same passage. The translation contradicts his astute remarks on the active and passive types of adjective, which properly warn readers not to conflate the types of passive and active adjectives, as Cicero's Latin tends to do.[37] The predicate adjective "inapprehensible," as a relative disposition of putative things or objects in the Stoic account, qualifies things in virtue of their relation to the animals purportedly capable of giving and withholding assent to impressions. That relation is considered negative because, on the critical examination of the Stoic account of the apprehensive impression originally undertaken by Arcesilaus, the "things" serving the causal function in Zenonian impressionism fail to interact with mortal animals partaking in reason so as to produce the kind of impressions worthy of infallible assent.

---

[36] Brittain, *Philo*, 4, 138–9, and 144–5.
[37] Brittain, "Introduction," xlii.

Minimal Eudaimonism

In prior formulations, I noted that it is typical of modern historiographers to reconstruct Arcesilaus's anti-Stoic arguments as primarily epistemological. One particular effect of this reconstructive focus is now ready for further commentary. Epistemological readings effectively eliminate from reconstruction the *reductio* holding (the Stoic view of) nature responsible for the inapprehensibility of things and inaction.[38] Epistemological centrism has thus made it difficult to identify the accusation against Stoic nature as evidence that Zeno's conception of a harmonious and orderly totality comes under attack by Arcesilaus. Recall that Zeno and his early followers refer to φύσις as "designing fire" (D.L. 7.156), or sometimes as that which "holds the totality together, other times as the force or principle of coming-to-be, growth, and passing-away (D.L. 7.148)." Nature as "designing" fire is considered generative in the active sense of imparting a kind of seed (σπέρμα), which contains the reasons and the causes of all things (Aristocles *apud* Euseb., *Praep. ev.* 15.14.1–2 (= *SVF* 1.98 part, LS 46G)). In a brief summary of what appears to be Zeno's cosmogony in Diogenes Laertius (D.L. 7.136–7 (*SVF* 1.102, part)), one reads:

> And just as [in animal procreation] the seed is enveloped in the womb, so god the seminal reason of the world remains as such in the moisture, modifying to its ends the matter, with a view to the next stage in the process of the coming-to-be of the world. Thereupon he created first of all the four elements, fire, water, air, earth. They (the elements and their generation) are discussed by Zeno in his treatise Περὶ τοῦ ὅλου.

Canonical Stoics would have wanted to deny, of course, that nature is, or could be, a principle of subverting the possible harmony of the totality of what is (D.L. 7.89), thereby rendering life impossible to live.[39] The providence and forethought of expert nature are part of the metaphysical background motivating the Stoics to retaliate against the Academy with an inaction objection. The accusation that emerges in response to the inaction objection spells out what is for the Stoics an untenable thesis, namely, that their own conception of nature is responsible for perverting and corrupting all life, including but not limited to the mortal life of rational animals. The accusation against the agency of nature derives from

---

[38] For an exception to this tendency to eliminate the *reductio*, see Allen, "Carneadean Argument," 245.
[39] For discussion of the seminal principles in relation to early Stoicism, see Ilsetraut Hadot, "Getting to Goodness: Reflections on Chapter 10 of Brad Inwood, *Reading Seneca*," in *Seneca Philosophicus,* ed. Jula Wildberger and Marcia L. Colish (Berlin: Walter De Gruyter, 2014), 11–20.

critical examination of the causal conception of Stoic apprehension, and the thesis that nature conceals truth by making things inapprehensible reduces the causal conception to an absurd contradiction.

As standardly reconstructed, Arcesilaus's arguments motivate nothing more than a simple epistemic *reductio ad absurdum*. *Reductio ad absurdum* arguments set out by granting the premises under examination and proceed until they come to absurd or impossible conclusions, thus showing the provisional views to be problematic or false. But in the present study, Arcesilaus's attack on the causal conception of apprehension involves a number of metaphysical premises, and the attack proceeds to bind those premises conceptually to absurd conclusions. The absurdity is doubly pernicious for the Stoa, for not only does the animal suspending assent about all things lack apprehension and knowledge, the apprehension needed to act and make moral progress, according to Stoic orthodoxy, but also the animal suspending assent about all things now seems to live in a world held together by a force actively concealing the truth by making all things inapprehensible. Under such conditions, it is impossible to live the Stoic life of virtue.

The record in Sextus of Arcesilaus's reply to the problem of action differs in important ways from the subtle traces in Cicero. Rather than revert to an accusation against the Stoic view of nature, Sextus reports that Arcesilaus followed up his polemical arguments by invoking the criterion of the "reasonable" (τὸ εὔλογον). The invocation of this notion seems to sketch a positive account of how to suspend assent about all things and regulate "actions generally" (κοινῶς τὰς πράξεις). With this appeal, Arcesilaus seemingly reduces the robust notion of perfect action (τὸ κατόρθωμα/*recte factum*) to the more pedestrian notion of τὸ καθῆκον. That is to say, Arcesilaus seems to suggest that the one suspending assent can act rightly and regularly pursue with practical insight the reasonable course of action. After eliminating the possibility of the sage's perfect action, Arcesilaus would then be redeeming, or perhaps rehabilitating, a component of Zeno's Grand End theory of action.[40] One notion being redeemed here is that of "the reasonable," or the "reasonable justification" of action.

However, there is no indication in Sextus to suggest that this new iteration of action is meant to fulfill the metaphysically luxuriant promise of Zeno's Grand End theory. The theory of perfectly right action depends upon the core assumptions of Zeno's metaphysical realism: that there is such a thing as a unified

---

[40] Cf. Hans von Arnim, "Arkesilaos von Pitane," in *Paulys Realencyclopädie der classischen Altertumswissenschaft*, ed. Georg Wissowa (Stuttgart: Alfred Druckenmuller, 1895), 1165.

whole called the world, and that it is structurally comprised of individual bodies relatively disposed to being apprehended and known. Zeno's Grand End theory of action envisions the appropriate actions of mortal animals partaking in reason arising from the fundamental apprehensibility of causally efficacious bodies. On the basis of apprehensive impressions received from individually apprehensible bodies, it is considered necessary for the progressive achievement of virtue to harmonize the actions of the mortal animal partaking in reason with nature as the benevolent force of the world. While Zeno and the early Stoics understand appropriate action in terms of a Grand End theory, the pedestrian notion introduced by Arcesilaus is conceptually detached from the Stoic supposition that the rationality of mortal animals, in either their perfect or imperfect action, is the kind of rationality that is actually responsive by means of giving assent to a totalizing ontology centralized by apprehensible bodies. Recall that Arcesilaus's anti-Stoic arguments reveal that individual bodies are relatively disposed to being inapprehensible. Hence, the rational response ought to involve declining assent because of the inapprehensibility of things. Arcesilaus's appeal to the reasonable justification therefore takes the concept of right action in an altogether different direction. In this appeal, the Stoic "world" as a coherent and unified whole exhibiting rational order is no longer invested with explanatory and normative power, thus the invocation of a notion of "justification" (ἀπολογία, M. 7.158) radically different from its Stoic iteration. The possibility of justifying such actions indicates at the very least that the assumptions governing the ontology of Stoic apprehension are no longer necessary for the pursuit of happiness.

Nevertheless, it might seem strange to find Arcesilaus formulating (even in outline) an account of action from the remains of anti-Stoic argument. One recent scholar asks: Why would Arcesilaus give, *gratis*, a positive account of action, especially one using a core component of Zeno's ethics, namely, the rational responsiveness of reasonable justification? It would make little sense for Arcesilaus to have responded in this positive manner after he had undermined Zeno's theory of virtuous action. Why, then, "did he [Arcesilaus] not leave him [the Stoic] to stew? We are invited to imagine he first knocked his opponent to the ground and then gave him a hand up again. And that is a most unGreek idea."[41] If Arcesilaus attacked the robust Zenonian notion of τὸ καθῆκον as Cleanthes had alleged, again it seems puzzling to find Arcesilaus recuperating a component of Stoic ethics in a positive way.

---

[41] Maconi, "*Nova Non Philosophandi Philosophia*," 247–9; Hankinson, *Sceptics*, 274–6.

One influential approach to resolving the issue ascribes to Arcesilaus himself a commitment to the aim and method of pure refutation. This *de dicto* specification of ascribed commitment advances no further in ascribing any positive beliefs or commitments to Arcesilaus other than a commitment to refutation. That is to say, as Pierre Couissin has defended, that "the sole purpose" of Arcesilaus's critique was to "demonstrate that knowledge, as the Stoics conceived it, apprehension (*katalēpsis*), which is their criterion of truth, does not exist."[42] According to this restricted form of *de dicto* ascription, Sextus portrays Arcesilaus as merely using Zenonian propositions and premises in order to wound and attack the doctrine of apprehension. Strangely, on this view, Arcesilaus need not have been committed to the arguments making use of those propositions and premises to fulfill his commitment of refuting the Stoic theory of knowledge. This purely destructive strategy could be what Cleanthes recognizes in charging Arcesilaus with destroying (in argument) the doctrine of appropriate action. Accordingly, under no pressure to commit to a view of the conduct of life after undermining apprehension, Arcesilaus advances the same destructive strategy against the Stoic theory of action. Borrowing a component of Zeno's ethical theory, Arcesilaus uses τὸ εὔλογον against Zeno to humble the sage. On this interpretation, Arcesilaus has no stake in any practical criterion outside of refuting the Stoic theory of knowledge, for the claim is that Arcesilaus does not have any commitment or belief of his own other than a commitment to proving that the Stoic theory of knowledge is inconsistent and useless for action. In his discussion of τὸ εὔλογον, Couissin identifies the ethical dimension of this destructive strategy: "He [Arcesilaus] labored to prove that, contrary to Stoic doctrine, assent was not necessary for action and that in consequence, the Stoic theory of knowledge was not only inconsistent but useless."

Other scholars propose a different resolution. More ambitious in the *de dicto* ascription of commitment and belief, this approach ascribes to Arcesilaus the motive and method of arguing for his own positive view. This mode of *de dicto* interpretation takes Sextus's testimony as a basis for the specification that Arcesilaus himself was actually committed (to some degree) to the practical criterion of the reasonable. The criterion of the reasonable recuperates, on this approach, an Aristotelian notion of voluntary action, and it has no conceptual ties to Zeno's corresponding catalogue of precepts.[43] Right actions are simply

---

[42] Pierre Couissin, "Le Stoïcisme de la Nouvelle Académie," *Revue d'historie de la Philosophie* 3 (1929): 241–5, trans. Jennifer Barnes and Myles Burnyeat as "The Stoicism of the New Academy," in *The Skeptical Tradition*, ed. Myles Burnyeat (Berkeley: University of California Press, 1983), 37–40.

[43] Ioppolo, *Opinione e scienza*, 131–4; see also Frede, "Two Kinds of Assent," 135–6.

those that can be given a "reasonable justification" after the action has been performed. Plutarch seems to reconstruct Arcesilaus's reasoning in a similar way (*Adv. Col.* 1121f–1123b (> F 75 Vezzoli)). It is far from clear, however, that such reasoning derives from Arcesilaus, given that Plutarch stops short of ascribing the conclusions of the reconstructed reasoning to Arcesilaus himself.[44] Assuming that a positive *de dicto* ascription of the reasonable to Arcesilaus is otherwise on the right track, the passage from Sextus could be taken to support the claim that Arcesilaus generally acted in conformity with his positive view of action. It might follow, then, that his invocation of the reasonable functions as a revealing self-description of how he went about regulating "actions generally" (κοινῶς τὰς πράξεις), including, perhaps, his use of a Socratic method to critically examine early Stoic doctrine. In that broad and inclusive sense of action, Arcesilaus's revival of a strictly oral method modeled on Socratic cross-examination potentially qualifies as a "reasonable" course of action. Although he sought to undermine in oral argument Zeno's defense of appropriate action, on this constructive account Arcesilaus also articulated his commitment to a revised notion of reasonable action.

In my view, the two reconstructions of Sextus's testimony sketched above remain in an interminable deadlock of speculative *de dicto* reconstruction. Sextus's testimony is the only source to report on Arcesilaus's explicit appeal to the reasonable. By itself, the report fails to establish or support a conclusive historiographical *de dicto* ascription, and it is certainly not sufficient evidence for historiographers to decide between purely refutative or positive commitments.[45] Rather than speculate about what Arcesilaus himself actually believed, or acknowledged committing himself to, it is worth pursuing an altogether different historiographical approach. This third way takes Arcesilaus's method of reasoning to preclude definitive *de dicto* ascription beyond provisional acceptance. In other words, given that Arcesilaus's revival of a Socratic style of interrogation seems to entail the inscrutability of the commitments and beliefs that he himself would acknowledge as his beliefs, the present study insists on another type of

---

[44] Krämer, *Platonismus und hellenistische Philosophie*, 43; H. J. Mette, "Zwei Akademiker heute: Krantor von Soli und Arkesilaos von Pitane," *Lustrum* 26 (1984): 92; Maconi, "*Nova Non Philosophandi Philosophia*," 251 n54.

[45] David N. Sedley, "Three Platonist Interpretations of the 'Theaetetus,'" in Gill et al., *Form and Argument*, 89, correctly observes the compatibility of the positive and negative interpretations on offer, what he designates the *ad hominem* (Couissin) and the constructive or positive interpretations (Ioppolo). It is worth recalling Lucullus's caricature of an Academic describing his chosen method (Cicero, *Acad.* 2.60): "He [the Academic] says, 'it is not our practice to disclose our view.'" Other passages in Cicero allude to this [Academic] self-description (*Acad.* 2.8–9, *Tusc.* 5.33, 83, *Div.* 2.150).

historiography: *de re* interpretation *de traditione*. This type of interpretation grants priority to mediated *de re* specifications of the theses derived from the oral arguments that Arcesilaus formulated against the ontology of Stoic apprehension.

While recognizing how difficult it might be for engaged interlocutors to determine whether their Socratic interrogator is really committed to an open and explicit affirmation of the arguments and conclusions articulated in the interrogation, it is also important to recognize that independent of this difficulty the oral method of interrogating the premises and principles of a philosophical interlocutor holds educational potential for those submitting to the interrogation. In the course of having an oral dialogue with a doctrinally elusive interrogator, the interrogated is nonetheless able to reflect and improve on their own views and arguments. Likewise, Arcesilaus's interlocutors were presumably able to reflect on the metaphysical inapprehensibility of things, and that view's consequences, for example, the impossibility of Stoic virtue. Arcesilaus's introduction of right action invited interlocutors to abandon the absurd metaphysical commitments of canonical Stoicism and the explanatory impotence of those commitments for the realization of acting rightly. Given the introduction of a non-metaphysical notion of right action, the key component of what is designated here *minimal eudaimonism*, systematic explanations of the supreme rationality of the world, and its constituent parts, become useless extravagances for the pursuit of happiness. The notion of right action introduced by Arcesilaus is minimalist in the sense that it dispenses with systematic explanations of how "things" really are, or what grounds what, in a totalizing structure of things. *Minimal eudaimonism* focuses exclusively on action and the practical application of the reasonable to the prospects of living well, abandoning the grand metaphysical views and principles associated with disciplinary holism. Again, the possibility of considering such an approach to action arises not from what Arcesilaus acknowledges or believes about Socrates or the ethical life, but rather from the way his method of contentious reasoning demonstrates the inapprehensibility of individual bodies and the consequent impossibility of Stoic ethics. This model of historiographical interpretation observes the significance of Arcesilaus's Socratic revival independent of considering what Arcesilaus took himself to be doing vis-à-vis Socrates, or the so-called Socratic method. The state of historiographical uncertainty regarding his commitments is not a direct consequence of the precarious nature of the sources, nor is it the consequence of conflicting and unscrupulous ancient reporting. The uncertainty is, rather, a consequence of the elusive method that Arcesilaus revived by accepting oral argument as the way of conducting philosophical investigation.

Pursuing the *de re* interpretation *de traditione* of Arcesilaus's revival of oral argument, the concluding chapters explain how this practice of interrogation, in confrontation with the ontology of Stoic virtue, effectively disrupts the tradition of Old Academic ethics. The next step of the reconstruction expands the argument against the historiographies of epistemological centrism, and the assumptions governing the posit of an isolated problem-area of epistemology (Stoic or Academic), which control and direct the historiographical task of specifying what is novel about the philosophical orientation of the early Hellenistic Academy.

4

The Old Academy's Traditional Hierarchy of Goods

Recent historiographers attribute a "revolution" or "radical change of direction" to the Hellenistic Academy under the directorship of Arcesilaus. In fact, epistemological specification is the most common way of presenting this Academic change of direction. Scholars maintain the thesis that Arcesilaus's "turn," or "change," in the Academy's philosophical orientation is primarily epistemological.[1] The final two chapters of this study reject the Epistemological Novelty Thesis. Along the way, I defend an alternative account of change.

The alternative account identifies an element of philosophical continuity between Arcesilaus's anti-Stoic arguments and the latest phase of the so-called Old Academy, represented in the early Hellenistic period by Arcesilaus's predecessor Polemo.[2] In short, both Polemo and Arcesilaus contest Zeno's ethics. The continuity of a shared opponent has important implications for grasping the essential features of Arcesilaus's Socratic revival, and the profound change of direction that this revival brings to the Academy.[3] Beyond the problem-areas of epistemological reconstruction, I examine Polemo's ethical orientation and demonstrate the structural dependence of Polemo's ethics on certain metaphysical principles adopted by Speusippus and Xenocrates. Arcesilaus

---

[1] Schofield, "Academic Epistemology," 323; Richard Bett, "Socrates and Skepticism," in *A Companion to Socrates*, ed. Sara Ahbel-Rappe and Rachana Kamtekar (Malden, MA: Wiley-Blackwell, 2009), 306.
[2] For the language of "revolution" to characterize Arcesilaus's epistemological novelty, see Jacques Brunschwig and David N. Sedley, "Hellenistic Philosophy," in *The Cambridge Companion to Greek and Roman Philosophy*, ed. David N. Sedley (Cambridge: Cambridge University Press, 1983), 176. For "radical change of direction," see John Dillon, *The Heirs of Plato: A Study of the Old Academy (347-274 BC)* (Oxford: Oxford University Press, 2003), 178.
[3] More than a century ago, Hirzel (*Untersuchungen*, t. 3, 38) anticipated the heterodox account of continuity defended in this chapter. Hirzel's claim, largely ignored by recent scholars, is that Polemo's preoccupation with ethics prepares the Old Academy for the innovations of Arcesilaus. However, both Hirzel and modern scholarship overlook Polemo's adherence to a plurality of goods, and the corresponding hierarchical ordering of those goods which depends on the principles of Old Academic metaphysics.

momentarily recedes into the background, to foreground the more immediate task of specifying *de re* the systematic worldviews of the Old Academy. This foregrounding should lay the foundation for the Concluding Analysis. At that point, the theme of Arcesilaus's continuity with Polemo emerges, supplying the key to specifying Arcesilaus's novelty.

Scholars agree that Arcesilaus initiates some kind of change in philosophical orientation soon after Zeno begins to teach and attract his own entourage of talented disciples. Approximate dating of this early phase of Academic change is not a contentious issue; for the earliest "Zenonians" are known to have gathered in the *stoa poikilê* in the Athenian agora around the beginning of the third century BCE. In agreement with a general consensus, the present study asserts that Arcesilaus's polemic with early Stoic philosophy is at the core of his philosophical activity. This much remains uncontroversial. However, in the two-volume sourcebook of principal texts and fragments of the Hellenistic philosophers, Anthony A. Long and David N. Sedley make use of the term "revolution" to account for Arcesilaus's alleged reversion to the early dialogues of Plato, and his unremitting opposition to Zeno's empiricist theory of knowledge.[4] Emboldened by a misreading of Cicero's *Academica*, proponents of epistemological centrism occasionally opt for the term "revolution" to describe the epistemological orientation of the Hellenistic Academy, which involves not only an attack on Stoic epistemology but also "the systematic renunciation of knowledge as Plato's true legacy."[5]

I shall concentrate on two principal difficulties with conventional iterations of the Epistemological Novelty Thesis. This chapter postpones treatment of the first difficulty—the standard epistemological reading of Cicero's *Academica*—to address more immediately the general hazard of historical exclusion. That is to say, the epistemological framework currently excludes from its frame of historiographical reconstruction the metaphysical conditions of knowledge posited by Academics prior to Arcesilaus. On the odd occasion proponents of the Epistemological Novelty Thesis actually refer to the Old Academy, or Old Academic theories of knowledge, the thesis still fails to thematize the systematic connections between the Academy's metaphysical commitments and their varied views on knowledge. Those systematic connections are continually ignored by

---

[4] LS 1, 5, and 445–8.
[5] Brunschwig and Sedley, "Hellenistic Philosophy," 176. For additional references to scholarship taking a similar epistemological approach, see Charles E. Snyder, "On the Teaching of Ethics from Polemo to Arcesilaus," *Études platoniciennes* 14 (2018): § 1, n6, https://doi.org/10.4000/etudesplatoniciennes.1260.

conventional accounts of Arcesilaus's epistemological turn. Excluding these connections from historiographical accounts of Arcesilaus's change of direction renders such accounts dubious and incomplete.[6]

Polemo on Happiness

I begin the alternative account with an examination of Zeno's relation to Polemo. Zeno's motivations to study in the ambit of the early Hellenistic Academy are unknown. Motivations aside, Zeno's attempt to unify the tripartition of philosophy into a coherent rational whole reflects a deviation from the Academy's orthodox understanding of φύσις, which is sustained in the Academy from Speusippus down to Polemo, including the latter's associate, Crantor of Soli (c. 336–276/5).[7] However, the source of Polemo's disagreement with his former student appears to be a very specific issue. At first glance, the disagreement seems completely unrelated to Zeno's tripartition of philosophical λόγος. In raising an objection against Zeno, Polemo was narrowly concerned with his former student's proposed method of teaching ethics: in particular, the ethical role of dialectical theorems in guiding students to virtue. Diogenes Laertius reports (4.18 (= Fr. 101 Gigante)):

> Polemo regularly said (ἔφασκε) that one should practice in concrete actions and not in dialectical theorems (ἐν τοῖς πράγμασι γυμνάζεσθαι καὶ μὴ ἐν τοῖς διαλεκτικοῖς θεωρήμασι), just as those who absorb some technical treatise (τι τέχνιον) on harmony without practicing an instrument resemble those who are wondrous in questioning (τὴν ἐρώτησιν) but in conflict with themselves in disposition (διάθεσις).

---

[6] Peter Adamson, in a judicious review of John Dillon, *The Roots of Platonism: the Origins and Chief Features of a Philosophical Tradition* (Cambridge: Cambridge University Press, 2019), 84, identifies three potential hazards that any interpreter of the so-called Platonic tradition between Plato and Plotinus ought to avoid when reconstructing "satisfying" historical narratives. Adamson fails to mention the most obvious hazard: ignoring ancient source materials in the service of a generic "cream-skimming" picture of the Platonic tradition. As a result, this doxographical hazard makes a claim about "novelty" without submitting to interpretation the ancient evidence concerning what precedes the novelty. Proponents of the Epistemological Novelty Thesis succumb to this doxographical hazard when specifying the historical development of the Academy's epistemological "turn." Peter Adamson, "Review of John Dillon, *The Roots of Platonism*," *The International Journal of the Platonic Tradition* 14 (2020): 84–6.

[7] On the coherence of Stoicism as a whole, see P. Hadot, "Les divisions des parties," 209–12; Pierre Hadot, "Philosophie, discours philosophiques, et divisions de la philosophie chez les Stoïciens," *Revue Internationale de Philosophie* 45, no. 178.3 (1991): 208–9.

Relying on a comparison to training in musical harmony, Polemo objects to a certain method of ethical training. The comparison is worth examining alongside the appeals made to musical training by Xenocrates and Aristotle. To prepare for that examination, Polemo's statement will need further comment. Polemo's objection against dialectical theorems fails to name Zeno as the specified target. Nevertheless, the pedagogical tendency in question here is, as Sedley contends, a near-perfect match for the kind of training that Zeno is famous for prescribing: training that requires the formation and comprehension of dialectical theorems for progress in virtue.[8] Zeno's syllogism against drunkenness is a case in point. In this syllogism, both major and minor premises are evaluative (and descriptive) in the sense that each proposition refers to what is "reasonable" to do in certain situations. Following Sedley, on this point, Polemo's intended opposition to dialectical theorems of the Zenonian sort seems narrowly ethical, such that the key issue motivating Polemo's objection is a concern over "practical ethics." In this sense, Polemo opposed the prescription of a particular method for learning how to become virtuous. The opposition is evidently limited to the ethical part of Zeno's system, and while the function of the dialectical part of Stoic logic might be an issue for Polemo, it is challenged only for its decisive role in the ethical sphere. If one thus takes Polemo as rejecting the ethical requirement of dialectical syllogistic as conceived by Zeno, then perhaps one should refrain from taking Polemo here as rejecting dialectic, or dialectical reasoning, as such. An additional source seems to supplement a narrow ethical construal of the rejection.[9] Philodemus presents Polemo as having juxtaposed dialectical question and answer against the "training" one receives "in actions or deeds" (ἐν τοῖς πράγμασιν γυμάζεσθαι, *Acad. hist.* col. 14.4). Polemo praises the latter and disparages the former, but perhaps such a comparison is only meant to evaluate question and answer as its relates to ethical training. That is to say, training in the logic of question and answer is generally held to be, at the very least, ethically inferior to the improvements gained by the training one receives in actions or deeds. The issue motivating Polemo's opposition seems to be the requirement of studying, for the sake of progress in virtue, anything like the formal structures of descriptive and evaluative propositions of Zeno's syllogistic reasoning. On this construal, Polemo's narrow opposition would be consistent with what is known of Academic ethics preceding the Hellenistic period. For

---

[8] Sedley, "Stoic-Platonist Debate," in Ierodiakonou, *Topics in Stoic Philosophy*, 145–9.
[9] Also relevant is the passage in Plutarch (*St. rep.* 1045f–1046b (= Fr. 122 Gigante)), referring to Chrysippus as saying: "dialectic was treated seriously by Plato and Aristotle and their successors down to Polemo and Strato, but most of all by Socrates."

Plato and his early successors in the Academy do not compose or require the study of a comprehensive catalogue of syllogisms to assist those in training with "reasonable" courses of action.

At *De fin.* 4.19–21, Cicero alludes to Zeno's "secession" from Old Academic teaching in the area of ethics, and later refers to his ethical *controversiae* with Polemo (*Zenonem cum Polemone disceptantem, De fin.* 4.45 (= Fr. 128 Gigante), cf. 4.44, 4.60: Zeno's ethical disagreement is there designated a *verbis discrepare*). The term *controversia* does not necessarily imply an actual encounter of criticism and response between the two philosophers. One implication of the term is simply that there was a difference of opinion, which Polemo seems to have "regularly" expressed.[10] Cicero himself presents Zeno's deviation from an Old Academic view of the good (including Polemo's) as a mere terminological variance and accuses Zeno of inexplicably discarding the terminology of bodily and external "goods" to describe imperfect reasonable actions (*De fin.* 4.25–6). In light of these departures, Cicero admits his confusion over Zeno's "secession" from the eudaimonist tradition. In Cicero's view (4.3), the Academic tradition of defining a conception of happiness is even upheld by Aristotle and Theophrastus. Cicero's charge of "secession" is one of several textual indications that Cicero himself may have agreed, at least partially, with Antiochus's historical views (*De fin.* 5.7–8, *Acad.* 1.34) of a eudaimonist tradition of Academic ethics from Speusippus to Polemo.[11] In partial agreement with those views, Cicero includes the Academic Crantor (*Acad.* 2.135, cf. 1.34), but also Aristotle (cf. *De fin.* 5.14) and Theophrastus (*Acad.* 2.131, 139). Cicero is nonetheless reluctant in *De fin.* 4 to attribute any actual motivation on the part of Zeno, beyond mere semantic quibbling, to explain why he abandoned defining the things originally recommended by nature as goods. Unlike Antiochus, Cicero confines himself to reproaching Zeno for failing to clarify the cause of his terminological disagreements with this tradition of eudaimonism. Having said that, Zeno incurs Cicero's charge of distorting the teaching of ethics by making it an excessively pedantic enterprise, thus convoluting the ordinary meaning of words with an inordinate regard for conceptual distinction and petty syllogistic theorems (4.7). In the same spirit as Polemo's objection to dialectical theorems, Cicero

---

[10] On the semantics of ἔφασκε ("regularly said") at D.L. 4.18, see Krämer, *Platonismus und hellenistische Philosophie*, 33.
[11] Woldemar Görler, "Cicero und die 'Schule des Aristoteles,'" in *Kleine Schriften zur hellenistisch-römischen Philosophie*, ed. Christoph Catrein, *Philosophia Antiqua*, v. 95 (Leiden: Brill, 2004), 204. A cautionary approach is, of course, wise when studying Cicero's use of sources. As Görler himself remarks in a relevant context: "Hier ist behutsame Interpretation geboten, denn Cicero hat nicht einfach übersetzt." Woldemar Görler, "Review of *The Philosophy of Antiochus*, ed. David Sedley," *Elenchos* 33 (2012): 376.

portrays the Stoic founder as the one and only punctilious verbarian among fellow eudaimonist philosophers, seduced by the "grandeur and magnificence of words" (4.60).

There is, however, another way to specify the underlying reasons for Polemo's pithy rejection of early Stoic ethics. Unlike Sedley's approach, this mode of historiographical specification is not limited to what Polemo intentionally selected for criticism, that is, the role of dialectical argument in Zenonian ethics. Sedley's interpretation is almost entirely devoted to the important task of specifying *de dicto* what Polemo took it that he was committing himself to by rejecting Zenonian ethics.[12] Again, *de dicto* specifications tend to focus historical reconstruction on how a given figure understood the content of what he was claiming or rejecting. To adapt the formulation of Bernard Williams, Sedley's *de dicto* interpretation *looks sideways* to the context of how Polemo understood the content of the view he regularly rejected and his reasons for such rejection. In this context, historiographical *de re* interpretation sets out to reconstruct the underlying philosophical reasons at the core of the disagreement independent of determining the content of what Polemo took himself to be rejecting. *De re* specification shifts the emphasis of reconstruction from the specification of how Polemo understood his opposition to the type of pedagogical commitment implemented by Zeno to a specification of the auxiliary principles and commitments motivating Polemo's rejection of Zenonian virtue ethics. Keeping this mode of *de re* specification in mind, consider one of the central principles of Zeno's demand for a kind of dialectical rigor in the gradual process of learning how to become virtuous: the principle of disciplinary holism, which holds that evaluative propositions and conclusions converge or "mingle" with propositions and conclusions associated with the other parts of philosophical discourse (logic and physics). Diogenes Laertius documents what was considered the broad scope of Stoic logic, and the systematic view of philosophical λόγος implicitly challenged by Polemo and Cicero: "for all things (πάντα γὰρ τὰ πράγματα) are discerned by means of the theory of logical arguments, whether they belong to the domain of physics or ethics" (D.L. 7.83). This alternative approach to reconstructing Polemo's opposition specifies the structural implications of an

---

[12] While Sedley adopts the model of *de dicto* specification in the interpretation of Polemo's objection, he does take a decisive step in the direction of *de re* interpretation. In this direction, Sedley surmises that Polemo's opposition may point to another, unacknowledged issue of disagreement, which allegedly belongs to the subfield of "moral psychology," or what I prefer to specify as the metaphysical principles of moral psychology (see Chapter 3, n8 on the historiographical specification of "moral psychology"). Sedley, "Stoic-Platonist Debate," in Ierodiakonou, *Topics in Stoic Philosophy*, 152.

Academic rejecting the mingling of logic, or the dialectical part of logic, with the techniques of ethical training.

Polemo succeeds Xenocrates of Chalcedon around 314 BCE. He presides as head of the Academy well into the next century (*c.* 270/69). Sources on Polemo are fragmentary and mostly anecdotal. He wrote a number of treatises, all of which are now lost. However, biographical reports of his dissolute youth are prominent in many ancient sources: for example, in Diogenes Laertius (4.16–17 (= Fr. 16 Gigante)), Philodemus (*Acad. hist.* col. 13 (= Fr. 15 Gigante)), and Augustine (*Ep.* 144 (= Fr. 33 Gigante)). Philodemus and Diogenes Laertius explicitly cite Antigonus of Carystus (*fl.* late third century BCE) in the course of conveying accounts of Polemo's drunken exploits prior to entering the Academy. Xenocrates's lecture on the virtue of moderation inspires Polemo's moral awakening, and shortly thereafter he joins the Academy. Evidently, Xenocrates has an important role in helping Polemo later become a model of emotional austerity for the next generation of Academics. Diogenes Laertius reports that Polemo "emulated Xenocrates in all respects" (κατὰ πάντα ἐζηλωκέναι τὸν Ξενοκράτην, D.L. 4.19, cf. Philodemus, *Acad. hist.* col. 14.41–5). And it seems that he followed his teacher in deciding on moral grounds for a diet of vegetarianism (Clement, *Strom.* 7.32 (= Fr. 112 Gigante)). Remarkably transformed from his association with Xenocrates and the Academy, Polemo famously surpasses his associates with his own equanimity and moderation. He is appointed the successor of his beloved mentor, and eventually becomes the longest serving scholarch of the Academy at Athens. After choosing to live his philosophical life almost exclusively within the institutional grounds of the Academy, Polemo was reportedly honored by the city for his "love of what is noble" (τὸ φιλογενναῖον, D.L. 4.19). Biographical accounts of his philosophical life suggest that as scholarch he promoted close bonds among his associates and cultivated his own loving relationships with younger associates. As he is reportedly known for having "emulated" and "loved" (ἐρασθῆναι, D.L. 4.19) Xenocrates, Polemo's promotion of intimacy with Academic associates apparently set in earlier than his directorship. Later, as scholarch, emulation seems to function as a means of keeping younger associates physically close to one another, for during this time his associates reportedly resided together in nearby huts and to the study halls of the Academy.

More importantly, Polemo's definition of ἔρως attests to the close pedagogical bonds cultivated in the early Hellenistic Academy. According to Plutarch, Polemo defined ἔρως as "service to the gods for the care and salvation of the young" (*Mor.*, 780d (= Fr. 113 Gigante)). Implementing this notion of love for the sake of taking care of the young, Polemo's approach to education seems to harmonize with the figure of a divinely guided Socratic lover, promoting a model of care for the young depicted in various Platonic dialogues. In order to understand the educational culture of the early Hellenistic Academy, recent scholarship concentrates on *Alcibiades* 1, *Theaetetus*, and the pseudo-Platonic *Theages* as the inspirational sources of Polemo's return to a Socratic style of education.[13] Polemo reportedly cultivated intimate relationships with Crantor, the first exegete of Plato's *Timaeus* (Proclus, *In Pl. Tim.* 1.76), as well as Crates of Athens (D.L. 4.17, 4.21–2, Philodemus, *Acad. hist.* col. 15.31–46), his housemate and later for a brief period his successor, shortly before Arcesilaus becomes scholarch. Upon meeting Polemo and Crates, a young Arcesilaus acclaimed Polemo and Crates the divine remnants of a Golden Age (D.L. 4.22, *Acad. hist.* col. 15.4–10), uttering divine words from daimonic lips. Young Arcesilaus abandoned the Peripatetic school—where he had previously earned the esteem of Theophrastus for his argumentative abilities (D.L. 4.29–30 (< F 107 Vezzoli))—soon after encountering Polemo and his associate.

Polemo promoted a version of eudaimonist ethics, which is to say, an ethics based on the view that attaining εὐδαιμονία ("happiness") is for human beings the end, or overall purpose, of life. Alexandrian Church Father Clement reports that Polemo maintained the following view (*Strom.* 2.22 (= Fr. 123 Gigante)):

> Polemo, the associate of Xenocrates, seems to be of the view that happiness (εὐδαιμονίαν) consists in self-sufficiency in respect of all goods, or of the most and greatest [of the goods] (ἀγαθῶν πάντων, ἢ τῶν πλείστων καὶ μεγίστων). For he affirms that happiness can never be achieved apart from virtue, while virtue is sufficient for happiness even if bereft of bodily and external goods.

Polemo presumably defended this conception of the good life in his treatise *On Life according to Nature* (Περὶ τοῦ κατὰ φύσιν βίου). The title of this lost work is also preserved by Clement, and it could be the original source of Clement's passing reference to Polemo's vegetarianism—although it is unlikely Clement had direct access to the original. Cicero repeats on several occasions that for Polemo the highest good is a "life according to nature" (*secundum naturam vivere*,

---

[13] On ἔρως in the educational culture of Polemo's Academy generally, but also as it relates to the *Theages*, see Harold Tarrant, "Socratic *Synousia*: A Post-Platonic Myth," *Journal of the History of Philosophy* 43 (2005): 142–5. On the possible link between Polemo's Academy and *Alcibiades* 1, see John Dillon, "A Platonist *Ars Amatoria*," *The Classical Quarterly* 44, no. 2 (1994): 390n7. Cf. Harold Tarrant, "Piecing Together Polemo," *Mediterranean Archaeology* 19/20 (2006/07): 228–32; Harold Tarrant, "Improvement by Love: From Aeschines to the Old Academy," in *Alcibiades and the Socratic Lover-Educator*, ed. Marguerite Johnson and Harold Tarrant (London: Bristol Classical Press, 2012), 158–63; Tiziano Dorandi, "Le Vie de Polémon," *Aitia* 5 (2015), http://aitia.revues.org/1183.

De fin. 2.34 (< Fr. 127 Gigante), *De fin.* 4.6 (= Fr. 129 Gigante), 4.45–51 (< Fr. 130 Gigante). And in what is certainly a rare reference to the content of Polemo's *scripta*, Cicero claims that "in his writings Polemo points out" (*indicant scripta Polemonis, Acad.* 2.131 (= Fr. 96, 125 Gigante)) that one could live honorably while enjoying the first things nature recommends to human beings. According to Clement, Polemo associated his own regime of vegetarianism with the moral goal of living "according to nature" (κατὰ φύσιν), on the understanding that the consumption of animal flesh is unsuitable for animals with a rational soul, for the flesh of animals is associated with "the souls of irrational [creatures]" (ταῖς τῶν ἀλόγων ψυχαῖς, Clement, *Strom.* 7.32 (= Fr. 112 Gigante)).

Given that virtue is for Polemo sufficient for happiness even without the possession of external and bodily goods—a conception of happiness *qua* highest good dependent on the orthodox Academic distinction between soul and body—it follows for Polemo that the goods more directly associated with the rational soul rank superior to goods of the body. Although Polemo's vegetarian regime is based on the distinction between the rational souls of animals and the nonrational souls of other animals, it remains unclear whether he had bifurcated (or perhaps trifurcated) the human soul into rational and irrational components. There is, however, one provocative clue indicating that he affirmed not only the metaphysical irreducibility of soul to the body, but also that Polemo held "mind" to be an important power of the soul. The clue is found in a controversial passage of Cicero's *Academica*, in which Varro admits to reiterating the historical views of Antiochus concerning the Old Academy (*vetus Academia*) and Peripatetic schools. This passage requires further examination, but for present purposes it should suffice to note that Cicero's Varro ascribes the following view to Polemo, among others: "that *mens* (mind) alone deserves credence because it alone discerns what is always simple, uniform, and same as itself" (*Acad.* 1.30).[14] Given Clement's testimony above, that which ascribes the reasoning in Polemo's *On Life according to Nature* against the consumption of animal flesh to Xenocrates as well, it seems less controversial to allege, as Varro does, that both Polemo and Xenocrates defended similar or nearly identical ethical theories, according to which φύσις ("nature") and the rational soul have important normative

---

[14] Philippson is right to caution. Cicero may be offering a controversial interpretation of Polemo's writings. Robert Philippson, "Das 'erste Naturgemässe,'" *Philologus* 87, no. 4 (1932): 447. Pohlenz also observes that Cicero's interpretation of the *scripta* may be controversial, claiming that Cicero seems to agree with, if not reproduce, Antiochus's own views of Polemo and his writings. In any case, Cicero's agreement with Antiochus on Polemo is not sufficient to dismiss the possibility that Cicero was familiar with Polemo's writings and the views expressed in them (from sources other than Antiochus). Max Pohlenz, *Grundfragen der stoischen Philosophie* (Göttingen: Vandenhoeck & Ruprecht, 1940), 20.

functions in the account of happiness. Additional testimony informs readers of a nearly identical Old Academic point of view on happiness. Plutarch, in his polemic with the Stoics, states that Zeno followed both Xenocrates and Polemo in assuming that "nature and that which is according to nature (τὴν φύσιν καὶ τὸ κατὰ φύσιν) are the elements of happiness" (*Comm. not.* 1069f (< Fr. 124 Gigante, Fr. 151 IPD)).[15] Moreover, there is Aristotle, who states unambiguously that Xenocrates held that one cannot be happy unless and until one's soul is in a good state, for the soul of each human being is the δαιμῶν of that individual being (*Top.* 2.6, 112a32 (= Fr. 154 IPD), cf. *Top.* 7.1, 152a5–12, 25–30 (= Fr. 158 IPD)).

The Basic Explanatory Framework of Old Academic Ontology

Xenocrates's views on the human soul can be further discerned from his view of daimonic life. According to Xenocrates, daimons are situated in a mediating position within his triadic hierarchy of reality.[16] As sublunary beings, daimons move among humans, but unlike them the movements of daimonic life also border on the realm of the heavens. On this model, the "nature" of the daimonic participates in both human affection and divine power. Xenocrates's view of daimonic life is similar to the view held by Plutarch, for whom "the divine element of the daimon shares its lot with the 'nature' (φύσις) of the soul and the sense-perception of the body" (Plutarch, *Def. or.* 416c–d (= Fr. 142 IPD)). Thus, for Xenocrates and Plutarch, daimons have a composite nature structurally analogous to the divided or partitioned souls of human beings. Daimons supposedly partake in the experience of psychic "disturbances," which arise from the affections of bodily sense-perception. Yet, Xenocrates credits humans and not daimons with the discovery of philosophy. Through the lifelong pursuit of *sophia*, the complex soul of the human is capable of putting an end to its psychic "disturbances" (τὸ ταραχῶδες, Ps. Galen, *Hist. philos.* 8 (= Fr. 171 IPD)).[17] On this view, the rational portion of the human soul corresponds to the divine

---

[15] For the fragments of Xenocrates, see Margherita Isnardi Parente, ed., *Senocrate e Ermodoro: Testimonianze e frammenti*, rev. ed. Tiziano Dorandi (Pisa: Edizioni Della Normale, 2012) (= IPD).

[16] For discussion of the composite nature of daimons in Xenocrates, see Hermann S. Schibli, "Xenocrates' Daemons and the Irrational Soul," *The Classical Quarterly* 43, no. 1 (May 1993): 147–53.

[17] On Xenocrates's use of the term ταραχῶδης and its later usage by Hellenistic philosophers, see Phillip Sidney Horky, "Speusippus and Xenocrates on the Pursuit and Ends of Philosophy," in *Brill's Companion to the Reception of Plato in Antiquity*, ed. Harold Tarrant, Danielle A. Layne, Dirk Baltzly, and François Renaud (Leiden: Brill, 2018), 43. For discussion of this term in relation to Plato and Aristotle, see Isnardi Parente and Dorandi, eds., *Senocrate e Ermodoro*, 330.

part of the human. Of course, the essentially composite nature of the human soul should not be taken to eliminate the possibility that Xenocrates divides the soul into more than two parts.[18]

Is there anything important to be said about the role of the concept of "nature" (φύσις/κατὰ φύσιν) in Xenocrates's ethics? Additionally, is it worth considering whether the concept has for Xenocrates the ethical importance it later receives from Polemo and Zeno? For too long, these issues have seemed irrelevant to an account of Arcesilaus's novelty. The argument of this chapter, however, is that such questions pertain to the correct specification of Arcesilaus's break from conventional Academic ethics. Once again, an important passage to examine in this context comes from Clement (*Strom.* 2.22 (= Fr. 150 IPD), cf. Fr. 123 Gigante):

> Xenocrates of Chalcedon defines happiness as the possession of proper virtue (κτῆσιν τῆς οἰκείας ἀρετῆς) and the resources with which to service it. Then as regards the proper seat of this, he plainly says the soul; as the motive causes of it he identifies the virtues; as the material causes, in the sense of parts, fine actions and good habits and attitudes; and as indispensable accompaniments, corporeal and external goods. (trans. Dillon, slightly modified)[19]

For Xenocrates, the possession of corporeal and external goods contributes to the possession of proper virtue. Inferior goods are necessary for the superior good of proper virtue. In relation to the instrumental role of inferior goods in Xenocrates, Polemo's conception of happiness seems to reflect a considerable deviation. Again, for Polemo it appears that goods of the soul (presumably, "the greatest of goods") are the only goods necessary for happiness; this conception of necessity relieves the rational soul from the need to procure either external goods or corporeal goods for happiness. However, testimony from Seneca seems to challenge the claim that Polemo deviates from his predecessor in this respect (*Ep.* 85.18 (= Fr. 166 IPD, Fr. 78e Tarán)): "Xenocrates and Speusippus think that one can become happy by virtue alone, but it is not the case that what is honorable is the only good."[20] Setting Speusippus aside for

---

[18] Citing Ps. Olympiodorus, *In Pl. Phd.* 74 (2.107–9 Westerink), D. A. Rees, "Bipartition of the Soul in the Early Academy," *Journal of Hellenic Studies* 77, no. 1 (1957): 118, argues that we should refrain from attributing a simple bipartition (the rational and irrational) to Xenocrates and Speusippus, in view of the possibility that both Academics divide the irrational into additional subparts. As I suggest below, there are reasons to believe that the rational is also subdivided (especially by Xenocrates) into different powers in accordance with the different kinds of cognizable beings.

[19] John Dillon, "The Origins of Platonists' Dogmatism," ΣΧΟΛΗ 1, no. 1 (2007): 29–30.

[20] In his letter to Lucilius, Seneca writes: *Xenocrates et Speusippus putant beatum vel sola virtute fieri posse, non tamen unum bonum esse, quod honestum est.* The source of Seneca's remark, according

a moment, Seneca evidently believes that on the topic of virtue, Xenocrates defends an early version of the sufficiency of virtue thesis—a thesis similar to Polemo's view of the goods, and perhaps yet another source of inspiration for Zeno's defense of the sufficiency of virtue thesis. Seneca implies that the two Academic scholarchs recognize a plurality and hierarchy of goods, which Zeno and his Stoic followers later reject. Admittedly, on the issue of "nature" and its conceptual role in Xenocrates's doctrine of happiness, the passage from Clement is far from decisive. Cicero's remarks on Polemo's *scripta*, on the other hand, and the *vetus Academia* (*Acad.* 2.131) are more suggestive. For there it appears that the superior good, which is rendered consistent with enjoying the first natural things, is attributed to Polemo, but not only Polemo. Again, it is a hierarchical view of goods that the Old Academics reportedly share (2.132); and it is a hierarchical view of goods that Aristotle and Theophrastus allegedly endorse. On the more controversial issue of including Aristotle in this way of thinking, Plutarch's perspective noted above should be kept in mind (*Comm. not.* 1069e–f (= Fr. 151 IPD < Fr. 124 Gigante)): "From what [principles] do Aristotle and Theophrastus begin, and what do Xenocrates and Polemo take as their principles? And has not Zeno followed them in their assumptions (τούτοις ἠκολούθησεν ὑποτιθεμένοις) that *nature* and *that which is according to nature* are the elements of happiness" (italics added)? Plutarch also believes, it seems, that Zeno followed Polemo and Xenocrates (as well as Aristotle and Theophrastus) by taking φύσις and τὸ κατὰ φύσιν as principles or elements of happiness.[21]

According to Aristotle, a triadic classification of goods is a standard and widespread ethical view. That is to say, no one would dispute that the happy soul ought to possess all three kinds of good (*Pol.* 7.1, 1323a24–7), not even philosophers offering otherwise disparate theories of the happy life (*EN* 1.8, 1098b12–20), including Xenocrates. The assemblage of sources on Xenocrates and Polemo examined here—passages from Aristotle, Cicero, Seneca, Plutarch, and Clement—gathers evidence in support of a fundamental agreement between Polemo and his Academic teacher on the existence of a plurality of

---

to Isnardi Parente, is likely Cicero. Margherita Isnardi Parente, *Speusippo: Frammenti* (Naples: La Scuola di Platone I, 1980), F 88, http://rmcisadu.let.uniroma1.it/isnardi/fronte.htm

[21] Postponing a moment the examination of Speusippus's use of the phrase κατὰ φύσιν in his definition of happiness (Clem., *Strom.* 2.133 (= Fr. 77 Tarán, Fr. 123 Gigante)) allows me to note agreement with Leonardo Tarán: from the definition of happiness recorded by Clement, Cicero (*Tusc.* 5.30, 39, 87 (= Frs. 78a–c Tarán), *Leg.* 1.37–8 (= Fr. 78d Tarán), and Plutarch (*Comm. not.* 1065a (= Fr. 79 Tarán)), it is reasonable to conclude that Speusippus maintained some doctrine of the hierarchical plurality of goods. Leonardo Tarán, *Speusippus of Athens: A Critical Study with a Collection of the Related Texts and Commentary* (Leiden: Brill, 1981), 436.

hierarchical goods. In the light of these sources, it becomes clear that Polemo and his beloved Xenocrates promoted the life of εὐδαιμονία by partitioning and ranking a plurality of goods.

An early expression of the hierarchical classification of goods can be found in Plato's *Laws* 1 (631b-d). In that dialogue, the unnamed Athenian distinguishes between divine goods of the soul, which are the virtues, and inferior human goods, such as health, beauty, bodily exercise, and the acquisition of wealth accompanied by good judgment. Among the superior divine goods, "wisdom" (φρόνησις) is "authoritative" (ἡγεμονοῦν), whereas the moderate disposition of the soul "with intellect" (μετὰ νοῦ) is second in rank, with justice and courage to follow. Note, for later reference, that this assortment of superior divine goods is considered ethically superior "by nature" (φύσει). Later in the *Laws* (697a-c), a triadic classification is presented in terms of psychic goods, corporeal goods, and those goods associated with wealth and property.[22] There is no doubt that Old Academic and Peripatetic adherence to the plurality of goods (ἡ ἀρετή-τὰ σωματικά-τὰ ἐκτός) has conceptual roots in Platonic dialogues. The hierarchical classification of this plurality is based on a certain metaphysical view of νοῦς ("intellect") and the way in which "intellect" is supposed to function in relation to hierarchical conceptions of the world as a whole. Old Academic conceptualizations of εὐδαιμονία, and their respective hierarchical classification of goods, are fundamentally based on a metaphysical distinction between the soul and the body. Furthermore, the traditional conceptualizations of the soul and the body in the Old Academy emerge as key parts of larger, and more comprehensive, explanatory frameworks associated with their ontological hierarchy of beings as a whole. Eudaimonist ethics for both Speusippus and Xenocrates, and their gradable plurality of goods, presupposes the larger explanatory framework of an ontology of virtue. The identification of inferior goods assigns certain items *qua* goods to the structural level of perceptible being. Individual souls with reason, or intellect, encounter the perceptible phenomena of non-psychic goods, including the individual soul's encounter with its own body and bodily components. Traditional Academic accounts of the goal of human life imply the metaphysical assumption that the world itself is an ordered whole, or totality, which can be systematically studied and structurally explained. The constituent parts and principles of reality as it really is are considered more or less intelligible, and in one way or another, the parts and principles

---

[22] Cf. *Laws* 726a-729b, 743c-e, 870a-b. For the interchangeable use of φρόνησις and σοφία in the *Laws*, see 689d2, d4, d5, d7, 696c8, and 710a6. As stated below, Xenocrates later develops a distinction between the two terms.

are structurally related within the whole. The evaluative ranking of psychic and non-psychic goods involves a conception of goodness that is already there, which is to say, an absolute conception of goodness as it really is independently of the beliefs, thoughts, or attitudes of individual human souls. Individual souls are inevitably situated within the hierarchical structure of the totality of beings. It is important not to lose sight of the fact that it is from within such a basic metaphysical framework that Speusippus and Xenocrates (as well as Aristotle and Theophrastus) formulate their various hierarchical classifications of goods.[23]

The basic explanatory framework of their ontological systems enables Speusippus and Xenocrates to account for the higher-level reality of intelligible beings with an appeal to a pair of supreme incorporeal principles: the One and Multiplicity for Speusippus, the Monad and Dyad for Xenocrates. The pair of opposing principles generates the derivative levels of being, as well as the principles of order and stability for each subsequent level of reality. Speusippus evidently understood the opposing principles as seeds or potencies of all lower-level beings: from mathematical numbers and magnitudes, to the soul or world-soul as a complex whole, individual souls with bodies, perceptible beings, and so on. It seems that Speusippus has an ontological process of derivation in mind, in which the products of the higher principles, the mathematical numbers, for example, become the derivative principles of the subsequent lower level (Arist., *Meta.* Λ 10, 1075b37–1076a4 (= Fr. 30 Tarán)).[24] Speusippus thus maintains, according to Aristotle's critical treatment, the implausible view that whatever is the cause of some quality in other things, the originating cause cannot have that quality itself in the same way. That would mean that if the One is the cause of the being and goodness for all other things, imposing limit and order on Multiplicity, then the One as the source of order and limit cannot itself be properly termed a being (Arist., *Meta.* N 5, 1092a14 (< Fr. 43 Tarán)) or a good

---

[23] As Gerson observes, the basic explanatory structure of early Academic ontology opens up various ways of explaining the intra-hierarchical order of the intelligible realm. While Speusippus and Xenocrates diverged in their formulations of the intra-hierarchical structure, as noted below, both adhered to a structurally basic explanatory framework. Academic disagreements within this basic framework regarding the structure of the intelligible realm are likely the source of Academic disagreements concerning the intra-hierarchy of the sensible, which then manifest different formulations of happiness and the plurality of goods. Such variations are minor in the sense that they remain consistent with, and internal to, the Academy's traditional endorsement of eudaimonism. On the Old Academy's adherence to ethical eudaimonism, cf. Gerson, *From Plato to Platonism*, 16–17, 133–62.

[24] Expanding on the work of Philip Merlan, Dillon, *Heirs*, 41–64, defends the coherence of Speusippus's ontology with the help of two passages from Iamblichus (*De communi mathematica scientia* 4, p. 15, 6–18, 12 Festa [hereafter *DCMS*] (= Fr. 28 Tarán)). For defense of Merlan's reading of *DCMS*, see John Dillon, "Speusippus in Iamblichus," *Phronesis* 29 (1984): 325–32; Philip Merlan, *From Platonism to Neoplatonism*, Third Edition, revised (The Hague: Martinus Nijhoff, 1968), 96–140.

(Arist., *Meta.* Λ 7, 1072b30-4 (= Fr. 42a Tarán)). The principle of Multiplicity is the cause of individuation and differentiation, and just as Speusippus denies that the One is good, so does he deny that Multiplicity is evil or bad. Moreover, Speusippus refuses to identify the One with Intellect, holding that "intellect (which is god) has its own 'peculiar nature' " (ἰδιοφυῆ, Stobaeus, *Ecl.* 1.1 (= Fr. 58 Tarán)). Aristotle criticizes ontological systems of derivation such as this, for in his mind such systems structurally resemble a bad tragedy, that is, a loosely connected whole strung together in a series of disjointed episodes. From this Academic perspective on the supposed totality of beings, including the world as a whole, Aristotle claims that disparate principles at each level correspond in some unclear, or unspecified, way to the highest principles of the One and Multiplicity.

Deviating doctrinally from the ontology of his predecessor, Xenocrates identifies the supreme principle of the Monad with Intellect (Aëtius, 1.7.30 (= Fr. 133 IPD), Favonius Eulogius, *Disp. de Somn. Scip.* 5.6, p. 17 van Weddingen (= Fr. 134 IPD)).[25] The Intellect is tasked with imposing limit upon the indefiniteness of the Dyad to produce both numbers and forms, such that everything else in the world is derived from Intellect and the Dyad: points, lines and planes, beings in the heavens, and all other perceptible beings. According to Aristotle's testimony (*Meta.* Z 2, 1028b24 ff. (= Fr. 23 IPD)), Xenocrates holds that numbers and forms have the "same nature" (φύσιν)—a view that seems to equate forms with ideal numbers. Theophrastus praises Xenocrates, perhaps inspired by Aristotle's criticism of Speusippus, for attempting to derive all beings from his first principles, all the way down to perceptible beings (Theophrastus, *Meta.* 6a23 (< Fr. 59 Tarán, Fr. 20 IPD)). But Theophrastus's text also informs us that Speusippus would pay little attention to the derivation of perceptible beings. Xenocrates, for his part, is said to define the idea or form as "the paradigmatic cause of what is eternally unified according to nature" (αἰτίαν παραδειγματικὴν τῶν κατὰ φύσιν ἀεὶ συνεστώτων, Proclus, *In Pl. Parm.* 888.18-19 (= Fr. 14 IPD)). This specification of form in terms of "nature" seems to eliminate the possibility of a form or idea (eternally) existing for artificial things or unnatural perversions.

Xenocrates's specification of soul as "number moving itself" (Arist., *De anima* 1.2, 404b27-30, see Frs. 85-117 IPD) suggests that soul is the exemplary mediating entity, composed of both intelligible and perceptible

---

[25] On Favonius Eulogius (fifth century CE) and his source on the relation between Monad *qua animus* (νοῦς, intellect)/*deus* (θεός, god) and the intellectual nature of numbers, see Hans Joachim Krämer, *Der Ursprung der Geistmetaphysik: Untersuchungen zur Geschichte des Platonismus zwischen Platon und Plotin* (Amsterdam: Verlag P. Schippers, 1964), 42-4.

elements. Infusing what is likely Middle Platonist terminology into his report of Xenocrates's conception of soul, the testimony of Nemesius of Emesa (late fourth century CE) indicates that for Xenocrates the soul, which is "among the things that can be numbered and among things which are multiple," possesses a discerning power that distinguishes things by assigning shapes and characters to each and separates out forms from other forms, bringing to light their differences both in terms of otherness and in terms of numerical count (*De nat. hom.* 2.102 (< Fr. 110 IPD)).[26] More generally for Xenocrates, the mediation of intelligible and perceptible realms means that there is a third realm: the "composite" (σύνθετος) of the intelligible and perceptible that Xenocrates identifies with the "opinable" (δοξαστή), which is heaven itself—"for it [heaven] is visible by sense-perception, but intelligible by means of astronomy" (Sextus Empiricus, *M.* 7.147 (< Fr. 2 IPD)).

Despite the deviation in explicating the process of ontological derivation, Speusippus and Xenocrates idealize the intellectual power of the soul and the epistemic access to intelligible beings that the intellectual power grants: mathematical numbers for Speusippus, and forms/numbers for Xenocrates.[27] For the present study, there is, however, a more relevant point of commonality. To reiterate, the structural hierarchy in the ordering of the totality of beings in each case prescribes a structural hierarchy in the ordering and classification of human goods. Speusippus and Xenocrates assign priority to goods of the soul (over bodily and external goods) due to a shared view of the superior power of the soul—specified either as the intellectual or reasoning part (λόγος/διάνοια)— and its own participation in the ordering principle of the One or Monad. Hence, for individual souls with reason or intellect, the psychological state of "the mean" is a sort of limited or measured state of being. Krämer observes the function of "the mean" in the general economy of Old Academic metaphysics (or what he designates more controversially, the system of Platonic philosophy).

---

[26] On Nemesius as a source for Greek philosophy, see Jaap Mansfeld and David T. Runia, *Aëtiana: The Method and Intellectual Context of a Doxographer*, Volume 1: *The Sources* (Leiden: Brill, 1997), 291–9. For discussion of Xenocrates's conception of soul in relation to Pythagoras, and the notion of the κριτικὸν ὄργανον ("discerning tool") in Plutarch (*De anima pro.* 1032c3–d5) and Alcinous (*Did.*, 154.10–18), see Phillip Sidney Horky, *Plato and Pythagoreanism* (Oxford: Oxford University Press, 2013), 74–7.

[27] As for the question of Intellect itself, it seems that for Speusippus goodness emerges only at the level of soul, or world-soul (*DCMS* 4, p. 16 Festa, 12–17, Aristotle, *Meta.* N 4, 1091a33–b19 (= Fr. 44 Tarán)), *Meta.* Λ 4, 1072b30, cf. Fr. 42a, Fr. 43, 44 Tarán). If transcendent Intellect is itself "beautiful" (κάλον) yet lacking the quality of goodness, and its contemplative activity is the source of the creative function of the world-soul (Ps. Iamblichus, *Theol. arith.* 83.1–5 (< Fr. 28 Tarán)), bringing order to the realm of perceptible beings, then it would seem that goodness is in some way a product of beauty. For defense of this view, see Merlan, *From Plato to Platonism*, 103–10; Krämer, *Geistmetaphysik*, 212–14; Dillon, "Speusippus in Iamblichus," no. 3, 327–8.

In this general economy, "the mean" is a state participating in the structure of unity in multiplicity. This observation may or may not apply to Plato himself, but it certainly applies to the testimonies transmitting the ontological systems of Speusippus and Xenocrates.[28] As Krämer notes, the state of the mean is ordered as an "equilibrium" (ἴσον) between the extremes of the too much and the too little, or the greater and the lesser (μεῖζον–ἔλαττον).

> The character of order that belongs to each good thing [psychic, the bodily, or external] is based, thus, on the limitation of multiplicity produced by unity; order is limited multiplicity (ὡρισμένον) and, so to speak, [it] is unity in multiplicity; it is, in addition, like the ontological *prius*—as for example the fundamental measure of a sphere of things—that is more knowable.[29]

Again, testimony for the doctrine of the mean in Speusippus and Xenocrates supports this metaphysical view of the priority of order and unity. To begin with, consider Cicero who states that the "the Old Academics [Speusippus, Xenocrates, Polemo, and Crantor] approved the existence of 'mean-states', and that for each emotion there is a natural measure" (*naturalem modum*, *Acad.* 2.135 (< Fr. 1 Mette), cf. *Tusc.* 3.71 (= Fr. 3b Mette), 4.38). To support this ascription to the Academic Crantor, Cicero invokes Crantor's consolatory work *On Grief* (Περὶ πενθούς, D.L. 4.27). Crantor studied with Xenocrates and Polemo, remained a dear associate of his younger contemporary Arcesilaus, and he is well known for initiating the tradition of exegetical commentary on Plato's dialogues. Extant fragments from *On Grief* are not sufficient to verify the accuracy of Cicero's reference to Crantor, which is presented as in agreement with Peripatetic and Old Academic positions on the ethical mean. Cicero claims, with notable confidence, to know Crantor's consolation treatise, praising the work as a little book of golden words, and one worth learning by heart (*Acad.* 2.135). Moreover, Crantor is reported to have maintained, according to a later source (*Cons. ap.* 104c (= Fr. 4 Mette)), that a "portion of evil is mingled with our nature at birth. For indeed, the seed was already mortal and shares in this

---

[28] Krämer, *Platonismus und hellenistische Philosophie*, 204–16, 220–30; Hans Joachim Krämer, "Die Ältere Akademie," in *Die Philosophie der Antike*, Bd. 3: *Ältere Akademie–Aristoteles–Peripatos*, ed. Hellmut Flashar (Basel: Schwabe, 1983), 27–8, 54.

[29] Hans Joachim Krämer, *Plato and the Foundations of Metaphysics: A Work on the Theory of the Principles and Unwritten Doctrines of Plato with a Collection of the Fundamental Documents*, ed. and trans. John R. Catan (Albany: State University of New York Press, 1990), 86. Translation is slightly modified. An expression of this specification of unity in multiplicity can be traced back to Plato's *Philebus* (e.g., 16c–d, 25d–26e), and it can be found in Plotinus, *Ennead* 1 2.2.15–18. John Dillon, "Speusippus on Pleasure," in *Polyhistor: Studies in the History and Historiography of Ancient Philosophy Presented to Jaap Mansfeld on his Sixtieth Birthday*, ed. Keimpe Algra, P. W. van der Horst, and David T. Runia (Leiden: Brill, 1996), 102, esp. n14 and n15.

cause through which there creep upon us defects of mind and the 'illnesses and myriad cares of mortals.'" Upon death, the good person departs a life that was "full of cares and calamities," and when the "right-minded" memorialize the loss of the beloved good person, they do not "devote themselves to grief beyond the natural measure of psychic pain, for grieving is barbaric and achieves nothing" (*Cons. ap.* 114d–e (< Fr. 6a Mette)).[30] At *Tusc.* 3.12, Cicero again cites Crantor, making an exception to his general wish not to be ill: "but if I am, and if some part of my body is to be cut open or even amputated, let me feel it. This absence of pain comes at a high price: it means being numb in body, and in mind scarcely human." Crantor's consolation work affirms, for Cicero, that the emotions ought to be kept within naturally prescribed limits, but not totally eradicated. If emotions are kept within certain natural limits, they are deemed useful for the overall goal of a happy life. Evidently, Cicero was not entirely dependent on Antiochus as his only source for an understanding of Crantor's consolatory remarks, or for the Old Academy more generally.[31] Cicero nevertheless seems to agree with an Antiochean view of Crantor, which maintains that Crantor's ethical views continue to preserve the traditional eudaimonist ethics of the Old Academy (*Acad.* 1.34, *De fin.* 5.7, cf. *Tusc.* 3.22, 3.71–4, 4.38–47). And more broadly, it seems that the character Cicero also agrees with Antiochus/Varro that it is a "mistake to say that the Academics of that time differed from the Peripatetics" (*Acad.* 1.22) on the triadic classification of goods (cf. *Acad.* 2.135).

Theophrastus ascribes to Speusippus the view that "the honorable [τὸ τίμιον = τὸ ἀγαθόν in this context] is something rare (σπάνιόν τι), which occupies 'the middle place' (περὶ τὴν τοῦ μέσου χώραν), but the rest he makes extremes and to each side of the center" (Theophrastus, *Meta.* 2a18–26 (= Fr. 83 Tarán)). Speusippus would thereby specify his conception of goodness in terms of an appeal to the "middle" (μέσον/ἴσον, Arist., *EN* 1153b7 (< Fr. 80a Tarán), cf. Frs. 80b–e, 81b Tarán) between the extremes. Aulus Gellius reports that "Speusippus and the whole of the Old Academy say that pleasure and pain are two mutually

---

[30] Daniel Babut, "Ἱστορία οἷον ὕλη φιλοσοφίας: histoire et réflexion morale dans l'œuvre de Plutarque," *Revue des Études Grecques* 88 (1975): 215–19, raises legitimate reasons to doubt Plutarch's authorship. In any case, at *Cons. ap.* 110a (= F 63 Vezzoli), the following statement is ascribed to Arcesilaus: "Arcesilaus remarks that 'death, which is said to be an evil, has this distinct from all other things that are thought to be evils, that when it is present it never grieves anyone, but when remote and in expectation only, then it afflicts us.'"

[31] Cf. Dillon, "Polemo, *grosser Schatten* of the Old Academy," in *Plato's Academy: Its Workings and Its History*, ed. Paul Kalligas, Chloe Balla, Effie Baziotopoulou-Valavani, and Vassilis Karasmanis (Cambridge: Cambridge University Press, 2020), 193 n10. Dillon overstates Cicero's reliance on Antiochus as the only source of information on the Old Academy "that he would bother using." The passage at *Acad.* 2.131 indicates that he probably used and relied on Crantor's golden little book, and perhaps the *scripta* of Polemo.

opposing evils, but that the good is what stands in 'the middle' of the two" (*NA* 9.5.4 (= Fr. 84 Tarán)). Attributing an ethical mean to Speusippus is moreover supported by Aristotle's critical treatment.³² Aristotle criticizes (*EN* 7.13, 1153b1–7 (= Fr. 80a Tarán)) Speusippus's attempt to undermine the view that pleasure is a good. In the testimony of later Aristotelian commentators, it is said that Speusippus identifies freedom from trouble as the good to which the extremes of pleasure and pain are opposed, an identification which seems to entail that Plato's successor upheld a doctrine of freedom from trouble as an intermediate state, or ethical mean. Indeed, Clement's succinct summary of Speusippus's conception of εὐδαιμονία seems to imply this view. Speusippus defines εὐδαιμονία as follows:

> the state complete (ἕξιν εἶναι τελείαν) in things according to nature (κατὰ φύσιν) or the possession of goods. While all humans have a desire toward this state, the good ones aim for being free from trouble (στοχάζεσθαι δὲ τοὺς ἀγαθοὺς τῆς ἀοχλησίας). In his view, the virtues generate happiness. (*Strom.* 2.133 (= Fr. 77 Tarán))

Recall that for Speusippus there is a mode of reasoning (τὸν ἐπιστημονικὸν λόγον, Sextus Empiricus, *M.* 7.145 (< Fr. 75 Tarán)) relevant to ethical life, which is also capable of accessing the reality of intelligible beings. Given Speusippus's posit of a plurality of goods, it seems that some goods rank higher—those essentially associated with non-psychic possessions—than other goods, such as wealth or bodily health (Plutarch, *Comm. not.* 1065a), which Aristotle, Xenocrates, and "the entirety of their school" understand as genuine (though inferior) goods, according to Cicero's view of the ethical alliance between the Old Academy and Peripatetics. On this view of the alliance, both schools would refrain from "calling them praiseworthy" (Cic., *De fin.* 4.49 (= Fr. 165 IPD)). Aristotle conceptually links happiness to a certain "activity" of the soul, which Speusippus fails to do, explicitly, emphasizing instead a link between happiness and certain "states" or "dispositions." That is, although Aristotle admits that his conception of happiness is broadly speaking in "harmony" with "those [like Speusippus and Xenocrates] who say that it is virtue or a certain virtue, for the activity in accord with virtue belongs to virtue" (*EN* 1.8, 1098b30–2), he immediately qualifies this "harmony" by noting a considerable exception to the consensus, saying:

---

³² On the potential conflict in the testimonies of Aristotle and Aulus Gellius on Speusippus, see James Warren, "Aristotle on Speusippus on Eudoxus on Pleasure," *Oxford Studies in Ancient Philosophy* 36 (2009): 273–80.

it makes no small difference whether one supposes the best thing to reside in possession (κτῆσις) or in use, that is, either in a "state" or an "activity" (ἐν ἕξει ἢ ἐνεργείᾳ). It is possible that a state is present while accomplishing nothing good—for one may be asleep or inactive in some other way, whereas this is not possible for the activity of the soul. Just as at the Olympic games, it is not the strongest who are crowned but those who compete (some of these in fact win), so also it is those who act correctly who attain the fine and good things of life.

By identifying happiness with a certain kind of activity, Aristotle expresses his disagreement, on one hand, with Speusippus's eudaimonist ethics, in which happiness is either a "complete state" or a "possession of goods," and on the other, with Xenocrates's eudaimonist ethics, in which happiness consists in the "possession of proper virtue."[33] Supposedly representing the views of Antiochus in Cicero's *De fin.* 5.58, Piso seems to reaffirm the importance of "activity" for an understanding of the highest good, stressing that "we are born to act" (*nos ad agendum esse natos*), and that among the heterogeneity of human activities (important and trivial), the activity of contemplation is most important.[34] This reaffirmation might be taken to oppose those Old Academics (Speusippus and Xenocrates, perhaps Polemo) who define the highest good by "possession" or "state." Although there is a notable difference for Aristotle between his conception of happiness and those of Speusippus and Xenocrates, for Cicero and his Antiochean representatives, there seems to be a lack of interest in underscoring this conceptual difference.

When Cicero does address Old Academic views of wisdom in *Tusculan disputations* (5.28–31 (> Fr. 78a Tarán), 5.39–40 (= Fr. 78b Tarán)), his account implies that for Speusippus, Xenocrates, and Polemo the wise man or sage is always happy, and that freedom from trouble is a necessary (but not a sufficient) condition of happiness. Tarán reasons, using these fragments as a basis, that for Speusippus "wisdom is the highest virtue."[35] With respect to conceptions of the highest virtue, the evidence is slightly more direct for Xenocrates. The latter distinguished between σοφία and φρόνησις in the following way: whereas "wisdom" (σοφία) is the "knowledge of first causes and of intelligible

---

[33] At *EE* 1219a38–9, Aristotle defines happiness as the *activity* of a complete life in accordance with virtue. For a helpful overview of the three Peripatetic definitions of happiness found in Stobaeus (*Ecl.* 2.7.18), and their relation to Aristotle and Theophrastus, see William W. Fortenbaugh, "Arius, Theophrastus and the *Eudemian Ethics*," in *On Stoic and Peripatetic Ethics: The Works of Arius Didymus*, Rutgers University Studies in Classical Humanities, vol. 1, ed. William W. Fortenbaugh (New Brunswick, NJ: Transaction, 1983), 212–16.

[34] Georgia Tsouni, "Antiochus on Contemplation and the Happy Life," in Sedley, *The Philosophy of Antiochus*, 142–6.

[35] Tarán, *Speusippus*, 436–7.

being," φρόνησις is both practical and theoretical, which is considered "human σοφία" (Clement, *Strom*. 2.5 (= Fr. 177 IPD)). "Human" σοφία is presumably the "proper virtue" (οἰκεῖα ἀρετή), which for Xenocrates constitutes human happiness. This could mean that (nonhuman) σοφία is the divine knowledge that god or other divine beings have of reality and of themselves—a kind of divine knowing either inaccessible to human beings or only partially attainable. Admittedly, the evidence is such that one can only speculate about how exactly Xenocrates distinguished divine and human σοφία or φρόνησις. Relevant to any possible specification of the distinction is an important passage in Sextus, which gives an overview of the structure of Xenocrates's ontology of knowledge(s). This passage is proof, it seems to me, that historiographical *de re* specifications of Old Academic epistemology are inextricably connected to specifications of Old Academic ontologies of knowledge and virtue. A strictly humanistic focus on a hypothetical notion of the epistemic subject—as is common in recent doxographies of Hellenistic epistemology—would be a very dubious reconstructive procedure for specifying the philosophical views of the Old Academy. Allow me to demonstrate briefly an alternative path, and what I mean by this inextricable connection.

Xenocrates distinguishes three kinds of epistemic power (ἐπιστήμη–δόξα–αἴσθησις), corresponding to three hierarchical levels of being (νοητή–δοξαστή–αἰσθητή, Sextus Empiricus, *M*. 7.147 (< Fr. 2 IPD)): the realm of the intelligible outside of heaven, or the super-celestial domain of Zeus, which is comprised of things relatively disposed to being known by the power of intellect, the realm of the opinable, referring to heaven itself, the spheres of the stars and planets, which is comprised of things relatively disposed to being known to a lesser degree by the power of opinion, and lastly the perceptible realm within heaven and the sublunary, including the earth, comprised more generally of things relatively disposed to being perceived by the power of perception. Again, the power of "opinion" (δόξα) is the power most suitable to the investigation of composite beings in the heavens, where stars and planets appear to be composites of the perceptible and the intelligible. In Xenocrates's ontology, the stars and planets are relatively disposed to being perceived, but they are also intelligible by means of the intellectual calculations of mathematical reasoning. The metaphysical composition of these objects renders them knowable by means of the scientific study of astronomy. In other words, the realm of the opinable, as structurally situated in Xenocrates's ontology, is comprised of composite beings cognizable by means of "epistemic sense-perception" (τὴν ἐπιστημονικὴν αἴσθησιν). This inferior form of knowing grasps beings relatively disposed to perception, and to participating "in the truth which accords with reason" (Sextus, *M.* 7.145 (< Fr. 75 Tarán)). In the ethical domain, the presence of the *epistemic* power of perception entails that individual human souls have at their disposal two powers for the attainment of goods in pursuit of happiness: the inferior power of perception, acquainting the soul (non-epistemically) with the physicality and mutability of sublunary objects, and the power of "reasoning" (λογισμός), or "the rational part of the soul" (τὸ λογικὸν τῆς ψυχῆς, Theodoret of Cyrrhus, *Gr. aff. cur.* 5.19 (= Fr. 126 IPD)): the part that supposedly "nourishes itself by means of learning" (Nemesius, *Nat. hom.* 2.72 (= Fr. 123 IPD)) and contributes to the soul's ascent to the intellectual grasp of intelligible beings, or to those beings transcending yet also inhering within the realm of the perceptible.[36] As relevant to this ascent, recall Xenocrates's view that the cause of the discovery of philosophy is the desire of putting an end to the troubles arising in the affairs of life (Ps. Galen, *Hist. phil.* 8 (= Fr. 171 IPD)). This view of the discovery of philosophy suggests that for Xenocrates the intellectual power of the human soul has at least two interrelated tasks to accomplish: alleviating the soul from trouble, that is, "practical wisdom" (τὴν μὲν [φρόνησιν] πρακτικήν, Clement, *Strom.* 2.5 (< Fr. 177 IPD)), and knowing first causes and intelligible realities, which accomplishes the end of "theoretical [human] wisdom," or "human wisdom" (τὴν δὲ [φρόνησιν] θεωρητικήν = σοφία ἀνθρωπίνη).

Sextus reports that Speusippus recognizes not only a mode of ἐπιστημονικὴ αἴσθησις ("epistemic sense-perception"), but also a mode of ἐπιστημονικὸν λόγον ("epistemic reason," *M.* 7.145–6 (= Fr. 75 Tarán)), which aims at the unerring grasp of intelligible beings. The distinction between "sense-perception" (αἴσθησις) and "reason" (λόγος) in Speusippus's ontology of knowing should not be taken to disqualify the possible coordination of reason and sense-perception, according to which the sense-perception of mutable bodies is mediated by the power of reason. Reason is thus able to direct a mode of grasping mutable objects participating in the truth. Briefly taking a step back: notice one key difference between the way that modern epistemology tends to separate the question of epistemic access from the question of *what there is*, and the way that Speusippus and Xenocrates, for example, conceive of the different powers of individual human souls with perception and reason: for these ancient thinkers, a general metaphysics, or ontology, is methodologically and conceptually inseparable from the specification and coordination of different epistemic powers and modes of

---

[36] On Theodoret (fifth century CE) as a source for Greek philosophy, see Mansfeld and Runia, eds., *Aëtiana* 1, 272–90.

access to *what there is*. The inextricable connection between the metaphysical and the epistemological applies no less to Speusippus and Xenocrates than it does to Zeno and the early Stoa. For present purposes, the point of taking a step back here is to foreground what is suppressed from the reconstructions of epistemological centrism: the ontological systems foundational to the various Academic accounts of the soul's powers are also foundational to the Old Academy's hierarchical classification of goods. More succinctly, the hierarchical structure of the plurality of goods is determined by the hierarchical structure of reality. Despite the deviation of Xenocrates's tripartite division of reality from the proposed structure of Speusippus's general metaphysics, two features of similarity are noteworthy. First, the layers of reality include a level of perceptible beings, which as a class is comprised of beings relatively disposed to a hybrid mode of reasoning/sense-perception. It is worth examining, in this connection, Speusippus's example of expert activity relative to the lower level of perceptible beings. Second, it is clear that some doctrinal formulation of two-opposing first principles governs the way that each scholarch conceives of the world as a living whole and of the corresponding epistemic powers assigned to the world's hierarchical levels. The postulation of two-opposing first principles governs Old Academic metaphysics, and it determines the order and rank of ethical goods for individual human souls striving to possess as many goods as humanly possible.

To clarify the coordination of reasoning and sense-perception, Speusippus invokes the example of a well-trained musician: "the fingers of the flute-player or harpist possess an expert activity (τεχνικὴν μὲν εἶχον ἐνέργειαν), which is, however, not brought to completion primarily through the fingers themselves, but fully developed from coordinated training through reasoning" (ἐκ τῆς πρὸς τὸν λογισμὸν συνασκήσεως ἀπαρτιζομένην). The sense-perception of the expert musician develops the capacity of actively grasping the harmonious and the non-harmonious, but the perceptual grasping is "not self-produced" (οὐκ αὐτοφυῆ). Rather, the grasp of perceiving occurs as a result of the "training" (συνασκήσεως) administered by the guidance of reasoning. As Tarán observes, epistemic sense-perception "naturally [φυσικῶς] shares in the cognitive experience derived from reason, which leads to the unwavering discrimination of its objects" (ibid.).[37] The example of expertise in musical sense-perception

---

[37] Agreeing with Tarán, *Speusippus*, 431–5, esp. 433 n257, I see no reason to doubt Speusippus's authorship of the passage appealing to the example of the expert musician. See also John Dillon, "Theories of Knowledge in the Old Academy," *Lexicon Philosophicum: International Journal for the History of Texts and Ideas*, Special Issue (2018): 45–6. Dillon sensibly revises Tarán's analysis by arguing that Speusippus upgrades the status not of all sense-perception (as Tarán claims), but only those sense-perceptions that have been trained and informed by reason.

sheds light on the potential use and misuse of sense-perception for the overall goal of life, and the way that Speusippus conceptualizes the project of ethical training, in particular, the training involved in "aiming" (στοχάζεσθαι, Clement, *Strom.* 2.133 (< Fr. 77 Tarán)) at the "mean" in particular situations. The example of musical training emerges again in testimonies of Polemo's ethics, and, more famously, in Aristotle's ethical writings. For review, recall that Polemo stresses, in his analogy with the technical proficiency of learning to play a musical instrument, the importance of practical training for the purpose of living in agreement with nature. In fact, the avowed preference for training in action over dialectical theorems in the teaching of ethics bears a remarkable resemblance to an Aristotelian approach to learning how to become virtuous.

Consider the passages where a doctrinal convergence between Aristotelian and Polemonian virtue ethics is particularly salient: especially, as it bears on the priority of action and training for the attainment of psychic goods. (1) At *EN* 1.3, 1095a5–6, dismissing the youthful lack of experience in the actions of life, Aristotle affirms the priority of action as the basis of ethical progress. And again, at 1095b4–7, Aristotle presses the point that ethical progress depends, not on knowing why something is such and such, but on the student cultivating the right habits through action. (2) At *EN* 2.1, 1103b6, Aristotle uses an analogy with musicianship to reiterate the priority of action—an analogy resembling the content of Polemo's rejection of Zenonian ethics and Speusippus's appeal to musical training, which takes place under the guidance of reason. In Aristotle's example, it is through "playing the lyre that one becomes a good lyre player," just as through one's "dealings with others" one can become virtuous. Here Aristotle states that the branch of philosophy being implemented throughout *EN* is οὐκ θεωρίας ἕνεκα (1105b2, 1107a29–32), which is to say, this mode of philosophy is "not [undertaken] for the sake of theorizing" about virtue, but rather for the sake of becoming good. (3) Finally, the practical dimension of ethical progress leads Aristotle to thematize the value of examples for ethical improvement and then to recommend the emulation of actions of those who are virtuous (1171b12). The priority of action and the displacement of theory, or knowing why, from a foundational role in ethical progress are combined in the moral efficacy of character sketches, which promote the emulation of exemplary actions, as Aristotle himself sketches in Books 3–5, reminding readers and those who already more or less partake in a virtuous disposition what a particular virtue in a given situation may look like (1143b5). So while it is probably true to say that no one before Antiochus and Cicero assimilated the ethics of Aristotle and Polemo as two representatives of a continuous and unified eudaimonist tradition, the following statement is also true. The shared eudaimonist commitments on the part of Aristotle and Polemo, and their formulations of a triadic hierarchy of goods (*De fin.* 4.16, 20–44), give Cicero and Plutarch philosophical grounds for affirming one facet of Antiochus's controversial history. In other words, the continuity of ethical doctrine as it pertains to the Old Academy and Peripatos is a credible view of the history. The sources are clear on this one point, at least; Aristotle shares with Polemo and the latter's Academic predecessors a basic eudaimonist outlook, which uses a classificatory scheme to rank the plurality of goods.

Set against this hierarchical classification, and the plurality it affirms, Zeno's eudaimonist outlook represents a rather stark contrast. Both Cicero (*De fin.* 4.3–7 (> Fr. 153 IPD, Fr. 7 Gigante), *De fin.* 4.16, 20–44) and Plutarch (*Comm. not.* 1069e-f) were evidently aware of this contrast.[38] For review, recall that the notion of "good" is manifold and hierarchical for Speusippus, Xenocrates, Aristotle, and Polemo.[39] Aristotle acknowledges the plausibility of this general Pythagorean approach, which posits "the One in the column of goods, and it is indeed they [Pythagoreans] whom Speusippus seems to follow" (*EN* 1.6, 1096b5–8 (= Fr. 47a Tarán)). Speusippus would thus acknowledge many goods, although he seems to deny that there is any single good comprehending the manifold of analogical goods.[40] In other words, the analogical conception of goods is irreducible to any kind of unique and uniform principle for all levels of being. Yet, Aristotle is also critical of Speusippus for the way that his ontology derives an abundance of higher and lower goods from first principles. It is worth examining a transition in Aristotle's reasoning against Speusippus as it moves rather seamlessly between ethical and metaphysical issues.

---

[38] Tarán, *Speusippus*, 212–13, supposes that *De fin.* 4.2, 3–7, has "little evidential value in so far as Speusippus and Aristotle are concerned." The sole reason adduced to support this dismissal of the passage: "Cicero mentions Speusippus, Aristotle, Xenocrates, Polemo, and Theophrastus as philosophers who anticipated the Stoics' tripartite division of philosophy into logic, physics, and ethics (cf. *De fin.* 4.4, 8 ff.)." Since "this [Stoic] division was also frequently ascribed *without good reasons* to Plato himself," the passage is too hastily deemed as otherwise uninformative. One may readily agree that ascribing the tripartite division of philosophy to Plato is misleading, and yet still recognize that the passage has value as it reinforces Clement's testimony (*Strom.* 2.133 (= Fr. 77 Tarán)), which Tarán takes as informative (*Speusippus*, 436), indicating that Speusippus—similar to Aristotle and Theophrastus, but unlike Zeno—subscribed to a eudaimonist ethics that recognizes a plurality of goods.

[39] For Crantor's adherence to a plurality of goods, see Sextus Empiricus, *M.* 11.51. On Theophrastus and the doctrine of the plurality of goods, see Cicero, *Tusc.* 5.24–5 (= 493 Fortenbaugh), *Acad.* 1.33–4 (497 Fortenbaugh). William W. Fortenbaugh, *Theophrastus of Eresus, Commentary Volume 6.1: Sources on Ethics (with contribution on the Arabic material by Dimitri Gutas)* (Leiden: Brill, 2011), 438.

[40] Tarán, *Speusippus*, 347–50. Also, Gerson, *From Plato to Platonism*, 136–7: "Pythagoreans and Speusippus in effect maintained that there are different kinds of goods as well as different kinds of ones; that is, the Good is not one thing."

A number of conceptual absurdities follow, according to Aristotle, from identifying the two-opposing principles with the good and the bad, respectively. He reasons that if one equates the principle of the One with the Good, then each and every unit will be a good, and then there will be an absurd abundance of goods in the world. Moreover, if the One is the Good, the opposing principle must be the Bad itself, and given that all things result from the One and its contrary, all things will participate in the Bad (with the exception of the One), including numbers and magnitudes (*Meta*. N 4, 1091b33, Λ 10, 1075b1). Aristotle alleges that, to avoid these absurdities, Speusippus detaches goodness and beauty from the One, positing instead that they are born later "from the procession of nature" (προελθούσης τῆς φύσεως, *Meta*. N 4, 1091a35 (< Fr. 44 Tarán)). Aristotle suggests that Speusippus compared "the principles of the world to that of animals and plants, on the ground that the more complete always comes from what is indefinite and incomplete—this being his reason for stating that this applies to the two-opposing principles as well, so that the One itself is not even a thing or being" (*Meta*. N 5, 1092a11–17 (= Fr. 43 Tarán)). The procession of nature is not temporal for Speusippus, given his reported denial (in the interpretation of the *Timaeus*) of a temporal process of creation (Frs. 61a–b Tarán). Rather, the procession of nature is conceived by means of a comparison with geometrical construction. Clues to Speusippus's conception of the "procession of nature" have been found in Iamblichus (*DCMS* 4, p. 16).[41] In one chapter in particular, it is said that Speusippus maintains that as "nature proceeds further from the primary level, first it is beauty that makes its appearance [originating at the metaphysical level of mathematicals], and secondly, the good, when the elements are at a still larger remove" (*DCMS* 4, p. 16, cf. 4, p. 18). The bad, however, emerges only at the end of nature's procession, in the fourth and fifth levels of being, not directly from those levels but as the result of a failure to tame natural things. Presumably, the emergence of the bad is an indication that the formal principle of unity fails to completely master the materiality and complexity of sensible bodies. The first being generated from the interaction of the two-opposing principles is number, which Speusippus seems to designate as the number one, and a derivative principle at the level of mathematical numbers. The number one unites with the principle of multiplicity to produce a series of numbers up to the number ten. But what remains obscure is how the geometrical level of beings, and its first principle, namely, the point, is supposed to proceed from numbers, or the derivative principles of the numerical level of reality. If

---

[41] Merlan, *From Platonism to Neoplatonism*, 118–20.

each sphere of being has its own pair of first principles, then it is difficult to understand how the being of one level is supposed to contribute to the being of another. It would seem that Speusippus explains the linkage between the levels of being by asserting some sort of analogy between the various levels.[42] The overall coherence of nature and the totality of beings appear to depend on the analogical structure of opposing principles at each level. Aristotle's reproach against this plurality of disjointed parts with principles at each level attributes a basic flaw to Speusippus's ontological conception of the totality of beings. Aristotle prefers the ontological view that

> all things are ordered in relation to one thing (πρὸς μὲν γὰρ ἓν ἅπαντα συντέτακται), just as in a household, in which the freemen are least at liberty to act at random but all or most things are ordered, while slaves and wild animals contribute little to the common good but for the most part at random; for such is the principle of each of these, which is their nature. I mean, for example, that all these must come together if they are to be distinguished; and this is what happens in other cases in which all the members participate in the totality. (*Meta.* Λ 10, 1075a19–25, cf. 1075b38–1076a3)

Aristotle's disagreement with Speusippus on first principles and the abundant plurality of goods eventually leads him to rebuke the overall structure of his ontology. As Speusippus supposedly maneuvers to avoid the absurd conclusions that follow from identifying the One and the Good, he is led to a view of the totality of beings that is structured by disjointed levels. That is, in Aristotle's view at least, the being of the whole is disjointed in the sense that Speusippus posits levels of being independent of one another, with distinct derivative principles for each level, "making the being of the whole (τὴν τοῦ παντὸς οὐσίαν ποιοῦσιν, *Meta.* Λ 10, 1076a1) a plurality of disjointed parts with many principles." Aristotle finally ridicules this view as an unwanted polyarchy, or the rule of many, appropriating Homer's monarchist saying (*Il.* 2.204) to reject Speusippus's ontology: "The rule of many is not good; let one thing be the ruler" (*Meta.* Λ 10, 1076a4). Yet, as Merlan contends, it is fair to say that a plurality of principles is also present in Aristotle.[43] In place of the two-opposing principles of the One and the Indefinite Dyad, Aristotle posits the two (or three) principles of form and matter/privation. In fact, this doctrine of principles is, one might say, also analogical, in the sense that there is no one single form for all beings nor is

---

[42] On Aristotle's tendency, in this critical context, to suppress any mention of Speusippus's concept of τὸ κοινόν/ὅμοιον, see Julius Stenzel, "Speusippos," *RE* 3, A 2 (1929): 1664–5. Cf. Krämer, *Platonismus und hellenistische Philosophie*, 177 n304.

[43] Merlan, *From Platonism to Neoplatonism*, 119–20.

there a single mode of privation for all beings. As Aristotle himself admits, the principles of distinct things are in one sense distinct, but in another sense, if one is to speak "universally and analogically, the same for all" (*Meta.* Λ 4, 1070a32, 1070b16: "the principles cannot be the same for all things, except by analogy, that is in the sense in which one might say that there are three principles: form, matter, and privation").[44]

Bipolar Notions of Nature

Speusippus's notion of φύσις ("nature") is manifold and hierarchical. Take, for instance, his view of mathematical numbers. While reportedly denying the identity of forms and numbers, he asserts that number has a φύσις, that is, it is endowed with an essential nature.[45] Speusippus is said to affirm in the second half of his treatise *On Pythagorean Numbers* that the number 10, or the Decad, is the "most natural (φυσικωτάτην) and most perfective of beings (τελεστικωτάτην τῶν ὄντων), because it is, in itself and not based on our thoughts, or because we postulate that it happens to be so, a kind of productive form of the finished products of the world, and set before the god who created the world as the most completely perfect paradigm" (Ps. Iamblichus, *Theol. arith.* 82.10 (< Fr. 28 Tarán)). Although mathematical numbers, including their properties and relations, have independent existence, they remain present in all other finished beings. Among numbers, number 10 is the perfect or complete number because it comprises all the structural relations between numbers, hence it also contains all the ratios and harmonies among animate things. The mathematical realism of numbers assigns them ontological priority over all other beings. In conformity with this testimony, Aristotle's treatment of these issues has Speusippus affirming the reality of mathematical numbers and magnitudes separate from the soul and from lower-level perceptible beings, in addition to affirming the realist claim

---

[44] Krämer correctly traces Aristotle's conception of "one according to analogy" (see also *Meta.* Δ 6, 1016b32–1017a3) back to Plato, Speusippus, and the Old Academy. Hans Joachim Krämer, "Grundbegriffe akademischer Dialektik in den biologischen Schriften von Aristoteles und Theophrast," *Rheinisches Museum für Philologie* 111, no. 4 (1968): 300–3.

[45] Passages in Aristotle are the source for the view that Speusippus denied the separate existence of ideas or forms, and that he also denied the identity of numbers and ideas (Arist., *Meta.* Z 2, 1028b18–24 (< Fr. 29a Tarán), M 1, 1076a19–29 (> Fr. 32 Tarán), see also Frs. 33–6 Tarán). For a slightly different view on Speusippus, cf. Dillon, *Heirs*, 48–54. Dillon argues that Speusippus repositioned the forms in his ontology by associating them with the creative function of the world-soul, the effective transmitter of forms to the sensible realm. In response, Bonazzi, *Il Platonismo*, 13–14, n37, objects on the grounds that the passages from Aristotle on Speusippus clearly show that Speusippus altogether abandoned the forms.

that number has its own "peculiar nature" (καθ' αὑτὴν φύσιν οὖσαν, *Meta.* N 2, 1090a12–13). Speusippus invokes the notion of φύσις to explain the endowed essence of the world as created by god.

In a similar way, but to different purposes, Aristotle himself invokes the notion of φύσις in the study of things that come to be to refer to the endowed essence of a given being, or what a being really is. Moreover, Aristotle would invoke the notion of φύσις to identify what a thing or being ought to be ("achievement").[46] This bipolarity in Aristotle's notion of φύσις is expressed explicitly in applications of the notion to matter, on one hand, and to the form or shape that a being or thing achieves (*Phys.* 2.1), on the other. Likewise, the notion of φύσις in the reports on Speusippus is bipolar; evidently, he refers to the nature of number itself, but also to a natural state of achievement with his conception of happiness as a complete state, to be achieved through the cultivation of natural states and activities, and the possession of goods "in agreement with nature" (ἐν τοῖς κατὰ φύσιν ἔχουσιν ἢ ἕξιν ἀγαθῶν, Clement, *Strom.* 2.133 (< Fr. 77 Tarán)).

It is said that Xenocrates reinstates the forms into his ontological hierarchy of beings, and identifies the essential "nature" of forms with mathematical numbers, holding that both have the essential endowment of "one nature" (μίαν φύσιν, Arist., *Meta.* M 1, 1076a21). Plutarch moreover indicates that Xenocrates conceives of happiness as a state of achievement, with the view that one should strive to live in accordance with nature (*Comm. not.* 1069e–f). Xenocrates's Academic associate Crantor reportedly refers to φύσις in the sense of essential endowment, maintaining that soul is a composite of an "intelligible nature" (τῆς νοητῆς φύσεως) and an "opinable nature" (τῆς δοξαστῆς φύσεως, Plutarch, *De anima pro.* 1012d (< Fr. 10 Mette)). Perceptible bodies are given by Crantor a "passive and changeable nature" (τὴν [φύσιν] περὶ τὰ σώματα παθητικὴν καὶ μεταβλητήν). Considering what Crantor meant by the composite of the dual-natured soul, one might be reminded here, as Dillon contends, of "something very like the Xenocratean Monad and Dyad; a deconstructed Demiurge inevitably becomes nothing other than a cosmic Intellect . . . while the passive and changeable element which is 'about bodies' (περὶ τὰ σώματα) can hardly be anything else than the Unlimited Dyad, or, in Aristotelian terms (accepted by now freely in the Academy), Matter." Dillon conjectures that while Crantor may

---

[46] In what follows, I take the term "bipolarity" from Lloyd P. Gerson, *Aristotle and Other Platonists* (Ithaca, NY: Cornell University Press, 2005), 285. Bipolarity expresses some "conceptual space between endowment and achievement." Since the concept of endowment can refer to the matter out of which a thing is generated (*Meta.* Δ 4, 1014b27–34), or the form that a certain thing has, one can speak furthermore of "endowment" in more than one way.

have expressed himself differently, it is nevertheless "hard to see that he is at serious odds with Xenocrates."[47] Dillon's reasoning is that Crantor's view of the composite soul, divided by its intelligible and opinable natures, resembles other Academic views on the coordination of reasoning and sense-perception: the doctrine of epistemic sense-perception held by Speusippus, in particular, and subsequently, Xenocrates's conception of opinion. For Crantor (and apparently his unidentified followers), "the soul's peculiar function is to make judgments of intelligible and perceptible beings and the differences and similarities occurring among these beings within their own kind and in relation of either kind to the other" (1012f2–1013a3). In view of this metaphysical mixture of the intelligible and perceptible, it seems that individual human souls are held to be composed in such a way that with the right training and guidance human souls are able to achieve insight into the nature of things, individually and in relation to one another. On this basis, one can conclude that the bipolarity of φύσις is certainly not unique to Aristotle or Speusippus; reasonably, one can enlist both Xenocrates and Crantor in the Academic custom of employing the notion of φύσις in at least two ways, in so far as a given human soul is endowed with an intellectual nature, which in turn enables the soul to ascend and think what it ought to think, that which is, generally speaking, beyond a given perceptible body.

However, the evidence is not sufficient to confidently ascribe bipolarity in the notion of φύσις to Polemo himself. The testimonies on Polemo and his Academic predecessors cited above sanction, it seems to me, a more modest reconstruction. The varied expressions of virtue ethics ascribed to the Old Academy (Speusippus, Xenocrates, Polemo) and certain Peripatetics (Aristotle, Theophrastus) involve a commitment to at least one of the following conjunction of principles. These principles comprise the necessary conceptual background for specifying the innovation of the New Academy under Arcesilaus. First, independent of any consideration of what the aforementioned Old Academic and Peripatetic philosophers themselves said in reference to their commitments and doctrines, these eudaimonists maintain—with the possible exception of Polemo—a particular variety of disciplinary holism.[48] Again, disciplinary holism is the principle that no area of philosophical study can be fully comprehended apart from a comprehensive understanding of the

---

[47] Dillon, *Heirs*, 223.
[48] A similar view of holism is defended by Lloyd P. Gerson, "Platonism in Aristotle's Ethics," *Oxford Studies in Ancient Philosophy* 27 (2004): 228. Gerson defends the hermeneutical principle of doctrinal holism. Additionally, Gerson ascribes this principle to Aristotle; on my view, ascription also extends to the scholarchs of the Old Academy (with the possible exception of Polemo), as well as early canonical Stoicism (though a different variety of doctrinal holism).

whole. The assumptions underlying ancient varieties of disciplinary holism are broadly realist: to name one, the assumption that there is such a thing as a living whole, that is, the unified world or cosmos that is there (or created there) *anyway*; or secondly, that the order and structure of this unified whole is relatively disposed to being systematically known and explained by human beings. Once again, both assumptions are fundamentally realist in the sense that each involves an "absolute conception" of reality, a conception of what is there *anyway*, namely, what is there independent of the activities, if any, of knowing and acting mortal animals. In other words, reality itself is an organized whole, or structural totality, made up of principles and parts, and its inhering structure of relations makes a systematic understanding of the constituent parts and principles of the whole epistemically possible for human beings. The conditions of epistemic possibility therefore depend on the world having an inherent structure.

Zeno and his successors adhere to a different version of the principle of disciplinary holism. What makes Zeno's holistic principle distinct from the Old Academic and Peripatetic variety is the specific way in which the former abandons the priority of noncorporeal principles. In the latter, corporeal and composite beings depend on the intelligibility of noncorporeals (mathematicals, ideal numbers and figures, or forms), and the unqualified simplicity of a first principle (the One or the Monad), even if the first principle is cast beyond οὐσία or the highest good. The simplicity of noncorporeal first principles is an altogether different ontological commitment than the corporeality of the active and passive principles out of which the Stoic world of individual bodies is created and preserved.

One of the most important principles for Old Academic and Peripatetic ethics is the notion of a power governing human beings in the pursuit of εὐδαιμονία. Let me specify this notion as the *intellectual principle* of εὐδαιμονία. It holds that the highest part of the soul is the divine part, and the power associated with divine being at the level of the composite soul is traditionally conceived as "intellect" (νοῦς/*mens*) or "thought" (διάνοια/*ratio*). Individual human souls are situated within the structural whole, or totality of beings, but since their souls are composites with an intellectual component, embodied human souls are idealized in view of the power of reasoning or thought: from the relatively lower-level powers of perceiving and judging the identity and difference of perceptible beings, up to the higher-level power of intellectual insight grasping the causes of beings more generally. The *intellectual principle* of Old Academic/Peripatetic ethics entails that the path of ethical progress for human beings is set by the layering of hierarchical levels structuring reality as a whole. Human beings take care of their own individual souls and pursue εὐδαιμονία by developing and maintaining its rational part, in a long-term project of care that the embodiment of the rational soul makes difficult, if not impossible, to sustain over the entire course of a mortal life.

Structurally analogous to Speusippus's hierarchical division of rational powers into epistemic reason and epistemic sense-perception, Xenocrates elevates theoretical wisdom over practical wisdom. Theoretical wisdom involves knowledge of first causes and intelligible realities. Adhering to a mathematical view of the world, the powers of epistemic reason and thought for Speusippus regiment the pursuit of the complete state of happiness; the achievement of this state entails the imposition of the principle of limit on the disorderly and troubling substratum of the unlimited. On the power of thought, consider Proclus's testimony, which ascribes to Speusippus the following account of the intellectual "hunt":

> Principles must in every case differ from what derives from them in being simple, indemonstrable, and self-evident (τῇ ἁπλότητι, τῷ ἀναποδείκτῳ, τῷ αὐτοπίστῳ). For generally, says Speusippus, of the things which *thought* (ἡ διάνοια) hunts after, some it sets up and prepares for the proceeding inquiry without having undertaken any sort of elaborate excursion, and it [thought] possesses a more vivid contact with these than sight has with visual objects; other things, because it is unable to grasp them immediately, *thought* attempts to hunt after by advancing on them step-by-step according to what follows after these. (*In Euclidem*, 179.12–22 (= Fr. 73 Tarán), italics added)

According to this testimony, Speusippus understands the double task of *thought* according to a contrasting set of objects that *thought* is primed to hunt after. *Thought* has the power to immediately grasp simple and indemonstrable mathematical principles, which are held to be ontologically prior to what follows; second, *thought* depends on those principles for "the hunt," to search for what it lacks immediate contact with, for example, the more complex geometrical propositions and constructed objects that depend for their construction on the simplicity of the point, line, and plane. It is helpful to recall that Speusippus, according to Aristotle, posits numbers, geometrical magnitudes, and soul in this order of being (*Meta*. Z 2, 1028b21–4 (< Fr. 29A Tarán), Λ 10, 1075b37–1076a4 (= Fr. 30 Tarán), N 3, 1090b13–21 (= Fr. 37 Tarán)), with numbers as the first entities (*Meta*. M 6, 1080b14–16 (< Fr. 33 Tarán), M 8, 1083a23–4 (< Fr. 34 Tarán)). As Speusippus refuses to identify νοῦς with the One, or highest good, νοῦς or *thought* is assigned its own peculiar nature, which means that it is assigned to a level of the hierarchy other than that of the One or highest good.⁴⁹ This derivative location in the hierarchy is furthermore suggested by Speusippus's claim that the objects composed of the intelligible and the perceptible in the heavens are visible, but by means of the study of astronomy these composite objects in the heavens are also intelligible. Speusippus reportedly insists on calling the derivative propositions concerning the intelligible entities of arithmetic and geometry θεώρημα ("theorems"), not πρόβλημα ("problems"), for it is said that he conceives of the intelligibles themselves as non-sensible, non-generated, and eternal (Proclus, In Euclidem, 2.8.78–9), although not as simple as the One, the principle of numbers.

The notion of simplicity represents the third common principle of Old Academic/Peripatetic ethics. This notion grants the intellectual power of the soul priority over the powers aimed at procuring the goods associated with composite being (external goods, corporeal goods). The basic idea of this principle is that the simple precedes the composite as the self-evident, or autoexplicable, stopping-point of explanation. Since each individual human soul is a composite being, the simplicity accessible to the intellectual part of the soul is a higher end, or good, than the activities or functions more closely associated with the composite of soul/body. With respect to the world-whole, there is a similar kind of complexity and thus a similar sort of priority, governed once again by a notion of simplicity. The world is therefore not only a unified whole, but also a composite of intelligible and sensible elements. The intelligibility of the whole requires an understanding of the intelligible principles holding the sensibility of the world together as an eternally existing unity.

For this tradition of eudaimonist ethics, the priority of the simple underlies a hierarchical division of goods. Psychic goods rank higher than external goods and those of the body in virtue of the soul's highest faculty: the intellect. Consider the way in which both Speusippus and Xenocrates conceptually link an epistemological ranking of psychic powers to an ontological hierarchy of beings, and how an ethical ranking of goods derives from this connection. The ordering of ethical goods is fixed and arranged hierarchically according to disciplinary holism(s). Which is to say, the epistemic powers of the soul are hierarchically gradable in accordance with the hierarchical stratification of reality as it really is, and the triadic classification of goods is hierarchically gradable according to the priority of the soul over the body. Following this

---

[49] Its non-identity with the One does not prevent νοῦς from being a part or power of soul (as it appears in Timaeus 30b3, 46d5–6). For discussion of this point, and the evidence independent of Timaeus, see Krämer, Geistmetaphysik, 214–18; Tarán, Speusippus, 378–9; Dillon, Heirs, 62–4.

schema of classification, the intellectual powers of the soul take priority over the assorted organs of perception. The superiority of thought corresponds to the metaphysical superiority of the first explanatory principles, and the complete state of virtue as a psychic good corresponds to the superior faculty of the soul, which is essentially endowed with the power of contemplating intelligible reality. Embodied souls endowed with the power of reason are subjected to the desires and affections accompanying the materiality of body, but they are also endowed with the capacity of exercising higher and lower powers of reason in pursuit of wisdom and knowledge.

Cicero's Varro attests to the significance of this principle of simplicity for the tradition under examination:

> Although it took its start from the senses, they maintained that the criterion of truth is not in the senses. *They* [Old Academics and Peripatetics] wanted the mind (*mens*) to be criterial of things, holding that it was the only power deserving our trust, because it alone discerned what was always *simple*, uniform and same as itself. (*Idea* was the term they used for this, the name Plato had already given it, and we can rightly use the word "form.") The senses were all blunt and feeble, in their view, and quite unable to apprehend the things people thought were subject to perception, because the latter were either so small that they were undetectable by the senses or moving so rapidly that nothing was one or constant or even self-identical because everything was continually slipping or flowing away. For this reason, *they* called the whole domain of things the opinable. (Cicero, *Acad.* 1.30–1, italics added)

The passage then goes on to identify Aristotle as "the first person to 'undermine' (*labefactavit*) the forms" (1.33).[50] Setting aside the controversial issue of what Varro or Antiochus means here by forms, or the precise meaning of the notion allegedly undermined by Aristotle, Varro's presentation of the *vetus Academia* ("Old Academy") is otherwise explicit: "Speusippus and Xenocrates, the first to take up the system and authority of Plato, and those who succeeded in the Academy, Polemo, Crates, and also Crantor, all were engaged in upholding the doctrines that they had received from their predecessors" (1.34).[51] The appeal

---

[50] On this passage, see G. R. Boys-Stones, "Antiochus' Metaphysics," in Sedley, *Philosophy of Antiochus*, 221–8.

[51] Crates's directorship lasts between two and five years. For approximate dating of his death (between 268 and 264 BCE), see Tiziano Dorandi, *Filodemo: Storia dei filosofici greci e latini. Platone e L'Academia* (PHerc. 1021 e 164) (Naples: Bibliopolis, 1991), 58. Crates wrote orations for political assembly and books on comedy, in addition to what was then emerging as the more traditional treatises of philosophy, all of which are no longer extant. No doctrinal innovations are attested in the two main reports on his life: D.L. 4.21–3, Philodemus, *Acad. hist.* cols. 15–17.

to simplicity and the criterion of truth, in this context, implies that the Old Academy and the Peripatos upheld doctrines attributing priority to the power of *mens* (νοῦς) over the senses, given the mind's special power to discern what is "always *simple*, uniform, and same as itself." As suggested above, Old Academic/Peripatetic notions of simplicity have ethical implications for ranking a plurality of goods. Both Aristotle and Theophrastus evidently associated one or more psychic goods with the power of *mens*/νοῦς (e.g., *Acad.* 1.19–20) as the power leading the soul to knowledge and virtue, so it can be maintained without much controversy that Aristotle and Theophrastus affirm the *intellectual principle* of εὐδαιμονία. It should be clear why Varro is inclined to include Aristotle and Theophrastus among those adhering to such a principle in their ethics. Varro states, in concluding his review of the Peripatetic trichotomy of goods (*animo, corpore, vita*), that "the greatest primary things of nature are the ones in the mind and in virtue itself" (1.22). Aristotle expresses his commitment to the *intellectual principle* of εὐδαιμονία, perhaps most forcefully, near the end of the *Nicomachean Ethics* (10.7):

> So since the intellect (νοῦς) is divine relative to a human being, the life according to this intellect, too, will be divine relative to human life. Thus we should not follow the recommendations of thinkers who say that those who are humans should think only of human things and that mortals should think only of human things, but we should try as far as possible to partake of immortality and to make every effort to live according to the best part of the soul in us; for even if this part be of small measure, it surpasses all the others by far in power and worth. It would seem, too, that each human is this part, if indeed this is the dominant part and is better than the other parts; so it would be strange if a human did not choose the life proper to himself but rather that proper to another. That which was said previously harmonizes with that which is being said now, that which is proper to each thing is by nature (τὸ γὰρ οἰκεῖον ἑκάστῳ τῇ φύσει) the best and most pleasant for that thing. So for a human being, too, the life according to intellect (ὁ κατὰ νοῦν βίος) is best, if indeed this especially is human. This life then is happiest. (*EN* 1177b30–1178a8)[52]

---

[52] On Theophrastus and the superiority of the life of intellect or contemplation, see the Scholium on *EN* 6.13, 1145a10–11 (461 FHS&G), Cod. Neapolitanus 2 D 22, sent. 18 (476 FHS&G), Cicero, *Ad Att.* 2.16.3 (481 FHS&G), Ps. Plutarch, *Plac. phil.* 874f (479 FHS&G), and Fortenbaugh's commentary (*Theophrastus*, 340–3, 743–4). On the limits of human intellectual activity according to Theophrastus, see Thomas Bénatouïl, "Théophraste: les limites éthiques, psychologiques et cosmologiques de la contemplation," in *Theoria, Praxis and the Contemplative Life after Plato and Aristotle*, Philosophia Antiqua, vol. 131, ed. Thomas Bénatouïl and Mauro Bonazzi (Leiden: Brill, 2002), 29–38.

Note the tacit bipolarity of the concept of "nature" (φύσις) in Aristotle's formulation of an intellectual principle. His reference to "that which is proper" to each thing "by nature" (τῇ φύσει) conveys a claim about what first and foremost the human ought to be, and ought to identify with, on the one hand; clearly, this notion of intellect as that which is proper to the human "by nature" refers, on the other hand, to a part that the human is naturally endowed with, or given, *qua* human. According to this iteration of the intellectual principle, the human beings who habitually identify with some active part of the composite soul/body other than its best part, in the course of choosing to cultivate powers that often procure some external or bodily good, risk depriving themselves of the superior good: "life according to intellect" (ὁ κατὰ νοῦν βίος).

In Polemo's definition of εὐδαιμονία, a version of the *intellectual principle* is undoubtedly more difficult to detect. It does seem that Polemo maintains a key realist assumption of the ontological systems promoted by his Academic predecessors, that is, the assumption that there is such a thing as "the world," but it is far from obvious how this realist assumption functions in relation to his virtue ethics. According to one source, Polemo asserts a version of the absolute conception of "the world" (κόσμος). For review, recall that absolute conceptions of reality typically posit the existence of the world as a being or whole that is there *anyway*. Polemo reportedly affirms not only that there is such a being as "the world," but he also declares that such a being is "god or (a) god" (Πολέμον τὸν κόσμον θεὸν ἀπεφήνατο, Stob., *Ecl.* 1.29 (= Fr. 121 Gigante)).[53] Once again, an absolute conception of the world involves a way of conceiving the world as it is independent of the observations, representations, or activities of human souls. The evidence is too scanty to effectively compare Polemo's absolute conception of the world to the metaphysical views of his Academic predecessors.

In any case, considering the specific kinds of metaphysical realism on the offer from the Old Academy, Zeno's corporealist view of first principles is undoubtedly groundbreaking. Reydams-Schils is certainly correct to emphasize the controversial nature of Varro's retrospective strategy of making Polemo and the Old Academy seem doctrinally Stoic and the early Stoa seem

---

[53] For discussion of Polemo, and the scant evidence of his cosmological realism, see Gretchen Reydams-Schils, "The Academy, the Stoics, and Cicero on Plato's 'Timaeus,'" in *Plato and the Stoics*, ed. A. G. Long (Cambridge: Cambridge University Press, 2013), 41–2. Reydams-Schils effectively challenges the heterodox interpretation of Sedley, which detects *inter al.* a view of god that anticipates the Stoic conception of an immanent god. Cf. David Sedley, "The Origins of Stoic God," in *Traditions of Theology*, ed. Dorothea Frede and Andre Laks (Leiden: Brill, 2002), 53–76. Margherita Isnardi Parente, "L'Accademia antica e le sue vicende filosofiche," *Rivista di Storia della Filosofia* 53, no. 2 (1998): 228, correctly states that there is very little in this fragment to support Polemo's originality in the area of cosmology or physics.

doctrinally Old Academic. Yet, Reydams-Schils shares an even more relevant insight. That is, however controversial Varro's presented history, it would have immediately sacrificed all credibility if Cicero's Varro (or Antiochus, for that matter) had taken the additional step of claiming that Polemo, or any other Old Academic, conceived of soul, reason, or intellect as either fundamentally corporeal or dependent on corporeal principles.[54] It is, I think, an important facet of this controversial history that Varro refuses to take such a step. The controversial history Varro presents retains a degree of credibility by not going too far in pushing the doctrinal alliance. In other words, the credibility of Varro's history is dependent on a certain level of historical generality. This is perhaps most evident—although not evident enough, given the generality—in Varro's overreview (1.24–9) of Old Academic physics: in particular, the discussion of "nature" and its relation to first principles. At the outset of what has become an important passage for potential reconstructions of Old Academic physics, Varro ascribes a manifold notion of *natura* to the Old Academy and the Peripatos (*Acad.* 1.24):

> When it came to nature (*natura* [= φύσις]), which *they* treated next, *they* spoke in such a way as to divide it into two things (*res duas*), so that one [thing] was active, the other [thing] at this one's disposal, as it were, and acted upon by it in some way. In the active one they held that that there was a power, in the one which was acted upon just as a kind of matter. (italics added; trans. Sedley, "Origins," in Frede et al., *Traditions of Theology*, 53)[55]

Here Varro undertakes a general overview of Old Academic/Peripatetic physics, according to which Speusippus, Xenocrates, Polemo, Crates, Crantor, Aristotle, and Theophrastus (1.33–4) preserve and defend one unified framework of disciplinary holism, which Socrates never himself approved (1.17). This holistic framework is then traced back to Plato and his initial formulations of doctrine. Plato's initial formulations (*prima forma*, 1.33) imply a form of disciplinary holism, but they are undeveloped. What emerges later, as a well-developed holistic

---

[54] Reydams-Schils, "The Academy," 50.
[55] Sedley argues that *Acad.* 1.24–9 provides a rare glimpse into what he calls the physics of Polemo's Academy (Polemo or Crates or both). Sedley eliminates Arcesilaus and Crantor (the latter defended the eternity of the world (Fr. 10 Mette), a view that allegedly conflicts with Varro's presentation of Academic physics) as possible sources for Cicero's presentation of Academic physics. This account challenges the consensus, which takes 1.24–9 as nothing more than Antiochus's unhistorical retrojection of Stoic physics onto early Academics and Peripatetics. Sedley, "Origins," 55–76. In defense of the consensus, see Gretchen Reydams-Schils, *Demiurge and Providence: Stoic and Platonist Readings of Plato's* Timaeus (Turnhout: Brepols, 1999), 128–32, and more recently, "The Academy," 48–58. For additional reservations regarding Sedley's reading, see Keimpe Algra, "Hellenistic Philosophy and Some Science," *Phronesis* 48, no. 1 (2003): 77–8.

system, fundamentally adheres to "Plato's authority" (*Platonis auctoritate*, 1.17, 1.33). Preserving disciplinary holism, but under two school names, "there was no difference between the Peripatetics and that Old Academy" (1.18). Again, obviously this is a controversial claim for Varro to espouse, and there is no intent to affirm or deny it in this study. Attention is fixed, rather, on key differences in doctrine that Cicero's Varro suppresses once Zeno is introduced into this broad philosophical alliance. When Varro's overview returns to Zeno, to supplement the controversial vision of a unified tradition that includes Stoic improvements, doctrinal differences in the tradition of eudaimonist ethics are diminished. On closer inspection, the credibility of Varro's Antiochean history becomes questionable with Zeno now in the picture. While Varro is willing to observe, and then minimize, a few doctrinal disparities between Zeno and the Old Academy with regard to "nature" and first principles, those disparities produce considerable deviations in the area of eudaimonist ethics that pass unmentioned. Not only does Varro downplay a number of Zeno's ethical deviations, but his account ignores entirely the way that these ethical deviations derive from Zeno's profoundly different conception of "nature."

For review, recall that for Polemo, the relatively inferior ethical status of natural goods, which he designates τὰ σωματικά, entails that the higher goods involve a form of intellectual activity irreducible to the body. Just as for Xenocrates, and before him Speusippus, the bipolarity of φύσις is determined by the irreducibility of soul to body, and the metaphysical priority of the soul informs the ethical classification and hierarchy of higher and lower goods. The present task is not to specify or reconstruct the content of Antiochus's history of philosophy, from its traces in Cicero, but it is important to specify why Varro's Antiochean history remains in a certain respect credible. Among other reasons, the speech is considered controversial because it seeks to unify what might otherwise appear to be two different systems of philosophy—the Old Academic and Peripatetic—into one explanatory framework. Nevertheless, in relation to the concept of philosophical system, a certain manner of doctrinal unity is defensible. Both schools uphold and make conceptual use of a bipolar notion of φύσις/*natura*: a bipolarity corresponding, I should add, to a bi-level metaphysical distinction between that which is noncorporeal and metaphysically separable from perceptible bodies and that which is corporeal. By contrast, the bipolarity of φύσις is repudiated by Zeno and his canonical successors and reconfigured in corporeal terms. For Old Academics, φύσις denotes, on one hand, that which is noncorporeal and separable from bodies; on the other, it denotes the essence of this or that composite being partaking of form and matter. Varro introduces

Zeno as someone venturing to issue a number of minor revisions, or corrections, to a unified tradition of disciplinary holism. That claim implies, however, that such corrections leave the internal relations among the disciplinary parts within the holistic system intact and unchanged. The result of such corrections is supposedly mere terminological alteration within each of the disciplinary parts (ethics, physics, logic). With the espousal of mere terminological alteration, which again implies that the cohesion of disciplinary holism remains unrevised, Varro's historical overview becomes too dubious to endorse. Varro alleges, in other words, that Zeno's alterations consist in minor revisions to the terminology that the Academics and Peripatetics traditionally relied on to articulate doctrines at the micro-level of the system's internal parts without producing any substantial deviating effect on the conceptualization of disciplinary holism.

To root my claim in the text, consider Varro's synoptic account of "nearly all of Zeno's disagreements" (1.42) with the Old Academy and Peripatos. Varro's micro-level focus on the parts of philosophy, I argue, fails to observe Zeno's profound alteration of disciplinary holism. By "blending" the tripartition of ethics-physics-logic, Zeno effectively abandons the kind of bipolarity in the notion of φύσις that harmonizes the basic hierarchical structures of Old Academic/Peripatetic metaphysics. One can state with conviction that no one before Zeno had tried to mix the three parts of philosophical *logos* into a coherent, systematic unity in the way that he envisioned.[56] Moreover, this blending of parts has substantial ethical implications, giving rise to a bold and revisionary ethical ideal of happiness: namely, that through "instruction and exercise" (ἄσκησιν, D.L. 7.8), mortal animals partaking in reason have the power to attain a corporeal state of perfect virtue. In fact, Zeno's ideal sage signals a substantial alteration of the traditional eudaimonism advanced by Old Academics and Peripatetics, but again it also manifests a profound alteration occurring at the holistic level of the old system. Cicero's own silence on this holistic change is also problematic.

Cicero responds to Varro's overview by agreeing that Stoicism should be considered a revision of the Academy (1.43), and not "some new system" (*novam aliquam disciplinam*). Elsewhere, Cicero notes (in response to Lucullus) that the Stoics divide wisdom, as "most philosophers do," into "three parts" (2.116). But Cicero fails on multiple occasions to observe the unprecedented novelty of

---

[56] At *De fin*. 4.3–6, Cicero in his own voice concedes Antiochus's (i.e., Varro's) historical view of the tripartition, using the concession as a premise in his argument against Zeno's unnecessary ethical deviation from Polemo and his predecessors (including Aristotle and Theophrastus). This passage in *De fin*. (4.3–6) is the only source to explicitly attribute the tripartition to Speusippus, Xenocrates, Polemo, Aristotle, Theophrastus, and Zeno. This broad alliance is left implied at *Acad*. 1.19 (cf. 1.34, where it is seems that Varro ascribes the division to Crantor and Crates), but not stated.

Zeno's transformation of disciplinary holism, which introduces a new version of holism and an altogether new ideal of wisdom. For the first time, Zeno conceives of disciplinary holism as a blending of the parts into a whole, and idealizes the potential embodiment of those unified parts in the sage's systematic knowledge of the world. The most important corollary of unifying the parts of wisdom in this way, for present purposes, is Zeno's reduction of first principles to bodies (Cic., *Acad.* 1.39 (= *SVF* 1.90), D.L. 7.134 (= *SVF* 2.300, LS 44B)). The active principle of nature is now conceptualized as corporeal, as is the passive principle—although the latter lacks quality or form. Disavowing Old Academic/Peripatetic notions of bipolarity, Zeno's notion of "nature" (φύσις/*natura*) repudiates the explanatory function of explaining the appearances or phenomena of lower-level corporeal beings by referring to high-level intelligible, noncorporeal principles. For Zeno and the early Stoa, divine λόγος is both a body and the active corporeal principle generating and pervading the finite totality of the world. As the active principle, it structures an unqualified passive principle *qua* body (or unqualified matter) to create and preserve the individual corporeal beings, which serve as constituent parts of the living natural body that is the world.[57] Cicero and his character Varro jointly conceal the extent to which this conceptual change to the principles of the whole substantially alters, for instance, the partition of ethics. The new disciplinary holism of Stoic philosophy entails a new way of conceptualizing the good, but again that innovation is not rehearsed by Varro.[58]

Preceding the overview of physics, Varro provides an account of the unity of the Old Academy and Peripatos as it applies narrowly to ethical doctrine (1.19–23). Here Varro continually refers to a plural subject, to identify the "Old Academics and Peripatetics" (1.21, cf. 1.17: *qui rebus congruentes nominibus differebant*). They begin investigations of the good life with appeals to nature, and declare that "one should obey nature in seeking the highest good, for the highest good which is the ultimate aim of all things is to be sought in nature and nature alone" (1.19). The ethical goal is therefore to obtain "everything natural in mind, body, and life" (*omnia e natura et animo et corpore et vita*). Uncontroversially, Varro here ascribes "three kinds of good" to Peripatetics and Old Academics: *animi bona*, *corporis bona*, and *bona vitae* (1.19) or *vitae adiuncta* (1.21). They share the view that the ethical end is to obtain all or "the greatest of the primary things nature recommends." The supreme goods are those associated with mind

---

[57] Lactantius, *Div. inst.* 4.9 (= *SVF* 1.160): "He [Zeno] designated the one who is responsible for the order in nature and who is the craftsman of world-reason (λόγος = *artificem universitatis*), calling him fate, necessity of things, god, and soul of Zeus." Cf. Tertullian, *Apol.* 21.

[58] Suggesting such whole-part entailment, see Reydams-Schils, "The Academy," 48.

or soul, and thus more directly associated with virtue than the lesser goods. Varro summarizes: "So the unanimous view of that ancient system of philosophy was this: while the happy life depends on virtue alone, it isn't the happiest life without the addition of bodily goods and those others mentioned above that are suitable for virtue" (1.22). The category of life goods, or goods in the service of life, includes circumstances ranging beyond what is considered, strictly speaking, natural. Although such accessories are more or less remote from the realm of the natural, they nevertheless contribute to the exercise of virtue (1.21, cf. *De fin.* 5.90–1, 68–9). Varro considers these goods to be *adiuncta*, not in the sense of being "external" to the soul, as Aristotle indicates;[59] rather, the implication of the plural term *adiuncta* is that such goods are subordinate and auxiliary in relation to what is essentially natural for the mind and for the body. Now, what is said about Zeno in relation to this ethical tradition? What does Varro say, in other words, about Zeno and the hierarchical classification of goods? Also, what sort of terminological alteration, according to Varro, does Zeno propose to this area of the ancient system?

To address these questions, first consider Varro's remarks on the ethical changes supposedly made by Theophrastus. The remarks are surprisingly instructive, especially when one compares his comments on Theophrastus's "violent" changes (*Acad.* 1.33) to his remarks on Zeno's ethical alterations. Unlike Zeno, Theophrastus denies that εὐδαιμονία depends solely on virtue, diminishing thereby the beauty and importance of virtue and disrupting "the authority of the old teachings." (Fortenbaugh conjectures that Cicero the author, resorting to what he had learned from Antiochus, may not have known Aristotle's considered view that bodily and external goods are important for living a happy life: unaware, even, of Aristotle's rejection of the view that a good man can be happy while experiencing extreme misfortune (*EN* 1.5, 1096a1–2, 1.9, 1100a5–9, 7.13, 1153b17–21)).[60] Otherwise, why would Varro's reproach take aim at Theophrastus and not Aristotle and Xenocrates—two philosophers in the unified tradition Varro praises, and the same philosophers who maintain the necessity

---

[59] Key passages for Aristotle's view of "external goods" (τὰ ἐκτὸς ἀγαθά): *EN* 1.8, 1098b12–16, 1099a31–33, *EN* 7.13, 1153a21–35, *Pol.* 7.1, 1323a21–35, *EE* 2.1, 1218b31–37, Ps. Aristotle, *Divisiones Aristoteleae* 1.1 (see also D.L. 3.80–1). In Plato's *Laws* (697b), the ranking of valuable things in the order of soul, body, and those things said to be about property and money, omits the modifier "external."

[60] Fortenbaugh, *Theophrastus*, 446–8 (497 FHS&G), 437–42 (493 FHS&G), and 448–9 (498 FHS&G). At *Acad.* 2.131–2, 134, Cicero summarizes Zeno's disagreement with the Old Academics and alludes to Theophrastus's views on goodness. He mentions Antiochus's view that "there are bad bodily and external circumstances, and yet believes that someone subject to all of them will be happy if he's wise." But notice here as well that the hierarchical classification of (inferior) goods goes unmentioned.

of possessing inferior goods for the attainment of virtue?) At any rate, now consider the treatment of Zeno's changes. The latter is praised for not being the sort of person "to cut the sinews of virtue." In fact, on Varro's view, Zeno elevates virtue by declaring its pure rationality, admitting nothing into the category of good other than virtue and giving it the name "noble" to denote the uniform, unique, and sole good (*Acad.* 1.35). Varro then summarizes Zeno's view that some things in accordance with nature are neither good nor bad, but are worthy of selection; whereas others of this kind are contrary to nature, and not worthy of selection (*Acad.* 1.36-7). And of those worthy of selection, Zeno supposedly assigns a degree of value to a subset of things in this larger intermediate set (of things neither good nor bad). In a very cursory fashion, Varro lists the other ethical revisions that Zeno makes (*Acad.* 1.38). Zeno's predecessors in the Old Academic and Peripatetic tradition claim that not every virtue resides in reason, for some virtues are held to be completed through lower natural dispositions and habit; by contrast, Zeno fixes all the virtues in reason. His eudaimonist predecessors hold that a certain set of (mixed) virtues are separable from one another, but Zeno believes that the separation and the subdivision of virtue into the rational and the nonrational are impossible. Varro's summary of the ethical corrections comes close to acknowledging Zeno's deviation from the traditional hierarchy of goods, but ultimately the summary omits Zeno's repudiation of the hierarchy.

In fact, stressing consistency in ethical doctrine from the Old Academy/Peripatos to the terminological corrections of early Stoic thought, Varro settles on suppressing in this context another one of the Stoic founder's most radical doctrinal innovations: namely, that the soul, or the governing faculty of the soul partaking in reason, is itself a body (*SVF* 1.136-8) comprised of "warm breath" (πνεῦμα ἔνθερμον, D.L. 7.157 (= *SVF* 1.135)). Zeno's conception of the soul is more closely affiliated with his physics; still, this conception once again has momentous ethical implications for certain mortal animals, for the psychic state of virtue is conceived by Zeno as a certain bodily state (Sextus, *M.* 11.23). As noted above, Varro does mention Zeno's minor variation from his eudaimonist predecessors in claiming that the intrinsic excellence of virtue resides in the state itself—not only in the exercise of the virtues. To recall, the tradition of Peripatetic and Old Academic philosophers divides the individual human soul into the rational and the nonrational, or partly rational components. Zeno, by contrast, identifies the human soul and its ἡγεμονικόν as entirely rational. When identifying this point of ethical contrast, Varro manages to conceal the underlying divergences, which again find clear expression in the ethical part of Zeno's disciplinary holism. With a radically altered conception of the soul partaking in reason, the struggle between virtuous and non-virtuous inclinations of the human soul is no longer one between two separate powers, as conceived by Speusippus, Xenocrates, Crantor, Aristotle, and Theophrastus, but rather a conflict of reason with itself. In the course of commenting on Zeno's attempt to diminish and narrow the range of the emotions and the nonrational, Varro once again understates Zeno's departure from the Old Academic-Peripatetic tradition. Whereas the preceding eudaimonist tradition held that the emotions and passions are natural and intractable features of the nonrational part of the human soul, Zeno advances the heterodox view that the emotions are voluntary, perverse forms of rational opinion, which the aspiring sage ought to abandon. Plutarch also brings out this contrast: "They [the Stoics] hold that the emotional power is not distinguished from the rational by some difference in its nature, but that it is the same part of the mind—I mean, that which they call intellect or the governing power" (*Virt. mor.* 441c (< LS 61B)).

Turning to the physical domain of Zeno's disciplinary holism, Varro does identify two points of alteration. Varro states:

> He [Zeno] also differed from the same thinkers in holding that it was impossible for a being to be acted on by something that is entirely without body, such as Xenocrates and other predecessors had pronounced the mind to be: neither what acts nor what it acts on could be noncorporeal. (1.39)

Zeno is said to have rejected the causal agency of a noncorporeal conception of mind. Nevertheless, Varro shies away from explicitly stating the ethical implications of Zeno's view that the rational agency of the soul (*animus*) is nothing other than body, as one should expect from the narrow contextual focus on physics. Varro states that Zeno's conception of natural things rejects Aristotle's addition of a fifth element, which Aristotle allegedly introduces to explain the origin of the senses and the mind. As Cicero explains elsewhere, Zeno posits god or fire as the one single corporeal element responsible for bringing everything into being (Cicero, *De nat. deor.* 1.39, 2.57–8 (= *SVF* 2.1077)). The causal primacy of the corporeal is a significant departure from Old Academic physics (leaving aside the evident contrasts with Aristotelian physics). Moreover, maintaining Zeno's view of causal efficacy, early Stoic physics repudiates the two-opposing principles of Speusippus and those of Xenocrates, consolidating the doctrine of two-opposing principles into the fundamental notions of body and designing fire. Nature is no longer separated into the metaphysical bipolarity of the intelligible and the sensible, as it is in the Old Academic-Peripatetic alliance. As a result, a new metaphysical bipolarity emerges: the active and passive principles of bodies. The opposition of two noncorporeal principles affirmed by the Old Academics is replaced by two corporeal principles. Varro's synoptic presentation of Zeno's "disagreements" with "the ancients" (1.39, cf. 1.24–9) in the domain of physics disguises the Stoic alteration of nature's bipolarity as a minor, insulated revision to physics; when, in fact, it profoundly alters the ethical part of the ancient system.

Again, when it comes to specifying the meaning of φύσις, disparate ancient sources demonstrate that for Speusippus, Xenocrates, Aristotle, and Crantor, the notion of φύσις is not entirely reducible to a body or a corporeal principle, or any other body referred to under the various appellations endorsed by Zeno and his successors, such as "designing fire" (D.L. 7.156), "fate," "Reason," or "Zeus" (D.L. 7.35), which refer either to what holds the totality of the world together as a unified whole or what causes terrestrial things to spring up (D.L. 7.148). The notion of φύσις generally designates for the Old Academy the essence of a being or thing, beings that are purely intelligible, universal, and noncorporeal, and composite beings partaking of the intelligible and corporeal. Aristotle certainly revises the doctrine of the separation of forms from sensible things, but he conceives of intellect as separable from soul and body. Polemo, in virtue of the ethical superiority of the rational soul (in comparison with the irrational souls of other animals), condemned eating the flesh of animals (*Strom.* 7.32 (= Fr. 112 Gigante)). Virtue is on his view sufficient for εὐδαιμονία even without the accompaniment of bodily and external goods. With an austere view of εὐδαιμονία, it seems that Polemo anticipates to some extent the monistic view of the good endorsed by Zeno, while at the same time maintaining the Old Academic-Peripatetic priority of an intellectual principle, according to which the noncorporeal part of the soul partaking in reason rules over the body. Hence, the power of the rational soul is not itself a body. Polemo therefore adheres to the sufficiency of virtue for happiness without rejecting the characterization of "first natural things" (τὰ πρῶτα κατὰ φύσιν/*prima a natura data*/*prima naturalia*) as goods of an inferior status. With Polemo's ethics in mind, the character "Cicero" says the following:

> Every living creature [. . .] cherishes above all its two major components, namely, mind and body, and the parts of each. Both mind and body have certain excellences; of these the young animal grows vaguely conscious, and later begins to discriminate, and to seek for the first natural endowments and shun their opposites. Whether the former category includes pleasure or not is a difficult question. But it seems to me the height of folly to think that it consists of nothing

except pleasure, with no room for the limbs or senses, for mental activity, bodily soundness or good health. This must provide the basis for any theory of goods and evils. Polemo, and before him Aristotle, held that the first endowments are those I just mentioned. (*De fin.* 2.33-4 (< Fr. 127 Gigante))

Given that Cicero explicitly assigns this view to Polemo, whose austere conception of εὐδαιμονία values the goods superior to those of the body, or first natural endowments, the implication is that even the most ethically austere of the Old Academy includes bodily goods within the category of first natural things, which involve *inter al.* the functioning of the limbs, bodily integrity, and so forth.[61] To reiterate, the evidence for Polemo's eudaimonist ethics, including his vegetarianism, demonstrates that while he acknowledges bodily goods as goods, he also seems to retain the priority of virtue as a noncorporeal good.

Recent scholarship has explored Polemo's educational stress on the Socratic side of Academic eudaimonism. Harold Tarrant argues, drawing on Polemo's definition of *erôs*, that at the time of Polemo's directorship, the Old Academy promoted a culture of education idealizing physical proximity and erotic relations among its associates. In such a setting, ethical progress is supposedly governed "by daimonic forces beyond the teacher's control." To make sense of this governance in the context of an institutional tradition of recognizing a scholarch or school director, Tarrant suggests that younger associates regarded their director as a successor of a "divinely inspired individual." As younger companions of Socrates benefit from the oversight of a divine force, younger associates of Polemo benefit from the daimonic influence of an inspired scholarch. Under this regime of moral cultivation, Tarrant conjectures that the practice of dialectical argument may have been "all but forgotten" as a means of ethical improvement. In response, Kurt Lampe accepts the Socratic spirit of Polemo's educational stress, but challenges the idea that such a stress might have displaced the role of question and answer. According to Lampe, Polemo's emphasis on love as service to the gods for the care and salvation of the young is a service perfectly consistent with the lover and the beloved regularly reasoning together in close physical proximity.[62] Verses from Antagoras's epitaph (D.L. 4.21) are taken by Lampe to support the possibility of Polemo defending and explicating his doctrines in the company of Academic associates: "Stranger, say

---

[61] Cicero the character thus agrees in part with the Antiochean position of Piso (*De fin.* 5.7-74), which is to say, the position that has come down to us mainly from Cicero *qua* author. At 5.14, Piso states that Polemo's ethical views coincided with those of Aristotle.

[62] Kurt Lampe, "Rationality, Eros, and Daemonic Influence in the Platonic *Theages* and the Academy of Polemo and Crates," *American Journal of Philology* 134, no. 3 (Fall 2013): 415-21.

that in this tomb lie god-like (θεουδέα) Crates and Polemo, men great-hearted in concord, from whose daimonic mouth[s] sprang sacred speech, and whose pure life of wisdom, obedient to unshakeable doctrines, prepared them for divine eternity." Ultimately, ancient evidence is not sufficient to settle the issue. For present purposes, it is wise to simply claim that Polemo's definition of ἔρως as divine service represents the aim of helping younger associates learn *inter al.* how to discern, procure, and prioritize a plurality of goods. As Lampe claims, Polemo's dismissal of Zenonian ethics and its dialectical requirement should not be taken as evidence of the disappearance of Socratic question and answer in the early Hellenistic Academy. His dismissal of a particular kind of ethical training more narrowly rejects the requirement that the teaching of practical ethics ought to depend on the study of dialectical syllogisms, as conceived by Zeno.

In my view, scholars have little reason to doubt that Polemo's conception of εὐδαιμονία affirms the Academy's hierarchical view of superior and inferior goods.[63] His educational stress on the "Socratic side of Plato" is informed by a standard ethical doctrine on the plurality of goods available, and the metaphysical priority of noncorporeal goods associated with the rational power of the soul. In conformity with the way in which the priority of the noncorporeal over the corporeal functions in the metaphysical worldviews of Speusippus and Xenocrates, Polemo's classification of goods is determined by the very same metaphysical priority. His pithy objection to Zenonian ethics suggests, then, that Polemo would oppose Zeno's peculiar variety of disciplinary holism, which carves up the study of the world as it really is into nonhierarchical domains of inquiry. However, there is no record of Polemo explicitly opposing, or engaging with Zeno's metaphysical realism more generally, and there is certainly no extant record of Polemo opposing Zeno's corporeal principles as they function to inform the latter's ethical program. Nevertheless, with the ascendancy of Arcesilaus in the early Hellenistic Academy, a new and improved strategy of Academic opposition to Zenonian ethics emerges. With Arcesilaus, the opposition to Stoicism takes aim at Zeno's general metaphysics, and for the first time, Academic opposition appropriates the premises and concepts of early canonical Stoicism to undermine its ontological conception of virtue.

---

[63] On the "Socratic side" of Polemo and his associates, consider the remarks of Anthony A. Long, "Diogenes Laertius: Life of Arcesilaus," *Elenchos* 7, Fasc. 1–2 (1986): 440–1.

Concluding Analysis

As a brief review of the preceding reconstruction, recall that Chapters 2 and 3 specify that Arcesilaus's arguments contest the metaphysical foundations of early Stoic eudaimonism. His arguments in fact show that early Stoicism espouses the absurd metaphysical theses of ἀκαταληψία and ἐποχὴ περὶ πάντων. Together the theses entail the absurd claim that life, on the Stoic view, cannot be lived. That is to say, Arcesilaus's arguments show that Zeno and his early canonical followers defend an ontology of nature that not only renders real individual bodies inapprehensible, but also in the humanistic domain of action it makes virtuous life impossible to live. The final task of this reconstruction has already begun to set the content of these arguments against the background of Arcesilaus's Academic predecessors. Initiating this task, the previous chapter identified Polemo's classification of ethical goods as a traditionally Academic iteration of eudaimonism.

The new direction Arcesilaus takes against Zeno makes no use of the metaphysical principles governing Academic ethics. For Polemo in particular, the metaphysical priority of the noncorporeal informs his targeted opposition to Zenonian ethics. The previous chapter is, one might say, an attempt to persuade historiographers to improve upon the myopic specifications of epistemological change in the early Hellenistic period. Alternatively, it initiates the attempt to conceptualize Academic change against the backdrop of the school's opposition to Zeno's ethics, which emerges prior to the rise of Arcesilaus as director and sets the stage for his later revival of a distinctly Socratic style of oral polemic. Arcesilaus expands on Polemo's targeted and rather pithy opposition to the dialectical dimension of Zeno's ethics, but the evolution of Academic opposition is what makes Arcesilaus's way of opposing Zeno's eudaimonism unprecedented.

Two features of Arcesilaus's opposition help bring about the early Hellenistic Academy's change of direction. Whereas Polemo pithily dismisses Zeno's regimentation of moral improvement through the study of dialectical theorems, Arcesilaus's arguments provisionally accept the premises and concepts of Zeno's physics in order to critically examine the structural ontology of apprehension.

Arcesilaus's *ad hominem* appropriation of early Stoic concepts reflects a new level of theoretical engagement with Zeno's philosophical views. Second, recall that Polemo's objection takes issue, above all other possible concerns, with a particular pedagogical method of training human beings to become virtuous. As argued above, Polemo's conception of εὐδαιμονία is conditioned by the metaphysical priority of the noncorporeal, which fixes the classification of goods into a hierarchy and controls the pedagogical method of training human beings for a virtuous life. With Arcesilaus's deduction of absurd theses (e.g., ἀκαταληψία) from Stoic concepts and arguments undermining early Stoicism as a coherently structured metaphysics, the scope of Academic opposition enlarges considerably. Thus, for the first time, Zeno's disciplinary holism finds itself under attack.

Cicero's Genealogy of the Academy

When confronted with the objection of "inaction," Arcesilaus shifts the blame to Zeno's conception of nature for making things inapprehensible and life impossible to live. Now it is true that Arcesilaus also ventures to propose a practical criterion, which is dissociated from the conception of the apprehensive impression. Such a proposal marks a third distinguishing feature of Arcesilaus's opposition. With the introduction of a revised notion of appropriate action, Arcesilaus prompts his Stoic adversaries, and interlocutors more broadly, to reflect on the possibility of appropriate action independent of assuming any absolute conception of reality. In other words, with this revised notion, it becomes clear that opposition to Zenonian ethics is no longer dependent on, or informed by, the underlying metaphysical principles associated with a hierarchical ranking of Academic goods. In defense of this alternative specification of change, I now return to what is typically invoked as a decisive source of evidence in support of the Epistemological Novelty Thesis: Cicero's *Academica*.

It is widely believed that Cicero's *Academica* presents, or at least relies on, Antiochus's conception of a "new" Academy. That conception seems to assert a thesis of Academic discontinuity, or rupture, initiated by Arcesilaus. In his own name, Cicero responds to the thesis with a rival account of the Academy's so-called *new* orientation (1.46). As representatives of Antiochus, Lucullus and Varro seek to reclaim the "authority of the ancients" (*Acad.* 2.13–18), contrasting the authoritative "old doctrines" of the Old Academy/Peripatos with Arcesilaus's subversion of those doctrines. Accordingly, Arcesilaus is presented as the first to systematically subvert the "authority of the ancients," and the first to break (1.43–6) the continuity of disciplinary holism from Plato to Polemo and Crates. From the Antiochean perspective, Arcesilaus's destruction of philosophical authority represents a doctrinal break from Aristotle and Zeno, just as it represents a break from the old teaching of Xenocrates or Speusippus.

Cicero, on the other hand, frequently declares his allegiance to the Academy as such, while avoiding the qualification of a "new" Academy. More often than not, he expresses his philosophical loyalty to an Academic tradition (*De nat. deor.* 1.11, *Tusc.* 2.4, *Off.* 2.8, *Acad.* 2.7), which Arcesilaus is said to have continued and improved. On the odd occasion Cicero alludes to a "new" or "most up-to-date" Academy (*Acad.* 1.46, cf. *Acad.* 1.13, 1.43), he tries to defend the outlines of an Academic continuity thesis that explicitly rejects the Antiochean history of Academic discontinuity. However, in reconstructing the Academic continuity thesis, proponents of Arcesilaus's epistemological novelty mistake Cicero's reconstructed defense for straightforward evidence of Arcesilaus's invocation of Socrates's claim to ignorance.

First note the truncated nature of Cicero's Academic history. At 1.44–6, Cicero sets aside the philosophical doctrines of Speusippus, Xenocrates, Polemo, Crantor, Crates, Aristotle, and Theophrastus from his account of a continuity thesis. Clearly, and just as dubiously, Cicero's strategy for defending Academic continuity involves ignoring the doctrines of the Academic scholarchs, opting instead for situating Arcesilaus and his manner of oral argument in relation to certain Presocratic philosophers, the Platonic Socrates, and Plato's writings more generally. Now, proponents of the Epistemological Novelty Thesis exclude from analysis the structural interdependency of disciplinary parts built into the holistic systems of Old Academic philosophy; in the previous chapter, I argue that Varro's synopsis of Zeno's terminological corrections manifests the very same neglect. What is more, Cicero's own defense of Academic continuity offers no improvement in this regard. In the context of articulating Academic continuity, Cicero appropriates the epithet of a "new" Academy, but the appropriation functions polemically to mitigate the alleged novelty of Arcesilaus's "rupture" from the Academic tradition. Crucial to this attempt to mitigate Arcesilaus's apparent novelty is his claim that Arcesilaus revives a Socratic method of oral argument, and that such a revival functions as a bridge between various Presocratics and Plato's dialogues. Cicero assigns this Socratic revival by Arcesilaus an essential role in the defense of an alternative vision of a continuous Academic tradition, which has its philosophical ancestry in Socratic interrogation.

Cicero's retrospective history of a continuous Academic tradition hinges on his own understanding of Socrates in the Platonic dialogues. His defense of the tradition has a basic conceptual structure. The conceptual structure holding the tradition together is purportedly a three-stage genealogy of increasing self-consciousness (*Acad.* 1.44–6). As it turns out, the account of genealogy itself manifests the third stage of genealogical development, as Cicero's genealogy brings the third and final stage of development to the latest summit of Academic self-consciousness. Cicero thereby includes himself (and the *Academica* itself) in the third stage of the tradition.

Very briefly, the first stage in the history of increasing self-consciousness dates back to Presocratic expressions of how obscure things are and how weak the human mind is; whereas, the second stage advances to the more self-conscious ignorance of Socrates and Plato, whose dialogues tacitly approve of Socrates's *confessio ignorationis*. Expressions regarding the universal obscurity of things in the first stage help motivate, according to Cicero's retrospective, Socrates's *confessio ignorationis* at the second stage of increasing self-consciousness. In the course of articulating the genealogical development from stage one to stage two, Cicero boasts of his intimacy with Socrates and Plato: "Can I speak more certainly about anyone? Indeed, I seem to have lived with them." His self-ascribed intimacy with Socrates and Plato gives him the conviction to claim that "Socrates thought that nothing could be known for certain" (2.74, cf. 1.45). Cicero's intimacy with Plato and the Platonic Socrates underpins his understanding of Arcesilaus's revival of the Socratic method of interrogation depicted in Plato's dialogues. From his experience studying Plato and Socrates, as if he had "lived with them," Cicero reconstructs a third and final stage as the continuation and culmination of Arcesilaus's revival. According to Cicero's retrospective, Arcesilaus takes the self-awareness of ignorance to a new level of reflection, surpassing Socrates's self-awareness of ignorance, thereby initiating a new stage of increasing self-consciousness. Cicero reasons as follows (1.45): "That's why Arcesilaus denied there is anything that can be known, not even that very thing (*illud ipsum*) which Socrates had allowed himself—the knowledge that he knew nothing."[1] Again, according to Cicero, Arcesilaus's higher-order

---

[1] *Acad.* 1.45: *itaque Arcesilas negabat esse quicquam quod sciri posset, ne illud quidem ipsum quod Socrates sibi reliquisset, ut nihil scire se sciret.* For useful comments on the Latin, see Burnyeat, "Antipater," 295 n49. At *De orat.* 3.67, Cicero contends that Arcesilaus took the claim that there is no certainty to be derived from the senses or the mind from "various books and Socratic discussions of Plato." But here again one should be more cautious in taking Cicero's retrospective view of Arcesilaus's reading of Plato as straightforward evidence of the way that Arcesilaus actually read Plato and of the way that Arcesilaus claimed to read Plato. Cf. Lévy, "La Nouvelle Académie," 144–7.

awareness surpasses Socrates's awareness in virtue of the former withdrawing the claim Socrates had affirmed: the claim to know that he knows nothing *except* this claim itself. Cicero is not claiming that Arcesilaus himself explicitly appealed to Socrates in this way; moreover, it should be clear to readers that Cicero is not claiming that one should conceive of Cicero's own specification of Socrates's claim to know that he knew nothing as the specification that Arcesilaus articulated or was committed to articulating. The specified content of Socrates's residual claim to know that he knew nothing is Cicero's way of making sense of the relation between Arcesilaus and Socrates. From Cicero's genealogy, there is simply no way to prove that Cicero's specification of Socrates's claim is a statement or commitment originally specified by Arcesilaus himself.

The mistake made by many epistemological centrists in the reconstruction of Cicero's Academic history is to assume that Cicero's reading of Socratic continuity represents what Arcesilaus thought or stated about his own view of a Socratic legacy.[2] Of course, it is logically possible that Cicero's history accurately specifies Arcesilaus's understanding of the Presocratics and Socrates. From Cicero's genealogical account, however, it is misleading to take such accuracy for granted.[3] Cicero's emphatic claim of intimate acquaintance with Socrates and Plato suggests the contrary. As Cicero presents the Platonic dialogues, Arcesilaus revives an oral style of argumentation, which preserves the following four features already present, allegedly, in Plato. Cicero declares, that in Plato's dialogues: "(1) nothing is affirmed, (2) many arguments are given on either side, (3) everything is under investigation, (4) and nothing is claimed to be certain" (1.46). Cicero's conception of Plato is, it seems to me, an essential resource for the bridge-building that Cicero undertakes in his effort to connect Arcesilaus to Socrates (and the Presocratics). At this moment in the *Academica*, Cicero is once again exhibiting his aspiration to defend the continuity of the Platonic school

---

[2] Burnyeat, "Antipater," 297; Brittain and Palmer, "New Academy's Appeals," 42 n7, 44, 48–9, esp. n12; Bett, "Socrates and Skepticism," 305–6. Anthony A. Long, "Socrates in Later Greek Philosophy," in *The Cambridge Companion to Socrates*, ed. Donald R. Morrison (Cambridge: Cambridge University Press, 2010), 365. Brittain, *Philo*, 178, claims that Cicero's Academic genealogy at *Acad.* 1.44–5 is the genealogy defended by Arcesilaus, and that Cicero "explicitly attributes" the genealogy to Arcesilaus. The basis for this claim is what Lucullus says at *Acad.* 2.15–16: "that Arcesilaus rose up to subvert philosophy, hiding behind the authority of those who had denied that anything could be grasped or known." At first glance, it seems plausible to infer from *Acad.* 2.15–16 that Arcesilaus himself often appealed to the Presocratics, but a closer look reveals that the appeals themselves offer no grounds for the additional claim that Arcesilaus "relied on a developmental view of history," or that such a view included an explicit appeal to Socrates's confession of ignorance.

[3] In addition to his own reading of Plato's dialogues, Cicero's genealogy may stem from his understanding of the now-lost books of Clitomachus, the Academic whom Cicero thinks correctly understood Carneades (as opposed to Philo) (*Acad.* 2.78).

and to consummate, by means of a highly selective genealogical account, "the most correct and improved" version of the so-called new Academy.

Cicero's genealogy constitutes his recorded response to the Antiochean defense of Plato's authoritative system, including the rebuke of Arcesilaus—that is to say, again, the reproach that Arcesilaus subverts the authority of a venerable holistic system. Cicero's response is an attempt not only to defend but also to preserve what he takes to be a different conception of *authority*: the authority of an Academic reception of Plato, from Arcesilaus and Carneades down to himself. This rival notion of authority is clearly not based on some authoritative system of doctrine. In fact, Cicero's sense of authority here excludes Old Academic doctrine from genealogical consideration. Cicero provides one of the earliest attempts to reconstruct how Arcesilaus might have defended an alternative conception of Plato's authority, a reconstruction that occurs in the context of defending his own conception of the Academy from Carneades down to himself, but clearly his historical vision of the Academy has almost nothing to say about the various doctrines affirmed by the so-called Old Academy.

Since Cicero cautiously avoids specifying in the *Academica* what Arcesilaus himself actually said about the authority of Plato, or his relation to Socrates, one might infer that Arcesilaus never explicitly referred (orally or in writing) to his own view of Socrates's confession of ignorance. This conclusion should be resisted. In fact, it would be just as incautious to defend this conclusion as it would be to claim that Cicero correctly specified Arcesilaus's own commitments in relation to Socrates, or what Arcesilaus said about his commitments in relation to Socrates. Simply put, even the most informative ancient sources are inconclusive on the matter of Arcesilaus's actual commitments. Considering the orality of the Socratic method of argument that Arcesilaus revived, there is nothing astonishing about this. Let me expand, in conclusion, on what this uncertainty means for the historiography of Hellenistic philosophy in general, and the framework of epistemological centrism.

Consider Philodemus's intriguing testimony: that Arcesilaus "at first defended an orientation maintained by the school from Plato and Speusippus until Polemo" (*Acad. hist.* 18.7, cf. Cicero, *De orat.* 3.67, *De fin.* 5.94). Living amid an erotic culture of instruction and close physical proximity to associates for nearly two decades before becoming scholarch of the Academy, it is unsurprising to read from an early source that Arcesilaus, in the early days of living with associates, defended a philosophical orientation of the Old Academy. Yet such orientation begs a number of questions. Unfortunately, the next several lines of Philodemus's text are lacunose, making it difficult if not impossible to decipher what may have delivered a fuller reckoning of this early adherence.[4] Once again, Cicero's genealogy of the "new" Academy is not much help in this regard; as already noted, the genealogy has no use for the philosophy of Polemo or Speusippus. Elsewhere, Cicero says that Arcesilaus devoted his inquiries to oral argument, cross-examining the views of his interlocutors (*De fin.* 2.2), while "not showing what he thought" (*De orat.* 3.67, cf. Philodemus, *Acad. hist.* 20.2–4). Cicero also specifies elsewhere that his inquiries were modeled on what generically is described as Socrates's "many-sided manner of reasoning" (*multiplex ratio*, *Tusc.* 5.11). Arcesilaus likewise examined all the claims affirmed in a cross-examination, presumably including all those claims Arcesilaus would provisionally accept to launch the many-sided cross-examination. Later testimony asserts, in figurative terms, the same general procedure. Arcesilaus would reportedly reverse himself time and again in the very same oral argument: "decapitating" or "severing" his earlier arguments into conflicting theses, like a many-headed Hydra (Eusebius, *Praep. ev.* 14.6.1). Diogenes Laertius appears to be more helpful in this context, suggesting that Arcesilaus deviated from Polemo and his Academic predecessors by conducting a "more contentious" mode of inquiry. That is to say, Arcesilaus was the "first to stir into motion the discourse handed down by Plato" (D.L. 4.28). From these sources, and the orality of his philosophical practice, it is at least clear that Arcesilaus evidently declined to follow his lover Crantor in the composition of exegetical commentary. In fact, in view of these snippets of testimony from Cicero, Diogenes Laertius, and Eusebius, it seems highly unlikely for Arcesilaus to defend or elaborate in oral argument anything like his own abiding interpretation of Plato's writings.

Sextus Empiricus, for his part, says that Arcesilaus's manner of argument and, more generally, his philosophical orientation have something in common with the investigations of the "skeptic," a term Sextus typically reserves (centuries after Arcesilaus's oral arguments were originally delivered) to designate Pyrrhonian philosophy. Prior to the introduction of technical Pyrrhonian terms, the Greek term σκέψις ordinarily meant "search" or "inquiry." It appears regularly in Plato in this less technical sense. In *Theaetetus*, for example, Plato uses the aorist infinitive, aorist imperative, aorist subjunctive, and future variants of the present middle/passive infinitive σκέπτεσθαι (144d9, 144e3, 145b3, 147a1, 148e2, 154e8, 157d3, 161d4, 165a4) to qualify and describe Socrates's mode of "cooperative inquiry" (κοινῇ σκεψώμεθα, 151e5). However, in Sextus Empiricus, the term denotes an "ability" to generate the suspension of belief, which is shadowed by

---

[4] Dorandi, *Filodemo*, 152–3, 59–62.

psychological tranquility (*PH.* 1.8). It is well known, but worth reiterating in this context, that there is no surviving testimony of Arcesilaus himself endorsing any sense of this term, or any other term, to characterize the form, method, or style of his oral investigations. In any case, attention to the conceptual differences between the technical and more pedestrian uses of the Greek σκέψις should steer historiographers away from assimilating the complexity of Arcesilaus's style of oral argument with the modes of argument explicated by Sextus as typically Pyrrhonian, modes that characteristically serve as a prelude to the psychological state of tranquility.[5]

Whereas Cicero's specification of the dispute between Arcesilaus and Zeno is informed by his genealogical understanding of the "new" Academy, Sextus Empiricus provides another kind of truncated perspective on the dispute. Sextus's account is informed by a Pyrrhonian way of conducting philosophical investigation (*PH.* 1.1). According to Sextus, Arcesilaus proceeded to propose, after having investigated Zeno's criterion of truth—extracting from the investigation of its premises (7.150–7) the anti-Stoic theses that bodies are ἀκατάληπτα ("inapprehensible") and that one ought to suspend assent about all [corporeal and incorporeal] things (ἐποχὴ περὶ πάντων)—a brief sketch of an account of how one might conceivably act without the regulation of the criterion. Sextus's testimony (*M.* 7.158) is limited to a clarification of the logical form and the conceptual content of Arcesilaus's argument against the Stoa. His Pyrrhonian perspective is perhaps most evident in the way that he isolates the logic and conceptual content of Arcesilaus's argument from its orality and dialogical context, and, most importantly, the legacy of this polemical practice of oral dialogue relative to the Old Academy. As a consequence of such isolation, Sextus's report should have limited evidentiary value for current historiographers. Sextus is, on my reconstruction, unable to conceptualize Arcesilaus's style of oral argument as a way of instigating interlocutors to consider a minimalist notion of right action, which is absolved from the metaphysical ambitions of a luxuriant Grand End theory. The Socratic style of Arcesilaus's reasoning effectively abandons the preceding pedagogical approach of Polemo and the metaphysical principles informing his Socratic approach to higher and lower goods, but ultimately one must look beyond Sextus and Cicero to specify this Academic novelty.

---

[5] On the connection in Cicero between arguing *contra omnia* (*De orat.* 3.80) and arguing *in utramque partem* (*De fin.* 5.10), see Castagnoli, "Hellenistic Academy," 185–7.

Bibliography

Adamson, Peter. "Review of John Dillon, *The Roots of Platonism*." *The International Journal of the Platonic Tradition* 14 (2020): 84–6.
Adorno, Theodor W. *Zur Metakritik der Erkenntnistheorie. Studien über Husserl und die phänomenologischen Antinomen*. Frankfurt am Main: Suhrkamp, 1971. Translated by Willis Domingo, *Against Epistemology: A Metacritique*. Cambridge: Polity Press, 2013.
Algra, Keimpe. "The Early Stoics on the Immobility and Coherence of the Cosmos." *Phronesis* 33, no. 2 (1988): 155–80.
Algra, Keimpe. "Hellenistic Philosophy and Some Science." *Phronesis* 48, no. 1 (2003): 71–88.
Algra, Keimpe. "Zeno of Citium: Some Notes and Two Case Studies." *Elenchos* 24, no. 1 (2003): 9–32.
Algra, Keimpe, Jonathan Barnes, Jaap Mansfeld, and Malcolm Schofield, eds. *The Cambridge History of Hellenistic Philosophy*. Cambridge: Cambridge University Press, 1999.
Allen, James. "Carneadean Argument in Cicero's Academic Books." In *Assent and Argument: Studies in Cicero's Academic Books*, edited by Brad Inwood and Jaap Mansfeld, 217–56. Leiden: Brill, 1997.
Allen, James. "Stoic Epistemology." In *A Companion to Epistemology*, 2nd ed., edited by Jonathan Dancy, Ernest Sosa, and Matthias Steup, 750–3. Oxford: Blackwell Publishing, 2010.
Althusser, Louis. *Pour Marx*, avec un avant-propos de Étienne Balibar. Paris: La Découverte, 2005. Translated by Ben Brewster, *For Marx*. London: Verso, 2005.
Annas, Julia. "Ethics in Stoic Philosophy." *Phronesis* 52, no. 1 (2007): 58–87.
Annas, Julia. *The Morality of Happiness*. Oxford: Oxford University Press, 1993.
Annas, Julia. "Stoic Epistemology." In *Epistemology: Companions to Ancient Thought* 1, edited by Stephen Everson, 184–203. Cambridge: Cambridge University Press, 1990.
Arnim von, Hans. "Arkesilaos von Pitane." In *Paulys Realencyclopädie der classischen Altertumswissenschaft*, edited by Georg Wissowa, 1164–8. Stuttgart: Alfred Druckenmuller, 1895.
Arnim von, Hans, ed. *Stoicorum Veterum Fragmenta*, 4 vols. Leipzig: Teubner, 1903–24.
Babut, Daniel. "Ἱστορία οἷον ὕλη φιλοσοφίας: histoire et réflexion morale dans l'œuvre de Plutarque." *Revue des Études Grecques* 88, fasc. 419–423 (1975): 206–19.
Bailey, D. T. J. "The Structure of Stoic Metaphysics." *Oxford Studies in Ancient Philosophy* 46 (2014): 253–309.

Barnes, Jonathan. "Medicine, experience and logic." In *Science and Speculation: Studies in Hellenistic Theory and Practice*, edited by Jonathan Barnes, Jacques Brunschwig, Myles F. Burnyeat, and Malcolm Schofield, 24–68. Cambridge: Cambridge University Press, 1982.

Bénatouïl, Thomas. "Force, fermeté, froid: la dimension physique de la vertu stoïcienne." *Philosophie Antique* 5 (2005): 5–30.

Bénatouïl, Thomas. "*Logos* et *scala naturae* dans le Stoïcisme de Zenon et Cleanthe." *Elenchos* 23, no. 2 (2003): 297–331.

Bénatouïl, Thomas. "Théophraste: les limites éthiques, psychologiques et cosmologiques de la contemplation." In *Theoria, Praxis and the Contemplative Life after Plato and Aristotle*, edited by Thomas Bénatouïl and Mauro Bonazzi, 17–40. Leiden: Brill, 2012.

Betegh, Gábor. "Cosmological Ethics in the 'Timaeus' and Early Stoicism." *Oxford Studies in Ancient Philosophy* 24 (2003): 273–302.

Bett, Richard, ed. *The Cambridge Companion to Ancient Scepticism*. Cambridge: Cambridge University Press, 2010.

Bett, Richard. "Carneades' *Pithanon*: A Reappraisal of Its Role and Status." *Oxford Studies in Ancient Philosophy* 7 (1989): 59–94.

Bett, Richard. "Socrates and Skepticism." In *A Companion to Socrates*, edited by Sara Ahbel-Rappe and Rachana Kamtekar, 299–312. Malden, MA: Wiley Blackwell, 2009.

Boeri, Marcelo. "Does Cosmic Nature Matter? Some Remarks on the Cosmological Aspects of Stoic Ethics." In *God and Cosmos in Stoicism*, edited by Ricardo Salles, 173–200. Oxford: Oxford University Press, 2009.

Bonazzi, Mauro. *Il Platonismo*. Turin: Einaudi, 2015.

Bonazzi, Mauro. "Plutarch on Pyrrhonists and Academics." *Oxford Studies in Ancient Philosophy* 43 (2012): 271–98.

Boys-Stones, George. "Antiochus' Metaphysics." In *The Philosophy of Antiochus*, edited by David Sedley, 220–36. Cambridge: Cambridge University Press, 2012.

Boys-Stones, George. "Plutarch on the Probable Principle of Cold: Epistemology and the *De primo frigido*." *The Classical Quarterly* 47, no. 1 (1997): 227–38.

Brandom, Robert. *Making It Explicit: Reasoning, Representing, and Discursive Commitment*. Cambridge, MA: Harvard University Press, 1994.

Brandom, Robert. *Tales of the Mighty Dead: Historical Essays in the Metaphysics of Intentionality*. Cambridge, MA: Harvard University Press, 2002.

Bréhier, Émile. *Histoire de la philosophie*, vol. 1 pt. 2. Paris: Presses Universitaires de France, 1961. Translated by Wade Baskin, *The History of Philosophy: The Hellenistic & Roman Age*. Chicago: University of Chicago Press, 1965.

Brennan, Tad. "Reasonable Impressions in Stoicism." *Phronesis* 41, no. 3 (1996): 318–41.

Brennan, Tad. *The Stoic Life: Emotions, Duties, and Fate*. Oxford: Oxford University Press, 2005.

Brennan, Tad. "Stoic Moral Psychology." In *The Cambridge Companion to the Stoics*, edited by Brad Inwood, 257–94. Cambridge: Cambridge University Press, 2003.

Brittain, Charles. "Arcesilaus." In *Stanford Encyclopedia of Philosophy* (Fall 2008 Edition), edited by Edward N. Zalta. https://plato.stanford.edu/archives/fall 2008/entries/arcesilaus/.

Brittain, Charles, trans. *Cicero: On Academic Scepticism*. Indianapolis, IN: Hackett Publishing Company, 2006.

Brittain, Charles. "Middle Platonists on Academic Scepticism." In *Greek and Roman Philosophy 100BC–200AD*, vol. 2, edited by R. W. Sharples and Richard Sorabji, 297–315. London: Institute of Classical Studies, 2007.

Brittain, Charles. *Philo of Larissa: The Last of the Academic Sceptics*. Oxford: Oxford University Press, 2001.

Brittain, Charles and John Palmer. "The New Academy's Appeals to the Presocratics." *Phronesis* 46, no. 1 (2001): 38–72.

Broadie, Sarah. *Ethics with Aristotle*. Oxford: Oxford University Press, 1991.

Brochard, Victor. *Les sceptiques grecs*. Paris, 1887.

Brouwer, René. *The Stoic Sage: The Early Stoics on Wisdom, Sagehood and Socrates*. Cambridge: Cambridge University Press, 2014.

Brunschwig, Jacques. "The Conjunctive Model." In *Papers in Hellenistic Philosophy*. Translated by Janet Lloyd, 72–91. Cambridge: Cambridge University Press, 1994.

Brunschwig, Jacques. "Epistemology." In *Greek Thought: A Guide to Classical Knowledge*, edited by Jacques Brunschwig and Geoffrey E. R. Lloyd with the collaboration of Pierre Pellegrin, translated by Catherine Porter, 72–93. Cambridge, MA: Harvard University Press, 2000.

Brunschwig, Jacques. "Introduction: The Beginnings of Hellenistic Epistemology." In Algra et al., *Cambridge History of Hellenistic Philosophy*, 229–59.

Brunschwig, Jacques. "On a Book-Title by Chrysippus: 'On the Fact that the Ancients Admitted Dialectic along with Demonstrations.'" *Oxford Studies in Ancient Philosophy*, Suppl. vol. (1991): 81–95.

Brunschwig, Jacques. "Stoic Metaphysics." In *The Cambridge Companion to the Stoics*, edited by Brad Inwood, 206–32. Cambridge: Cambridge University Press, 2003.

Brunschwig, Jacques. "Stoicism." In Brunschwig et al., *Greek Thought*, 977–96.

Brunschwig, Jacques and David N. Sedley. "Hellenistic Philosophy." In *The Cambridge Companion to Greek and Roman Philosophy*, edited by David N. Sedley, 151–83. Cambridge: Cambridge University Press, 1983.

Burnyeat, Myles F. "Antipater and Self-Refutation: Elusive Arguments in Cicero's *Academica*." In Inwood et al., *Assent and Argument*, 277–310.

Burnyeat, Myles F. "Idealism and Greek Philosophy: What Descartes Saw and Berkeley Missed." *The Philosophical Review* 91, no. 1 (1982): 3–40.

Burnyeat, Myles F. "The Origins of Non-Deductive Inference." In Barnes et al., *Science and Speculation*, 193–238.

Cappello, Orazio. *The School of Doubt: Skepticism, History and Politics in Cicero's Academica*. Leiden: Brill, 2019.

Castagnoli, Luca. "Dialectic in the Hellenistic Academy." In *Dialectic After Plato and Aristotle*, edited by Thomas Bénatouïl and Katerina Ierodiakonou, 168–217. Cambridge: Cambridge University Press, 2019.

Castagnoli, Luca. "How Dialectical was Stoic Dialectic?" In *Ancient Models of Mind: Studies in Human and Divine Rationality*, edited by Andrea Nightingale and David Sedley, 153–79. Cambridge: Cambridge University Press, 2010.

Caston, Victor. "Something and Nothing: The Stoics on Concepts and Universals." *Oxford Studies in Ancient Philosophy* 17 (1999): 145–213.

Chlup, Radek. *Proclus: An Introduction*. Cambridge: Cambridge University Press, 2012.

Clarke, Desmond. "The Epistemology of Descartes." In *Epistemology: The Key Thinkers*, edited by Stephen Hetherington, 90–110. London: Continuum, 2012.

Colvin, Matthew. "Heraclitus and Material Flux in Stoic Psychology." *Oxford Studies in Ancient Philosophy* 28 (2005): 257–72.

Cooper, John M. "Eudaimonism and the Appeal to Nature in the Morality of Happiness: Comments on Julia Annas, *The Morality of Happiness*." *Philosophy and Phenomenological Research* 55, no. 3 (1995): 587–98.

Couissin, Pierre. "Le Stoïcisme de la Nouvelle Académie." *Revue d'historie de la Philosophie* 3 (1929): 241–76. Translated by Jennifer Barnes and Myles F. Burnyeat, "The Stoicism of the New Academy." In *The Skeptical Tradition*, edited by Myles F. Burnyeat, 31–63. Berkeley: University of California Press, 1983.

Diès, Auguste, ed. *Platon, Œuvres Complètes*, t. VIII. 2e partie, Théétète. Paris: Les belles lettres, 2003.

Dillon, John. *The Heirs of Plato: A Study of the Old Academy (347-274 BC)*. Oxford: Oxford University Press, 2003.

Dillon, John. "The Origins of Platonists' Dogmatism." *ΣΧΟΛΗ* 1, no. 1 (2007): 25–37.

Dillon, John. "A Platonist *Ars Amatoria*." *The Classical Quarterly* 44, no. 2 (1994): 387–92.

Dillon, John. "Polemo, *grosser Schatten* of the Old Academy." In *Plato's Academy: Its Workings and Its History*, edited by Paul Kalligas, Chloe Balla, Effie Baziotopoulou-Valavani, and Vassilis Karasmanis, 188–99. Cambridge: Cambridge University Press, 2020.

Dillon, John. "Speusippus in Iamblichus." *Phronesis* 29 (1984): 325–32.

Dillon, John. "Speusippus on Pleasure." In *Polyhistor: Studies in the History and Historiography of Ancient Philosophy Presented to Jaap Mansfeld on His Sixtieth Birthday*, edited by Keimpe Algra, P. W. van der Horst, David T. Runia, 99–114. Leiden: Brill, 1996.

Dillon, John. "Theories of Knowledge in the Old Academy." *Lexicon Philosophicum: International Journal for the History of Texts and Ideas*, Special Issue (2018): 43–51.

Dorandi, Tiziano, ed. *Diogenes Laertius: The Lives of Eminent Philosophers*. Cambridge: Cambridge University Press, 2013.

Dorandi, Tiziano, ed. *Filodemo. Storia dei filosofici greci e latini. Platone e L'Academia* (PHerc. 1021 e 164). Naples: Bibliopolis, 1991.

Dorandi, Tiziano. "Le Vie de Polémon." *Aitia* 5 (2015). http://aitia.revues.org/1183.
Festa, Nicola, ed. *Iamblichus. De communi mathematica scientia*. Leipzig, 1891.
Fortenbaugh, William W. "Arius, Theophrastus and the *Eudemian Ethics*." In *On Stoic and Peripatetic Ethics: The Works of Arius Didymus*, Rutgers University Studies in Classical Humanities, vol. 1, 203–23. New Brunswick, NJ: Transactions Publishers, 1983.
Fortenbaugh, William W., ed. *Theophrastus of Eresus, Commentary Volume 6.1: Sources on Ethics (with contribution on the Arabic material by Dimitri Gutas)*. Leiden: Brill, 2011.
Frede, Michael. "Doxographie, historiographie philosophique et historiographie historique de la philosophie." *Revue de Métaphysique et de Morale* 97, no. 3 (1992): 311–25.
Frede, Michael. "Introduction." In *Rationality in Greek Thought*, edited by Michael Frede and Gisela Striker, 1–28. Oxford: Clarendon Press, 1996.
Frede, Michael. "The Sceptic's Two Kinds of Assent and the Question of the Possibility of Knowledge." In *The Original Sceptics*, edited by Myles F. Burnyeat and Michael Frede, 127–51. Indianapolis, IN: Hackett Publishing Company, 1997.
Frede, Michael. "The Sceptics." In *Routledge History of Philosophy*, vol. 2. *From Aristotle to Augustine*, edited by David Furley, 253–86. London: Routledge, 1999.
Frede, Michael. "Stoic Epistemology." In Algra et al., *Cambridge History of Hellenistic Philosophy*, 295–322.
Gabriel, Markus. "Zum Außenweltproblem in der Antike. Sextus' Destruktion des Repräsentationalismus und die skeptische Begründung des Idealismus bei Plotin." *Bochumer Philosophisches Jahrbuch für Antike und Mittelalter* 12 (2007): 15–43.
Gabriel, Markus. *An den Grenzen der Erkenntnistheorie. Die notwendige Endlichkeit des objektiven Wissen als Lektion des Skeptizismus*. Freiburg: Aber, 2008.
Gerson, Lloyd P. *Ancient Epistemology*. Cambridge: Cambridge University Press, 2009.
Gerson, Lloyd P. *Aristotle and Other Platonists*. Ithaca, NY: Cornell University Press, 2005.
Gerson, Lloyd P. *From Plato to Platonism*. Ithaca, NY: Cornell University Press, 2014.
Gerson, Lloyd P. "Platonism in Aristotle's Ethics." *Oxford Studies in Ancient Philosophy* 27 (2004): 217–48.
Gerson, Lloyd P. "Plotinus and the Platonic Response to Stoicism." In *The Routledge Handbook of the Stoic Tradition*, edited by John Sellars, 44–55. London: Routledge, 2016.
Gerson, Lloyd P. "What Is Platonism?" *Journal of the History of Philosophy* 43 (3): 253–76.
Gigante, Marcello. "Polemonis Academici Fragmenta." *Rendiconti della Accademia di Archeologia, Lettere e Belle Arti di Napoli* 51 (1976): 91–144.
Gigon, Olof. "Zur Geschichte der sogenannten Neuen Akademie." *Museum Helveticum* 1, no. 1 (1944): 47–64.

Glucker, John. *Antiochus and the Late Academy*. Göttingen: Vandenhoeck & Ruprecht, 1978.

Görler, Woldemar. "Älterer Pyrrhonismus, Jüngere Akademie, Antiochus aus Askalon, § 47 Arkesilaos." In *Die Philosophie der Antike 4: Die hellenistische Philosophie*, edited by Hellmut Flashar, 786–828. Basel: Schwabe, 1994.

Görler, Woldemar. "Cicero und die 'Schule des Aristoteles.'" In *Kleine Schriften zur hellenistisch-römischen Philosophie*, edited by Christoph Catrein, Philosophia Antiqua, v. 95, 194–211. Leiden: Brill, 2004.

Görler, Woldemar. "Review of *The Philosophy of Antiochus*, edited by David Sedley." *Elenchos* 33 (2012): 376–83.

Gourinat, Jean-Baptiste. "L'épistémologie stoïcienne." *Lexicon Philosophicum: International Journal for the History of Texts and Ideas*, Special Issue (2018): 123–44.

Gourinat, Jean-Baptiste. "Stoic Dialectic and Its Objects." In *Dialectic after Plato and Aristotle*, edited by Thomas Bénatouïl and Katerina Ierodiakonou, 134–67. Cambridge: Cambridge University Press, 2019.

Gourinat, Jean-Baptiste. "The Stoics on Matter and Prime Matter." In *God and Cosmos in Stoicism*, edited by Ricardo Salles, 46–70. Oxford: Oxford University Press, 2009.

Groarke, Leo. *Greek Skepticism: Anti-Realist Trends in Ancient Thought*. Montreal: McGill-Queen's University Press, 1990.

Hadot, Ilsetraut. "Getting to Goodness: Reflections on Chapter 10 of Brad Inwood, *Reading Seneca*." In *Seneca Philosophicus*, edited by Jula Wildberger and Marcia L. Colish, 9–42. Berlin: Walter De Gruyter, 2014.

Hadot, Pierre. "Les divisions des parties de la philosophie dans l'Antiquité." *Museum Helveticum* 36 (1979): 201–23.

Hadot, Pierre. "Philosophie, discours philosophiques, et divisions de la philosophie chez les Stoïciens." *Revue Internationale de Philosophie* 45, no. 178.3 (1991): 205–19.

Hadot, Pierre. "Zur Vorgeschichte des Begriffs 'Existenz': ὑπάρχειν bei den Stoikern." *Archiv für Begriffsgeschichte* 13 (1969): 115–27.

Hankinson, R. J. *The Sceptics*. London: Routledge, 1995.

Hankinson, R. J. "Stoic Epistemology." In *The Cambridge Companion to the Stoics*, edited by Brad Inwood, 59–84. Cambridge: Cambridge University Press, 2003.

Heidegger, Martin. "Die onto-theo-logische Verfassung der Metaphysik." In *Identität und Differenz* (GA 11), edited by Friedrich-Wilhelm von Herrmann, 51–79. Frankfurt am Main: Vittorio Klostermann, 2006. Translated by Joan Stambaugh, "The Onto-Theo-Logical Constitution of Metaphysics." In *Identity and Difference*, 42–74. Chicago: University of Chicago Press, 2002.

Heidegger, Martin. *Sein und Zeit*. Tübingen: Max Niemeyer Verlag, 1967. Translated by Joan Stambaugh, revised and with a foreword by Dennis J. Schmidt as *Being and Time*. Albany: SUNY Press, 2010.

Hirzel, Rudolf. *Untersuchungen zu Cicero's Philosophischen Schriften*, t. 3. Leipzig, 1883.

Horky, Phillip Sidney. *Plato and Pythagoreanism*. Oxford: Oxford University Press, 2013.

Horky, Phillip Sidney. "Speusippus and Xenocrates on the Pursuit and Ends of Philosophy." In *Brill's Companion to the Reception of Plato in Antiquity*, edited by Harold Tarrant, Danielle A. Layne, Dirk Baltzly and François Renaud, 29–45. Leiden: Brill, 2018.

Ierodiakonou, Katerina. "The Stoic Division of Philosophy." *Phronesis* 38, no. 1 (1993): 57–74.

Inwood, Brad. *Ethics and Human Action in Early Stoicism*. Oxford: Clarendon Press, 1985.

Inwood, Brad. "Review of J. Annas' *The Morality of Happiness*." *Ancient Philosophy* 15, no. 2 (1995): 647–65.

Inwood, Brad. "Rules and Reasoning in Stoic Ethics." In *Topics in Stoic Philosophy*, edited by Katerina Ierodiakonou, 95–127. Oxford: Clarendon Press, 1999.

Inwood, Brad. *Stoicism: A Very Short Introduction*. Oxford: Oxford University Press, 2018.

Inwood, Brad and Jaap Mansfeld, eds. *Assent and Argument: Studies in Cicero's Academic Books*. Leiden: Brill, 1997.

Inwood, Brad and Lloyd P. Gerson, eds. *The Stoics Reader: Selected Writings and Testimonia*. Indianapolis, IN: Hackett Publishing Company, 2008.

Ioppolo, Anna Maria. "Arcesilaus." In *Skepticism: From Antiquity to the Present*, edited by Diego Machuca and Baron Reed, 36–50. London: Bloomsbury, 2017.

Ioppolo, Anna Maria. "Arcésilas dans le *Lucullus* de Cicéron." *Revue de Métaphysique et de Morale* 57, no. 1 (2008): 21–44.

Ioppolo, Anna Maria. *Opinione e scienza: il dibattito tra Stoici e Academici nel III e nel II secolo a.C.* Naples: Bibliopolis, 1986.

Ioppolo, Anna Maria. "Presentation and Assent: A Physical and Cognitive Problem in Early Stoicism." *The Classical Quarterly* 40 (1990): 433–49.

Ioppolo, Anna Maria. *La testimonianza di Sesto Empirico sull'Accademia scettica*. Naples: Bibliopolis, 2009.

Isnardi Parente, Margherita. "L'Accademia antica e le sue vicende filosofiche." *Rivista di Storia della Filosofia* 53, no. 2 (1998): 215–34.

Isnardi Parente, Margherita. *Introduzione a Lo Stoicismo Ellenistico*. Rome: Editori Laterza, 1993.

Isnardi Parente, Margherita, ed. *Speusippo: Frammenti*. Naples: La Scuola di Platone I, 1980. http://rmcisadu.let.uniroma1.it/isnardi/fronte.htm

Isnardi Parente, Margherita, ed. *Senocrate e Ermodoro: Testimonianze e frammenti*, revised by Tiziano Dorandi. Pisa: Edizioni della Normale, 2012.

Khamara, Edward J. "Indiscernibles and the Absolute Theory of Space and Time." *Studia Leibnitiana*, Bd. 20, H. 2 (1988): 140–54.

Kidd, Ian G. "Posidonius and Logic." In *Les stoïciens et leur logique*, edited by Jacques Brunschwig, 273–84. Paris: J. Vrin, 2006.

Kirkland, Sean. *The Ontology of Socratic Questioning in Plato's Early Dialogues*. Albany: State University of New York, 2012.

Krämer, Hans Joachim. "Die Ältere Akademie." In *Die Philosophie der Antike 3: Ältere Akademie, Aristoteles, Peripatos*, edited by Hellmut Flashar, 1–165. Basel/Stuttgart: Schwabe, 1983.

Krämer, Hans Joachim. "Grundbegriffe akademischer Dialektik in den biologischen Schriften von Aristoteles und Theophrast." *Rheinisches Museum für Philologie* 111, no. 4 (1968): 293–333.

Krämer, Hans Joachim. *Plato and the Foundations of Metaphysics: A Work on the Theory of the Principles and Unwritten Doctrines of Plato with a Collection of the Fundamental Documents*, edited and translated by John R. Catan. Albany: State University of New York Press, 1990.

Krämer, Hans Joachim. *Platonismus und hellenistische Philosophie*. Berlin: De Gruyter, 1971.

Krämer, Hans Joachim. *Der Ursprung der Geistmetaphysik: Untersuchungen zur Geschichte des Platonismus zwischen Platon und Plotin*. Amsterdam: Schippers, 1964.

Lachterman, David Rapport. *The Ethics of Geometry: A Genealogy of Modernity*. New York: Routledge, 1989.

Lampe, Kurt. "Rationality, Eros, and Daemonic Influence in the Platonic 'Theages' and the Academy of Polemo and Crates." *American Journal of Philology* 134, no. 3 (2013): 383–424.

Lévy, Carlos. *Cicero Academicus. Recherches sur les Académiques et sur la philosophie cicéronienne*. Rome: École Français de Rome, 1992.

Lévy, Carlos. "La Nouvelle Académie a-t-elle été antiplatonicienne?." In *Contre Platon I. Le platonisme dévoilé*, edited by Monique Dixsaut, 139–56. Paris: Vrin, 1993.

Lévy, Carlos. "Les petits Académiciens: Lacyde, Charmadas, Métrodore de Stratonice." In *L' eredità platonica: studi sul platonismo da Arcesilao a Proclo*, edited by Mauro Bonazzi and Vincenza Celluprica, 53–77. Naples: Bibliopolis, 2005.

Lévy, Carlos. *Les philosophies hellénistiques*. Paris: Librairie Générale Français, 1997.

Lévy, Carlos. "Platon, Arcésilas, Carnéade, réponse à J. Annas." *Revue de Métaphysique et de Morale* 2 (1990): 293–306.

Lévy, Carlos. "Scepticisme et dogmatisme dans l'Académie: l'ésotérisme d'Arcésilas." *Revue des Études latines* 56 (1978): 335–48.

Locke, John. *An Essay Concerning Human Understanding*, edited by Peter H. Nidditch. Oxford: Clarendon Press, 1975.

Long, Anthony A. "Dialectic and the Stoic Sage." In *Stoic Studies*, 85–106. Berkeley: University of California Press, 1996.

Long, Anthony A. "Diogenes Laertius: Life of Arcesilaus." *Elenchos* 7, Fasc. 1–2 (1986): 431–49.

Long, Anthony A. "The Logical Basis of Stoic Ethics." In *Stoic Studies*, 134–55.

Long, Anthony A. "Socrates in Later Greek Philosophy." In *The Cambridge Companion to Socrates*, edited by Donald R. Morrison, 355–80. Cambridge: Cambridge University Press, 2010.

Long, Anthony A. "Zeno's Epistemology and Plato's *Theaetetus*." In Long, *From Epicurus to Epictetus: Studies in Hellenistic and Roman Philosophy*, edited by Anthony A. Long, 223–35. Oxford: Clarendon Press, 2006.

Long, Anthony A. and David Sedley. *The Hellenistic Philosophers*, 2 Vols. Cambridge: Cambridge University Press, 1987.

Machuca, Diego E. "Scepticisme, *apraxia*, et rationalité." In *Les raisons du doute: études sur le scepticisme antique*, edited by Diego E. Machuca and Stéphane Marchand, 53–87. Paris: Classiques Garnier, 2019.

Maconi, Henry [Jonathan Barnes]. "*Nova Non Philosophandi Philosophia*: A review of Anna Maria Ioppolo, *Opinione e Scienza*." *Oxford Studies in Ancient Philosophy* 6 (1988): 231–53.

Mansfeld, Jaap. "*Techne*: A New Fragment of Chrysippus." *Greek, Roman, and Byzantine Studies* 24 (1983): 57–65.

Mansfeld, Jaap. "Zeno and the Unity of Philosophy." *Phronesis* 48, no. 2 (2003): 116–31.

Mansfeld, Jaap. "Zeno of Citium: Critical Observations on a Recent Study." *Mnemosyne* 31 (1978): 134–78.

Mansfeld, Jaap and David T. Runia, eds. *Aëtiana: The Method and Intellectual Context of a Doxographer*, Vol. 1: *The Sources*. Leiden: Brill, 1997.

McDowell, John. *Mind and World*. Cambridge, MA: Harvard University Press, 1998.

Menn, Stephen. "The Stoic Theory of Categories." *Oxford Studies in Ancient Philosophy* 17 (1999): 215–47.

Merlan, Philip. *From Platonism to Neoplatonism*. Third Edition. The Hague: Martinus Nijhoff, 1968.

Mette, H. J. "Zwei Akademiker heute: Krantor von Soli und Arkesilaos von Pitane." *Lustrum* 26 (1984): 7–93.

Moore, George Edward. *Some Main Problems of Philosophy*. London: Routledge, 2013. First published 1953 by George Allen & Unwin Ltd.

Mouraviev, Serge. "Zeno's Cosmology and the Presumption of Innocence." *Phronesis* 50, no. 3 (2005): 232–49.

Nawar, Tamer. "The Stoic Account of Apprehension." *Philosopher's Imprint* 14, no. 29 (2014): 1–21.

Pasnau, Robert. *After Certainty: A History of Our Epistemic Ideals and Illusions*. Oxford: Oxford University Press, 2017.

Perin, Casey. "Academic Arguments for the Indiscernibility Thesis." *Pacific Philosophical Quarterly* 86, no. 4 (2005): 493–517.

Perin, Casey. "Descartes and the Legacy of Ancient Skepticism." In *A Companion to Descartes*, edited by Janet Broughton and John Carriero, 52–65. Oxford: Blackwell Publishing, 2008.

Perin, Casey. "Making Sense of Arcesilaus." *Oxford Studies in Ancient Philosophy* 45 (2013): 313–40.

Perin, Casey. "Stoic Epistemology and the Limits of Externalism." *Ancient Philosophy* 25, no. 2 (2005): 383–401.

Philippson, Robert. "Das 'erste Naturgemässe." *Philologus* 87, no. 4 (1932): 445–66.
Pohlenz, Max. *Grundfragen der stoischen Philosophie*. Göttingen: Vandenhoeck & Ruprecht, 1940.
Pohlenz, Max. *Die Stoa: Geschichte einer geistigen Bewegung*. Göttingen: Vandenhoeck & Ruprecht, 1959.
Quine, W. V. O. "Three Indeterminacies." In *Perspectives on Quine*, edited by Robert Barrett and Roger Gibson, 1–16. Oxford: Blackwell Publishing, 1990.
Reed, Baron. "The Stoics' Account of the Cognitive Impression." *Oxford Studies in Ancient Philosophy* 23 (2002): 148–80.
Rees, D. A. "Bipartition of the Soul in the Early Academy." *Journal of Hellenic Studies* 77, no. 1 (1957): 112–18.
Reid, James S., ed. *The Academica of Cicero*. London, 1874.
Reid, James S., ed. *M. Tulli Ciceronis, Academica*. London, 1885.
Reinhardt, Tobias. "Cicero and Augustine on Grasping the True." In *Philosophie in Rom – Römische Philosophie?: Kultur-, literatur- und philosophiegeschichtliche Perspektiven*. Beiträge zur Altertumskunde, vol. 358, edited by Gernot Michael Müller and Fosca Marinani Zini, 305–23. Berlin: De Gruyter, 2017.
Reinhardt, Tobias. "To See and to Be Seen: On Vision and Perception in Lucretius and Cicero." In *Roman Reflections: Studies in Latin Philosophy*, edited by Gareth D. Williams and Katharina Volk, 63–90. Oxford: Oxford University Press, 2016.
Reydams-Schils, Gretchen. "The Academy, the Stoics, and Cicero on Plato's 'Timaeus.'" In *Plato and the Stoics*, edited by A. G. Long, 29–58. Cambridge: Cambridge University Press, 2013.
Reydams-Schils, Gretchen. *Demiurge and Providence: Stoic and Platonist Readings of Plato's* Timaeus. Turnhout: Brepols, 1999.
Rorty, Richard. "The Historiography of Philosophy: Four Genres." In *Philosophy in History: Essays on the Historiography of Philosophy*, edited by Richard Rorty, J. B. Schneewind, and Quentin Skinner, 49–75. Cambridge: Cambridge University Press, 1984.
Schaffer, Jonathan. "The Action of the Whole." *Proceedings of the Aristotelian Society*, Supp. Vol. 87 (2013): 67–87.
Schwab, Whitney. "Skeptical Defenses Against the Inaction Objection." In *The Routledge Handbook of Hellenistic Philosophy*, edited by Kelly Arenson, 184–97. New York: Routledge, 2020.
Schibli, Hermann S. "Xenocrates' Daemons and the Irrational Soul." *The Classical Quarterly* 43, no. 1 (May 1993): 143–67.
Schofield, Malcolm. "Academic Epistemology." In Algra et al., *Cambridge History of Hellenistic Philosophy*, 323–51.
Schofield, Malcolm. "Antiochus on Social Virtue." In *The Philosophy of Antiochus*, edited by David Sedley, 173–87. Cambridge: Cambridge University Press, 2012.
Schürmann, Reiner. "Adventures of the Double Negation: On Richard Bernstein's Call for Anti-Anti-Humanism." *Praxis International* 3 (1985): 283–91.

Sedley, David N. "Antiochus as Historian of Philosophy." In *The Philosophy of Antiochus*, edited by David N. Sedley, 80–103. Cambridge: Cambridge University Press, 2012.

Sedley, David N. "Hellenistic Physics and Metaphysics." In Algra et al., *Cambridge History of Hellenistic Philosophy*, 353–411.

Sedley, David N. "The Origins of Stoic God." In *Traditions of Theology: Studies in Hellenistic Theology, Its Background and Aftermath*, edited by Dorothea Frede and Andre Laks, 41–83. Leiden: Brill, 2002.

Sedley, David N. "The Stoic Criterion of Identity." *Phronesis* 27 (1982): 255–75.

Sedley, David N. "The Stoic-Platonist Debate on *Kathêkonta*." In *Topics in Stoic Philosophy*, edited by Katerina Ierodiakonou, 128–52. Oxford: Clarendon Press, 1996.

Sedley, David N. "Three Platonist Interpretations of the 'Theaetetus.'" In *Form and Argument in Late Plato*, edited by Christopher Gill and M. M. McCabe, 79–103. Oxford: Clarendon Press, 1999.

Sellars, John. *The Art of Living: The Stoics on the Nature and Function of Philosophy*, 2nd ed. London: Bloomsbury, 2003.

Sellars, John. *Hellenistic Philosophy*. Oxford: Oxford University Press, 2018.

Sextus Empiricus. *Against the Logicians*. Translated and edited by Richard Bett. Cambridge: Cambridge University Press, 2005.

Sharples, R. W. *Stoics, Epicureans and Sceptics: An Introduction to Hellenistic Philosophy*. London: Routledge, 1996.

Shields, Christopher J. "Socrates among the Skeptics." In *The Socratic Movement*, edited by Paul Vander Waerdt, 341–66. Ithaca, NY: Cornell University Press, 1994.

Shogry, Simon. "Creating a Mind Fit for Truth: The Role of Expertise in the Stoic Account of the Kataleptic Impression." *Ancient Philosophy* 38, no. 2 (2018): 357–81.

Smyth, Herbert Weir. *Greek Grammar*, revised by Gordon M. Messing. Cambridge, MA: Harvard University Press, 1956.

Snyder, Charles E. "Arcesilaus and the Ontology of Stoic Cognition." *The Review of Metaphysics* 73, no. 3 (2020): 455–93.

Snyder, Charles E. "On the Teaching of Ethics from Polemo to Arcesilaus." *Études platoniciennes* 14 (2018). https://doi.org/10.4000/etudesplatoniciennes.1260.

Sparshott, F. E. "Zeno on Art: Anatomy of a Definition." In *The Stoics*, edited by John M. Rist, 273–90. Berkeley: University of California Press, 1978.

Spinelli, Emidio. "Ancient Stoicism, 'Robust Epistemology', and Moral Philosophy." In *Thinking about Causes: From Greek Philosophy to Modern Physics*, edited by Peter Machamer and Gereon Wolters, 37–46. Pittsburgh: University of Pittsburgh, 2007.

Stenzel, Julius. "Speusippos." In *Paulys Realencyclopädie der classischen Altertumswissenschaft* 3, A 2 (1929): 1636–69.

Stojanović, Pavle. "Epictetus and Moral Apprehensive Impressions in Stoicism." In *Epictetus: His Continuing Influence and Contemporary Relevance*, edited by Dane R. Gordon and David B. Suits, 165–95. Rochester: RIT Press, 2014.

Stojanović, Pavle. "Zeno of Citium's Causal Theory of Apprehensive Appearances." *Ancient Philosophy* 39, no. 1 (2019): 151–74.

Striker, Gisela. "*Ataraxia*: Happiness as Tranquility." *Monist* 73 (1990): 97–110.

Striker, Gisela. "On the Difference Between the Pyrrhonists and the Academics." In *Essays on Hellenistic Epistemology and Ethics*, 135–49. Cambridge: Cambridge University Press, 1996.

Striker, Gisela. "Κριτήριον τῆς ἀληθείας." In *Essays on Hellenistic Epistemology and Ethics*, 22–76.

Striker, Gisela. "The Problem of the Criterion." In *Essays on Hellenistic Epistemology and Ethics*, 150–65.

Striker, Gisela. "Sceptical Strategies." In *Essays on Hellenistic Epistemology and Ethics*, 92–115.

Tarán, Leonardo, ed. *Speusippus of Athens: A Critical Study with a Collection of the Related Texts and Commentary*. Leiden: Brill, 1981.

Tarrant, Harold. "Improvement by Love: From Aeschines to the Old Academy." In *Alcibiades and the Socratic Lover-Educator*, edited by Marguerite Johnson and Harold Tarrant, 147–63. London: Bristol Classical Press, 2012.

Tarrant, Harold. "Piecing Together Polemo." *Mediterranean Archaeology* 19/20 (2006/7): 225–32.

Tarrant, Harold. "Socratic *Synousia*: A Post-Platonic Myth." *Journal of the History of Philosophy* 43, no. 2 (2005): 131–55.

Thorsrud, Harald. "Arcesilaus: Socratic Skepticism in Plato's Academy." *Lexicon Philosophicum: International Journal for the History of Texts and Ideas*, Special Issue (2018): 195–220.

Thorsrud, Harald. "Arcesilaus and Carneades." In Bett, *Cambridge Companion to Ancient Scepticism*, 58–80.

Thorsrud, Harald. "Carneades." In *Skepticism: From Antiquity to the Present*, edited by Diego E. Machuca and Baron Reed, 51–66. London: Bloomsbury, 2018.

Trabattoni, Franco. "Arcesilao Platonico?" In *L'eredità platonica: studi sul platonismo da Arcesilao a Proclo*, edited by Mauro Bonazzi and Vincenza Celluprica, 13–50. Naples: Bibliopolis, 2005.

Tsouni, Georgia. "Antiochus on Contemplation and the Happy Life." In *The Philosophy of Antiochus*, edited by David Sedley, 131–50. Cambridge: Cambridge University Press, 2012.

Vezzoli, Simone, ed. *Arcesilao di Pitane: l'origine del Platonismo neoaccademico*. Turnhout: Brepols, 2016.

Vogt, Katja Maria. "The Hellenistic Academy." In *The Routledge Companion to Ancient Philosophy*, edited by James Warren and Frisbee Sheffield, 1142–73. New York: Routledge, 2014.

Vogt, Katja Maria. *Law, Reason and the Cosmic City: Political Philosophy in the Early Stoa*. Oxford: Oxford University Press, 2008.

Vogt, Katja Maria. "Sons of the Earth: Are the Stoics Metaphysical Brutes?" *Phronesis* 54, no. 2 (2009): 136–54.
Warren, James. "Aristotle on Speusippus on Eudoxus on Pleasure." *Oxford Studies in Ancient Philosophy* 36 (2009): 249–81.
White, Nicholas P. "Plato's Metaphysical Epistemology." In *The Cambridge Companion to Plato*, edited by Richard Kraut, 277–310. Cambridge: Cambridge University Press, 1992.
Williams, Bernard. *Descartes: The Project of Pure Enquiry*. London: Routledge, 2005.
Williams, Bernard. "Descartes and the Historiography of Philosophy." In *The Senses of the Past: Essays in the History of Philosophy*, edited and with an introduction by Myles F. Burnyeat, 257–64. Princeton, NJ: Princeton University Press, 2006.
Wittgenstein, Ludwig. *Tractatus Logico-Philosophicus*, translated by D. F. Pears and B. F. McGuinness. London: Routledge and Kegan Paul, 1961.
Woleński, Jan. "The History of Epistemology." In *Handbook of Epistemology*, edited by Ilkka Niiniluoto, Matti Sintonen, and Jan Woleński, 3–54. Dordrecht: Springer, 2004.
Zeller, Eduard. *Die Philosophie der Griechen in ihrer geschichtlichen Entwicklung*, pt. 3, vol. 1, 5th ed. Leipzig: O. R. Reisland, 1923.

Index of Subject

absolute conception of reality 19, 19 n.36, 22, 65, 65 n.19, 98, 165, 170, 182
absolute difference 19, 65–6, 82, 99
Academy
  early Hellenistic 23, 25, 133, 137, 141–2, 180–1
  New 9 n.21, 10, 164, 182–3, 186–8
  Old 22–4, 24 n.41, 34, 38, 133, 135–7, 135 n.3, 139, 143–4, 146–7, 148 n.23, 150–9, 152 n.31, 162 n.44, 164–80, 164 n.48, 175 n.60, 182–3, 186, 188
  and Peripatos 30, 38, 143, 147, 151–4, 159, 164–9, 171, 173–7, 182
Adorno, Theodor W. 19, 19 n.35
ἀκαταληψία (inapprehensibility) 7–12, 7 n.17, 9 n.21, 11 n.23, 18, 20, 22, 24, 53, 72–3, 72 n.28, 72 n.30, 77, 81, 84–5, 84 nn.45–6, 88–90, 94–7, 94 n.62, 102–3, 121–2, 127, 129, 132, 181–2
Annas, Julia 40 n.30, 52, 52 n.50, 58 n.6, 116 nn.23–4, 118, 118 n.26
Antiochus of Ascalon 28 n.3, 95, 139, 143, 143 n.14, 152, 152 n.31, 154, 158–9, 168, 171–2, 171 n.55, 173 n.56, 175, 175 n.60, 182
apprehension (κατάληψις) 1, 5–7, 5 n.14, 7 n.17, 11, 15–19, 22, 45–7, 55–6, 57 n.4, 58, 60 n.11, 61–2, 64, 66, 69–70, 71 n.26, 72–3, 72 n.30, 75, 81, 84, 88–90, 88 n.53, 92 n.59, 94, 96–100, 104–8, 112, 114–16, 120–1, 129–30, 132, 181
  causal conception 7–10, 12, 15, 24–5, 36 n.25, 46, 55–9, 58 n.6, 64 n.18, 64–5, 70, 77, 80–2, 85 n.46, 93–4, 96, 99–101, 103–4, 110, 119–21, 124, 128
  non-apprehension 11–14

appropriate action
  Grand End account 22, 107–8, 128–9, 188
  perfect and imperfect 21–2, 31, 101–2, 107–9, 109 n.15, 112–14, 120, 130
  revised notion 23–4, 101–3, 131, 182
ἀπραξία (inaction) 17–18, 21, 103, 103 n.4, 121–3, 127, 182
Arcesilaus
  ad hominem 14, 131 n.45, 182
  against Stoic ethics 5–6, 101–3, 121, 125, 130, 135
  against Stoic metaphysics 7, 9, 10 n.22, 16–18, 23, 25, 27–8, 46, 68–70, 71 n.26, 76–90, 100, 122, 127, 129, 132, 181–2 (see also indiscernibility arguments)
  against Stoic nature 17–18, 97, 121, 123–5
  critical epistemology 5–6, 13–15
  as epistemological skeptic 13–14, 17, 49
  novelty 24, 135 n.2, 136, 137 n.7, 145, 164, 183, 188
  right action 22, 30, 102–3, 102 n.2, 129–32, 188
  Socratic revival 22, 24, 24 n.41, 131–3, 135, 181, 183–4
Aristotle 28, 28 n.3, 34, 36 n.24, 38, 39 n.29, 52, 61 n.14, 138–9, 138 n.9, 144, 144 n.17, 146, 148–9, 153–4, 153 n.32, 154 n.33, 158–79, 159 n.38, 161 n.42, 162 nn.44–5, 164 n.48, 173 n.56, 175 n.59, 179 n.61, 181, 183–4
assent
  faculty or power 2 n.3, 9, 11–12, 17–18, 21, 27, 56–8, 60–1, 62 n.15, 63 n.16, 65, 71–5, 80–1, 84 n.46, 85–90, 87 n.52, 97–9, 102, 105–8, 112, 116, 119–21, 126, 128–30

Index of Subject

infallible 9, 60, 65, 67, 75, 80, 83–4, 84 n.45, 87–8, 126
  of sage/wise person 85–7, 86 n.50, 110 n.17, 188 (*see also* ἐποχὴ περὶ πάντων ("suspension of assent about all things"))
  system 22, 68, 108, 110
  weak assent 15 n.30
autoexplicable 21, 33, 44, 167

bipolarity, *see under* nature
Brandom, Robert 13 n.27, 46 n.44, 49 n.47, 58 n.8, 60 n.12
Brittain, Charles 1 n.1, 2 n.3, 11 n.23, 13 n.25, 15 n.29, 68 n.22, 69 n.23, 71 n.26, 72 n.29, 78 n.40, 84 n.46, 86–7, 86 n.51, 87 n.52, 88 n.53, 90–3, 90 n.55, 91 n.56, 92 n.60, 94 n.62, 96 n.64, 122 n.33, 126, 185 n.2
  and John Palmer 84 n.46, 97 n.65, 123–4, 126, 185 n.2
Brunschwig, Jacques 4, 4 n.9, 5 n.12, 33–4, 35 n.23, 36 n.24, 37, 46 n.43, 100, 117 n.25, *see under* Sedley, David N.

Carneades 2 n.2, 10 n.22, 72 n.27, 77, 122–3, 125–6, 185 n.3, 186
Chrysippus 8 n.19, 29 n.4, 31–2, 35, 37, 64 n.18, 66 n.20, 67, 105 n.10, 106, 106 n.11, 111–12, 117, 138 n.9
Cleanthes 35, 37, 56, 101, 101 n.1, 103 n.5, 106 n.11, 129–30
counterfactual possibility 18, 46, 61, 71, 73 n.32, 74, 76, 76 n.35, 78–80, 82–3
Crantor 137, 139, 142, 151–2, 152 n.31, 159 n.39, 163–4, 168, 171, 171 n.55, 173 n.56, 177–8, 183, 187
Crates of Athens 142, 168, 168 n.51, 171, 171 n.55, 173 n.56, 180, 183
criterion
  apprehensive impression 10, 31, 72, 85, 101, 105, 122, 125
  Arcesilaus 130–1, 182, 188
  knowledge 55 n.1, 60
  reasonable 102, 102 n.2, 128

truth 3 n.7, 28, 59, 59 n.9, 62, 103, 130, 168–9, 188

daimons/daimonic 142, 144, 179–80
Democritus 96, 121, 121 n.131, 124–5
dialectic
  dialectical theorems 117, 120, 137–40, 158, 180–1
  Stoic 29, 29 n.4, 31–2, 39–40, 59, 103, 138 n.9, 141, 181
disciplinary holism 23–4, 29–30, 132, 140, 164–5, 164 n.48, 167, 171–4, 177, 180, 182–3
  early Stoic 29–30, 117, 140
  Old Academic/Peripatetic 23, 164–5, 171–3
doxography 20–1, 28, 47, 51–3, 59, 77, 94, 114, 137 n.6, 155

epistemic possibility 1–3, 5, 5 n.14, 7, 9, 10 n.22, 13–14, 18, 21, 46, 53, 55, 70, 73–5, 73 n.32, 89, 94, 98, 104, 165
epistemic sense-perception 155–8, 157 n.37, 164, 166
epistemic subject(s) 2–3, 3 n.5, 7, 11, 17, 30, 40–1, 44, 70–1, 73–6, 78–80, 82–3, 93, 95–6, 104, 115, 155
epistemological centrism, *see under* epistemology
Epistemological Novelty Thesis 22–4, 24 n.41, 135–7, 137 n.6, 182–3
epistemology 2–6, 2 nn.2, 4, 5 n.13, 6 n.15, 9 n.21, 18, 20–2, 30, 39–46, 41 n.32, 49–50, 52–3, 57 n.4, 58 n.6, 84, 93–4, 96, 104–5, 156
  epistemological centrism 5–7, 11–15, 17–22, 40, 45–6, 49–50, 52–3, 60, 68–72, 74, 77, 84, 94, 96, 110, 115, 127, 133, 136, 157, 185–6
  Hellenistic 4–6, 24, 28, 98, 155
  Old Academic 155
  Plato's dialogues 19 n.34
  Stoic 1, 2 n.2, 3, 5–6, 5 n.14, 11, 14–15, 20, 28, 39–40, 40 n.30, 45–6, 45 n.42, 46 n.43, 49–50, 52–3, 57 n.4, 67 n.21, 69, 69 n.23, 73, 77, 87 n.52, 89, 91 n.56, 96, 104–5, 104 n.8, 114–16, 133, 136

ἐποχὴ περὶ πάντων ("suspension of assent about all things")   10 n.22, 11–12, 18, 20, 24, 75, 84–9, 84 n.45, 86 nn.49–50, 102–3, 102 n.2, 123, 181, 188
   total or universal suspension   12–15, 84–9, 84 n.45, 86 n.50
ἔρως   141–2, 142 n.13, 179–80
ethics   6 n.15, 30, 52, 104 n.8, 114, 116
   Aristotle and Peripatetics   147, 151–4, 154 n.33, 163–79, 175 n.59, 179 n.61
   early Stoic   5–6, 9, 18, 21, 23–5, 29–31, 34, 37, 67 n.21, 102–5, 104 n.8, 116–17, 116 n.23, 119–20, 129, 132, 139–40, 158–9, 159 n.38, 172–3, 180–2
   and epistemological theory   6 n.15, 104–5, 104 nn.7, 8
   ethics proper   116–19, 116 n.23
   moral psychology   104 n.8, 140 n.12
   Old Academic   23–4, 38–9, 133, 135, 135 n.3, 137–9, 147, 151–61, 159 nn.38–40, 164–7, 169–70, 172–5, 176–9, 181
   training   105–7, 113, 119, 138, 141, 158, 182
expertise (τέχνη)   105–7, 106 n.11, 116, 121, 157–8, 174 n.57
   expert activity   157–8, 157 n.37

fire   27, 127
   designing   106–7, 116, 127, 177
first principles   23, 31, 33–4, 39, 39 n.29, 149, 157, 159–61, 165, 170–2, 174
form(s)   23, 36 n.24, 149–50, 161–3, 162 n.45, 163 n.46, 165, 168–9, 178
Frede, Michael   1 n.1, 15 n.30, 20–1, 21 n.38, 27 n.2, 40 n.30, 45 n.42, 47, 50, 52 n.49, 66 n.20, 72 n.29, 75 n.34, 97–8, 130 n.43

Gerson, Lloyd P.   30 n.8, 33 n.18, 86 n.51, 148 n.23, 159 n.40, 163 n.46, 164 n.48
good(s)
   absolute conception   148
   analogical conception   159–60, 159 n.40

   bodily   23, 28, 139, 142–3, 145, 147, 150, 167, 169, 172, 175, 178–9
   divine   147
   external   23, 39, 139, 142–3, 145, 150, 167, 175, 175 n.59, 178
   first natural things   139, 146, 169, 178–9
   hierarchy of goods   23–4, 30, 39, 135 n.3, 142, 145–8, 146 n.21, 150–3, 157, 159, 159 nn.39–40, 167, 169, 172–6, 175 n.60, 179–82, 188
   highest/supreme   27, 142–3, 146–7, 154, 165–7, 174–5
   life   169, 174–5
   perceptible   111
   psychic   23, 39, 142–3, 145, 147, 150, 150 n.27, 158, 167–9, 179
   Zeno   176, 178
Grand End account, *see under* appropriate action

Hadot, Pierre   30, 30 n.7, 36 n.26, 137 n.7
happiness (εὐδαιμονία)   23, 39–40, 102–3, 102 n.2, 117, 119, 129, 132, 139, 142–8, 146 n.21, 148 n.23, 152–6, 154 n.33, 163, 169–70, 173, 175, 175 n.60, 178–80, 182
   intellectual principle   165–6, 169–70, 178
   minimal eudaimonism   22 n.40, 132
Heidegger, Martin   34, 34 n.20, 43–4, 43 n.38, 99
Hellenistic period   4, 46, 138
   early Hellenistic   21, 25, 135, 181
hierarchy of beings   11, 38–9, 144, 147–8, 148 n.23, 150, 155–7, 160–2, 165–7, 173
historiography
   doxographical (*see* doxography)
   historical and philosophical   47
   philosophical   47, 50, 66–7
   specification *de dicto*   13–16, 13 n.27, 46–51, 46 n.44, 53, 71 n.26, 130–1, 140, 140 n.12
   specification *de re*   13–16, 13 n.27, 15 n.31, 40, 45–52, 66, 69, 73, 88, 104, 110, 114–16, 132–3, 136, 140, 140 n.12, 155
   specification *de traditione*   48–9, 53, 66, 69, 104, 132–3

Index of Subject

humanistic viewpoint   2–5, 2 n.4, 5 n.14,
    7, 11–12, 13 n.25, 17–18,
    19 n.34, 20–1, 24, 27, 40, 45,
    49, 52, 68–9, 74–5, 84, 84 n.46,
    93–4, 98, 116–17, 121, 155, 181
humanistic/anti-humanistic   7, 10, 45

impressionism   8, 15–16, 18, 20, 56,
    64–5, 67, 71, 82, 93 n.61, 98,
    103, 105, 126
impressions (φαντασιαί)   1, 3, 8, 10 n.22,
    11–13, 16–18, 28, 29 n.4, 31–2,
    37, 50, 55–65, 58 nn.6–7, 60 n.11,
    63 n.16, 64 n.18, 67–72, 69 n.23,
    70 n.25, 72 n.28, 73–83, 78 n.40,
    84 nn.45–6, 87–99, 87 n.52,
    88 n.53, 91 nn.56–7, 104–13,
    106 n.11, 111 n.18, 119, 121–6
  apprehensive impression(s)   3, 3 n.7,
    7 n.17, 10–11, 16, 18, 28, 31–2,
    36 n.26, 58 n.7, 59–65, 60 n.11,
    61–5, 63 n.16, 64 n.17, 69 n.23,
    67–75, 77, 83–5, 84 n.45,
    86 n.51, 88, 90, 94–6, 98–9,
    101, 103, 106, 109–16, 109 n.16,
    112 n.20, 119–22, 125–6,
    129, 182
  impulsive   108–9, 111–14
  moral/evaluative (vs. descriptive)
    108–12, 109 n.16, 110 n.17,
    112 n.20, 120
  non-apprehensive   63 n.16, 68, 88,
    108, 113–14
inapprehensible beings (ἀκατάληπτα)
    7–10, 7 n.17, 10 n.22, 17, 77,
    81–2, 84–91, 84 n.46, 86 n.49,
    94, 122–3, 122 n.32, 125–6,
    128–9, 181–2, 188
  impressions   10 n.22, 87, 91, 91 n.56,
    94, 102–4, 122
  unclear or non-evident   10 n.22, 17,
    97, 122–3
incorporeal beings   12, 17, 19–20,
    34–8, 36 n.24, 61 n.13, 65–6,
    69, 69 n.23, 74, 84 n.46,
    88, 93–4, 98–100, 104, 116,
    148, 188
indiscernibility arguments   17–19, 25, 46,
    55, 61, 64, 66–80, 77 n.38, 82–5,
    88, 91, 97–100, 104

indiscernible beings   6, 8, 20, 46, 67–8,
    70–1, 74–80, 75 n.34, 82, 98
  impressions   70 n.25, 78, 82–3
individual bodies   6–9, 8 n.19, 12, 16–21,
    31, 34–9, 36 n.24, 56–61, 63–71,
    69 n.23, 71 n.26, 74–7, 80–3,
    84 nn.45–6, 87–94, 96–100,
    102–5, 108–11, 114–16, 118–21,
    118 n.27, 124, 129, 132, 165,
    177, 181, 188
intellect (νοῦς/*mens*)   143, 149 n.25,
    150 n.27, 167 n.49, 169,
    169 n.52, 177–9, *see also under*
    happiness
  thought (διάνοια/*ratio*)   118, 166
Ioppolo, Anna Maria   1 n.1, 9 n.21,
    14 n.28, 60 n.10, 72, 72 nn.29,
    31, 85 n.46, 97 n.65, 102 nn.2–3,
    120 n.28, 130 n.43, 131 n.45
Isnardi Parente, Margherita   69, 69 n.24,
    144 n.15, 147 n.20, 170 n.53

Lévy, Carlos   5 n.14, 71 n.26, 73 n.33,
    79, 79 n.42, 95 n.63, 101 n.1,
    184 n.1
logic   29, 29 n.4, 31–2, 34, 37, 39–40, 50,
    69, 103, 105, 107, 117, 119, 138,
    140–1, 159 n.38, 173
Lucullus   2–5, 77 n.37, 91–2, 92 n.59, 97,
    105, 121–4, 131 n.45, 173, 182,
    185 n.2

mean   150–3, 158
metaphysica generalis, *see* ontology
metaphysica specialis, *see* metaphysics
metaphysics   6–7, 6 n.16, 16, 18, 19 n.34,
    23–4, 33–5, 33 nn.16, 18,
    34 n.19, 36 n.24, 39, 42, 50, 61,
    67 n.21, 70, 71 n.26, 75 n.34,
    80–1, 90, 98, 98 n.66, 103,
    115, 124, 135 n.3, 150, 156–7,
    168, 173, 180, 182, *see under*
    realism
mortal animal partaking in reason   3,
    7–9, 12, 17–22, 24, 30–1,
    36–8, 37 n.27, 45, 50, 56–61, 63,
    65–7, 69, 74–6, 81–3, 84 n.46,
    87–90, 94, 96–8, 103–9, 112–16,
    118–21, 125–9, 165, 173, 176
music   138, 157–8, 157 n.37

nature 17–18, 28, 30–1, 35, 45 n.42, 55, 97, 102, 103 n.3, 105–8, 114–17, 118 n.27, 119–25, 127–9, 139, 142–7, 149, 153, 158, 160–3, 169–72, 174, 174 n.57, 176–8, 181–2
  bipolarity 163–4, 163 n.46, 170, 172–4, 177–8
noncorporeal being 23, 38–9, 172, 177–8, 180–1
  goods 179–80
  principles 30, 165, 174, 178
numbers 23, 148–50, 149 n.25, 160, 162–3, 162 n.45, 165–7

obtaining (ὑπάρχειν) 7–8, 12, 16–17, 36, 36 nn.24–6, 38, 45, 55–65, 67–71, 69 n.23, 75–7, 80–3, 84 n.46, 87–9, 97–100, 103, 105–6, 108–12, 110 n.17, 114, 119–20, 174
ontology 7, 30, 33 n.16, 35, 41–4, 50, 60, 103 n.3, 156
  dualistic or Platonic 5 n.14, 71 n.26
  Old Academic 148 nn.23–4, 148–51, 155–7, 159–62, 162 n.45, 164
  Old Academic/Peripatetic 38, 173
  Stoic 5 n.14, 7–9, 27 n.1, 33 n.18, 35–6, 38, 46, 61, 65, 81–2, 84 n.46, 88, 98–100, 102, 129, 180–1
ontology of knowledge
  historiographical framework 7, 17–18, 43–5, 93, 104, 136
  Old Academic 155–6
  Stoic apprehension 15, 17–18, 25, 46, 59, 69, 81–2, 88, 96, 100, 104–5, 112, 129, 132, 181
ontology of virtue
  Old Academic 147, 155
  Stoic 9, 104–5, 107–9, 133

Peripatetic 28 n.3, 142, 154 n.33, 164
Philo of Larissa 10, 122 n.32, 125–6, 185 n.3
physics 6, 69, 173
  early Stoic 20–1, 27 n.1, 29–30, 32, 32 n.13, 34–5, 37, 68–9, 71 n.26, 75 n.34, 96, 103–5, 104 n.7, 114, 117, 120, 140, 159 n.38, 171 n.55, 176–8, 181

Old Academic 170 n.53, 171, 171 n.55, 174, 177
Peripatetic 171, 174, 177
Plato 14 n.5, 19 n.34, 23, 24 n.41, 30, 36 n.24, 52, 55 n.1, 60–2, 71 n.26, 136, 137 n.6, 138 n.9, 139, 142, 144 n.17, 147, 147 n.22, 150–1, 153, 159 n.38, 162 n.44, 168, 171–2, 175 n.59, 179 n.62, 180, 183–7, 184 n.1, 185 n.3
Plotinus 5 n.14, 137 n.6, 151 n.29
Polemo 23, 24 n.41, 25, 28, 28 n.3, 39, 135–47, 135 n.3, 142 n.13, 143 n.14, 151, 152 n.31, 154, 158–9, 159 n.38, 164, 164 n.48, 168, 170–2, 170 n.53, 171 n.55, 173 n.56, 178–83, 179 n.61, 180 n.63, 186–8
Presocratic 34, 38, 96–7, 183–5, 185 n.2
provisional acceptance 15 n.31, 16, 16 n.32, 18, 67–9, 67 n.21, 69 n.23, 76–7, 80, 82, 84, 87–8, 124, 128, 131, 181–2, 187

realism
  epistemological 4
  metaphysical 19, 19 n.36, 23–4, 30, 57–8, 58 n.7, 60–1, 64–7, 82, 99–100, 103, 118, 128, 162–3, 165, 170, 170 n.53, 180
reasonable 101–2, 107–8, 113, 128–32, 138–9, 155
reductio ad absurdum 15, 70, 127–8, 127 n.38
relative disposition 7–9, 8 n.19, 12, 30, 35, 81, 81 n.43, 88–90, 96–7, 126, 129, 155, 157, 165
representationalism 55–6, 58–9, 100
representational purport/representational success 58, 58 n.8, *see also* impressions
Rorty, Richard 20–1, 52 n.51

Sedley, David 66 n.20, 73 n.33, 97–8, 98 n.66, 125, 131 n.45, 135 n.2, 138, 140 n.12, 170 n.53, 171, 171 n.55
  and Brunschwig, Jacques 135 n.2, 136 n.5

and Long, Anthony A.   9 n.21, 58 n.7, 136, 136 n.5
simplicity/simple   23, 38–9, 39 n.29, 72, 143, 165–9
skeptic   13–14, 187
   epistemological skeptic   5, 12–14, 13 n.25, 17, 22, 41, 49, 59 n.9
   ontological skepticism   17, 17 n.33, 71 n.26
Socrates   10, 40, 55 n.1, 62, 73–4, 76, 82–3, 84 n.46, 96, 132, 138 n.9, 179–80
soul
   Aristotle and Peripatetics   153–4, 165–75, 177–8
   Old Academic   30, 39, 143–50, 145 n.18, 150 n.26, 156–7, 162–72, 167 n.49, 174–5, 177–8, 180
      world-soul   148, 150 n.27, 162 n.45
   Plato   175 n.59
   Stoic   8, 35, 42, 55–7, 60–1, 63–5, 64 n.18, 67, 76, 99, 105–6, 108–11, 119, 174 n.57, 176–7
      hēgemonikon   56, 58, 103, 176
Speusippus   23, 28, 28 n.3, 38, 135, 137, 139, 145, 145 n.18, 146 n.21, 147–54, 148 nn.23–4, 150 n.27, 153 n.32, 156–64, 157 n.37, 159 nn.38, 40, 161 n.42, 162 nn.44–5, 166–9, 167 n.49, 171–2, 173 n.56, 177–8, 180, 183, 186–7
Stoic sage   12, 14, 27, 31–2, 57 n.4, 67 n.21, 68, 84–7, 86 n.50, 105–8, 113, 115–16, 119–21, 130, 154, 173, 177
Stoic tripartition of philosophy/philosophical discourse   10, 29, 31, 37, 40, 40 n.30, 45, 50, 55, 101, 121, 137, 157, 159 n.38, 173, 173 n.56

Tarrant, Harold   142 n.13, 144 n.17, 179
Theaetetus   55 n.1, 60–2, 64, 142, 187
Theophrastus   28, 28 n.3, 38, 139, 142, 146, 148–9, 152, 154 n.33, 159 nn.38–9, 164, 169, 169 n.52, 171, 173 n.56, 175, 175 n.60, 177, 183

Thorsrud, Harald   10 n.22, 16 n.32, 67 n.21, 72 n.30, 85 n.46, 98

Varro   62, 94–6, 143, 152, 168–78, 171 n.55, 173 n.56, 182–3
vegetarianism
   Polemo   141–3, 178–9
   Xenocrates and Polemo   141
virtue
   Aristotle and Peripatetics   158, 164, 167–70, 175–6
   Cynic   28
   Old Academic   23, 39, 141–3, 145–7, 153–5, 154 n.33, 158, 164, 167–70, 175–6, 178–80
   Stoic   9, 18, 21, 24–5, 32, 37, 40, 45, 45 n.42, 103–5, 105 n.9, 107, 111, 113, 117, 119, 128–9, 132–3, 137–8, 140–3, 173, 175–6

Williams, Bernard   19 n.36, 20 n.37, 46, 47 n.45, 57, 65 n.19, 73 n.32, 140
wisdom   29, 35, 40, 45 n.42, 68, 106–7, 116, 154–6, 166, 168, 173–4, 180
   φρόνησις   102 n.2, 120, 144, 147, 147 n.22, 156, 166
   theoretical and practical   154–6, 166
world   1–2, 4, 30, 33, 41, 43–5, 43 n.36, 44 n.39, 64 n.17, 92–4, 93 n.61, 116–17
   Old Academic   23–4, 30, 136, 147–9, 150 n.27, 157, 160, 162–3, 165–7, 170, 171 n.55, 180
   Stoic   4, 10, 17, 19, 22, 24, 27–8, 28 n.3, 30, 32–5, 38, 46, 55, 57, 59–60, 74, 92–4, 98, 100, 102–3, 106–7, 115, 117–21, 118 n.27, 124, 127–9, 132, 165, 174, 174 n.57, 178

Xenocrates   23, 28–30, 28 n.3, 38, 135, 138, 141–51, 144 nn.16–17, 145 nn.18–19, 147 n.22, 148 n.23, 150 n.26, 153–7, 159, 159 n.38, 163–4, 166–8, 171–2, 173 n.56, 175–8, 180, 183

Zeno 2 n.3, 3–4, 7–11, 8 n.19, 9 n.21,
        13–25, 22 n.40, 27–40, 27 n.1,
        29 n.4, 32 n.13, 33 nn.16–18,
        36 nn.24–6, 45–7, 49–50, 55–62,
        57 n.4, 58 n.7, 61 n.13, 64–75,
        66 n.20, 67 n.21, 77, 77 n.38,
        81–5, 88–9, 93–4, 98–103,
        105–6, 105 n.10, 105 n.11,
        107–8, 110–1, 113, 116–21, 124,
        126–31, 135–40, 144–6, 157–9,
        159 n.38, 165, 170, 172–8,
        173 n.56, 174 n.57, 175 n.60,
        180–3, 188

Zeus 3, 27, 155, 174 n.58, 178

Index of References

Aëtius
    1 proem. 2   29, 106
    1.7.30   149
    1.7.33   106
    4.12.1–5   64 n.18
    4.21.1–4   56

Alcinous
    Did.
    154.8–9   55 n.1
    154.10–18   150 n.26

Alexander of Aphrodisias
    In Top.
    1.8–14   32

Anon.
    In Pl. Tht.
    2.11–19   55 n.1

Arcesilaus
    Fragments (Vezzoli)
    F 35   15 n.30
    F 45   15 n.30, 121–2
    F 63   152 n.30
    F 72   103 n.5
    F 75   103, 131
    F 87   10, 77 n.38, 84–5, 88, 101, 103, 105, 122
    F 107   142
    F 112   101
    F 122   16
    F 124   10 n.22, 122–3
    F 125   15 n.30
    F 126   10 n.22, 15 n.30, 122

Aristocles
    apud Euseb., *Praep. ev.*
    15.14.1–2   127

Aristotle
    DA
    1.2, 404b27–30   149
    2.12, 424a17–26   61 n.14

EE
    2.1, 1218b31–7   175 n.59
    2.1, 1219a38–9   154 n.33

EN
    1.3, 1095a5–6   158
    1.4, 1095b4–7   158
    1.5, 1096a1–2   175
    1.6, 1096b5–8   159
    1.8, 1098b12–16   175 n.59
    1.8, 1098b12–20   146
    1.8, 1098b30–2   153
    1.8, 1099a31–3   175 n.59
    1.9, 1100a5–9   175
    2.1, 1103b6   158
    2.4, 1105b2   158
    2.7, 1107a29–32   158
    6.11, 1143b5   158
    6.13, 1145a10–11   169 n.52
    7.13, 1153b16–19   175 n.59
    7.13, 1153b1–7   153–4
    7.13, 1153b7   152
    7.13, 1153b17–21   175
    9.11, 1171b12   158
    10.7, 1177b30–1178a8   169–70

Meta.
    Δ 4, 1014b27–34   163 n.46
    Δ 6, 1016b32–1017a3   162 n.44
    Z 2, 1028b18–24   162 n.45
    Z 2, 1028b21–4   166
    Z 2, 1028b24 ff.   149
    Λ 4, 1070a32   162
    Λ 4, 1070b16   162
    Λ 4, 1072b30   150 n.27
    Λ 6–7   39 n.29
    Λ 7, 1072a31–5   39 n.29
    Λ 7, 1072b30–4   149
    Λ 10, 1075a19–25   161
    Λ 10, 1075b1   160
    Λ 10, 1075b37–1076a4   148, 166
    Λ 10, 1075b38–1076a3   161
    Λ 10, 1076a1   161
    Λ 10, 1076a4   161

Λ 10, 1076a2–6   39 n.29
M 1, 1076a19–29   162 n.45
M 1, 1076a21   163
M 6, 1080b14–16   166
N 2, 1090a12–13   163
N 3, 1090b13–21   166
N 4, 1091a33–b19   150 n.27
N 4, 1091a35   160
N 4, 1091b35   160
N 5, 1092a11–17   160
N 5, 1092a14   148

Phys.
2.1   163

Pol.
7.1, 1323a21–35   175 n.59
7.1, 1323a24–7   146

Top.
1.14, 105b19–25   28 n.3
2.6, 112a32   144
7.1, 152a5–12, 25–30   144

Arius Didymus
  apud Euseb., *Praep. ev.*
  15.20.2–3 56

  apud Stob., *Ecl.*
  1.19   32

Augustine
  Cont. Acad.
  2.6.14   86 n.50
  Ep.
  144   141

Aulus Gellius
  NA
  9.5.4   152–3

Cicero
  Acad.
  1.13   183
  1.15–42   95
  1.17   171–2, 174
  1.18   172
  1.19   28 n.3, 29,
                    173 n.56, 174
  1.19–20   169
  1.19–23   174
  1.21   175
  1.22   152, 169, 175
  1.24   171

1.24–9   171, 171 n.55
1.30   143
1.30–1   168
1.33   168, 171, 175
1.33–4   159 n.39, 171
1.34   139, 152, 168, 173 n.56
1.35   176
1.36–7   176
1.37   120
1.38   176
1.39   34 n.21, 37, 174
1.40   55
1.40–1   67
1.41   59, 92
1.43   173
1.44   10, 97, 121
1.44–5   94–6, 185 n.2
1.44–6   183–4
1.45   15 n.30, 86 n.50, 89,
          94 n.62, 95, 184, 184 n.1
1.46   10, 182, 183
2.7   183
2.8–9   131 n.45
2.12   123
2.13–18   182
2.14   97, 124
2.15   89, 91, 91 n.57
2.15–16   185 n.2
2.16   70, 77, 101 n.1
2.17   62, 92
2.18   55, 91, 91 n.57
2.21   3
2.23–5   103
2.31   103, 106, 121, 121 n.30
2.31–2   17, 103
2.32   97, 121, 123
2.33   62
2.36   62
2.39   17, 103, 103 n.4
2.40   91
2.40–1   91
2.45–6   62
2.48   55
2.50   77 n.37, 80
2.54–8   70, 77 n.37, 80
2.56   66
2.57   105
2.59   89
2.60   131 n.45
2.66   68, 105
2.67   86 n.50

2.68	87	4.44	139
2.74	184	4.45	139
2.75–7	105	4.45–51	143
2.76	91 n.57	4.49	153
2.77	55, 61, 67–8, 91	4.60	139
2.77–8	77 n.38	4.61	28
2.78	87, 185 n.3	5.7	152
2.81	78 n.41	5.7–8	139
2.84	78–80, 78 n.39, 78 n.40	5.7–74	179 n.61
2.84–5	77, 77 n.37	5.10	188 n.5
2.84–6	70	5.14	139, 179 n.61
2.85	66	5.58	154
2.99	121 n.30	5.68–9	175
2.112–13	91	5.79	28
2.115	105	5.90–1	175
2.122	78 n.41	5.94	186
2.131	139, 143, 146, 152 n.31		
2.131–2	175 n.60	*De nat. deor.*	
2.134	175 n.60	1.11	183
2.135	139, 151, 152,	1.39	177
2.139	139	2.21	27, 118
2.145	36, 121	2.22	33
		2.23–8	118 n.27
Ad Att.		2.57	106
2.16.3	169 n.52	2.57–8	177
13.19.3	95	3.22	118
De fin.		*De orat.*	
2.2	187	3.67	15 n.30, 184 n.1, 186–7
2.17	29 n.4	3.80	188
2.33–4	178–9		
2.34	143	*Div.*	
3.3	120	2.150	131 n.45
3.20–1	108		
3.58	108	*Leg.*	
3.59	107	1.37–8	146 n.21
4	139		
4.2	159 n.38	*Off.*	
4.3	28, 28 n.3, 139	1.6	113
4.3–6	28 n.3, 173 n.56	1.132	109
4.3–7	159, 159 n.38	2.8	183
4.4	159 n.38		
4.4–5	29	*Tusc.*	
4.6	143	2.4	183
4.8	159 n.38	3.12	152
4.14	28	3.22	152
4.14–18	28	3.71	151
4.15	28	3.71–4	152
4.16	159	4.38–47	152
4.19–21	139	5.11	187
4.20–44	159	5.24–5	159 n.39
4.25–6	139	5.30	146 n.21
		5.33	131 n.45
		5.39	146 n.21

5.83	131 n.45	7.58	66 n.20
5.87	146 n.21	7.61	36 n.24
		7.63	37, 63 n.16

Clement of Alexandria

Strom.
2.5	155–6
2.22	28, 142, 145
2.133	146 n.21, 153, 158, 159 n.38, 163
7.32	141, 143, 178

Crantor

Fragments (Mette)
Fr. 1	151
Fr. 3b	151
Fr. 4	151–2
Fr. 6a	152
Fr. 10	163, 171 n.55

David

Prol. philos. (Busse)
43.30–44.5	106 n.11
44.5	105 n.10

Diogenes Laertius

D.L.
3.80–1	175 n.59
4.17	142
4.18	139 n.10
4.19	141
4.21	179
4.21–2	142
4.21–3	168 n.51
4.22	142
4.27	151
4.28	187
4.29–30	142
7.4	107
7.8	173
7.35	178
7.39–41	29
7.40	29, 29 n.5, 117
7.41	29 n.4
7.42	31, 31 n.10
7.43	29 n.4, 31, 40
7.45–8	32
7.46	61 n.13, 63 n.16
7.50	61 n.13
7.52	60 n.11

7.83	32, 140
7.87	28
7.87–8	119
7.88	119
7.89	107, 127
7.92	110
7.107	107
7.108–9	113
7.132	34–5
7.134	31, 34 n.21, 174
7.135	34
7.136–7	127
7.140–2	32
7.148	127, 178
7.156	106, 127, 178
7.157	176
7.171	101
7.177	60 n.11
9.72	121 n.31

Epictetus
Diss.
1.20.15–16	119

Eusebius
Praep. ev.
14.4.15	86 n.50
14.6.1	187
14.6.1–3	16
15.14.1	34 n.21

Favonius Eulogius
Disp. de Somn. Scip. (van Weddingen)
5.6, p. 17	149

Galen
Qual. inc.
19.483	34

Homer
Il.
2.204	161

Iamblichus
DCMS (Festa)
4, p. 15	148 n.24
4, p. 16	150 n.27, 160
4, p. 18	160

Lactantius
Div. inst.
| 4.9 | 174 |

LS
26A	106
26B	29
28D	64, 66 n.20
28O	66 n.20
28P	66 n.20
33C	37
33F	37
33M	66 n.20
34H	38
34I	38
39A	61 n.13
39B	64 n.18
40B	55, 59, 67
40C	61 n.13, 63 n.16
40E	61 n.13, 64
40G	104 n.5
40H	61 n.13, 70 n.25
40J	77
41A	36, 121
41C	10, 84–5, 88
41H	57 n.4
42A	105
42F	62
44A	27 n.1, 32
44B	174
45A	34 n.21
45E	34
45G	34 n.21
46A	106
46G	127
51B, part	112
53H	56
53J	109
53Q	109
55B	58 n.7
59E	113
60R	111
61B	177
63A	119
68A	15 n.30, 89
68C	70, 77
68I	102
68R	121
68T	10, 125
69A	103
69B	101, 103

Marcus Aurelius
| 5.10.1–2 (Farquharson, 37) | 122 n.32 |

Nemesius
Nat. hom.
| 2.72 | 156 |
| 2.102 | 150 |

Numenius
apud Euseb., *Praep. ev.*
14.7.9	101 n.1
14.7.15	10 n.22, 122–3, 86 n.50
14.8.1–10	15 n.30
14.8.3–4	10 n.22, 122

Olympiodorus
In Pl. Gorg.
| 2.2 | 106 n.11 |
| 12.1 | 105 |

Philo
De immut. mundo
| 48 2.397 | 66 n.20 |

Philodemus
Acad. hist.
col. 13	141
col. 14.4	138
col. 14.41–5	141
col. 15.4–10	142
col. 15.31–46	142
cols. 15–17	168 n.51
col. 18.7	186
col. 20.2–4	187
col. 21.36–42	101 n.1

Plato
Laws
631b–d	147
689d2	147 n.22
689d4	147 n.22
689d5	147 n.22
689d7	147 n.22
696c8	147 n.22
697a–c	147
697b	175 n.59
710a6	147 n.22
726a–729b	147 n.22
743c–e	147 n.22
870a–b	147 n.22

Philebus
16c–d	151 n.29
25d–26e	151 n.29

Tht.
144d9	187
144e3	187
145b3	187
147a1	187
148e2	187
151e5	187
152b10–c1	55 n.1
154e8	187
157d3	187
161d4	187
165a4	187
178b3	55 n.1
178b5–7	55 n.1
208c–e	62
208c7	62
208c8	62
208d5–7	62
208e3–5	62

Timaeus
30b3	167 n.49
46d5–6	167 n.49

Plotinus
Enneads
1 2.2.15–18	151 n.29

Plutarch

Adv. Col.
1120c	86 n.50
1121f–1123b	131
1122a	103 n.4
1122a–e	103

Comm. not.
1059b–c	104 n.5
1065a	146 n.21, 153
1069e–f	28, 146, 159, 163
1069f	144
1073e	34 n.21
1074b–c	27 n.1
1077c	66 n.20

Cons. ap.
104c	151
110a	152 n.30
114d–e	152

De anima pro.
1012d	163
1032c3–d5	150 n.26

Def. or.
416c–d	144

Mor.
780d	141

St. rep.
1035c	117
1038c	111
1042e–f	111
1045f–1046b	138 n.9

Virt. mor.
441a	110
441c	177

Polemo
Fragments (Gigante)
Fr. 7	159
Fr. 15	141
Fr. 16	141
Fr. 33	141
Fr. 96	143
Fr. 101	137
Fr. 112	141, 143, 178
Fr. 113	141–2
Fr. 121	170
Fr. 122	138 n.9
Fr. 123	142, 145, 146 n.21
Fr. 124	144, 146
Fr. 125	143
Fr. 127	143, 179
Fr. 128	139
Fr. 129	143
Fr. 130	143

Proclus
In Euclidem
2.8.78–9	167
179.12–22	166

In Pl. Parm.
888.18–19	149

In Pl. Tim.
1.76	142

Ps. Aristotle
Divisiones Aristoteleae
1.1	175 n.59

Ps. Galen
  Hist. Phil. (Diels)
  5, 602.19   106
  8, 605   144, 156

Ps. Iamblichus
  Theol. arith. 82.10   162
  Theol. arith. 83.1–5   150 n.27

Ps. Olympiodorus
  In. Pl. Phd.
  74 (2.107–9
       Westerink)   145 n.18

Ps. Plutarch
  Plac. phil.
  874f   169 n.52

Seneca
  Ep.
  83.9   107
  85.18   145–6, 145 n.20
  94.18–19   113
  94.33–7   113
  94–5   113

Sextus Empiricus
  M.
  2.7   29 n.4, 31
  7.16   29
  7.16–19   28 n.3
  7.22–3   117
  7.145   153, 156
  7.145–6   156
  7.147   150, 155
  7.150–7   85–90, 86 n.50,
                      126, 188
  7.154   70, 77 n.38, 84
  7.155   10, 87–8, 122
  7.155–6   88–9
  7.155–7   86, 105
  7.156   86–7, 88 n.53,
                      89, 122
  7.156–8   86 n.49
  7.157   87, 89
  7.158   101–3, 102 n.2,
                      105, 188
  7.171   63 n.16
  7.194   56
  7.228–36   64 n.18
  7.248   61 n.13
  7.250–2   64
  7.253   61
  7.257   63 n.16
  7.402   61 n.13
  7.402–8   70 n.25
  7.403   63 n.16
  7.426   61 n.13
  7.408   63 n.16
  8.70   37
  8.98   38
  8.100   38
  9.78–85   118 n.27
  9.104   27, 118
  9.211   58 n.6
  9.332   27 n.1, 32
  10.218   34 n.21
  11.23   176
  11.51   159 n.39
  11.183   61 n.13
  11.200   120

  PH
  1.1   188
  1.8   188
  1.226   122
  1.232   86 n.50, 102
  1.232–4   102, 102 n.3
  1.233   102
  1.235   91 n.56, 122 n.32, 125–6
  2.4   61 n.13
  2.13   29
  2.51   55
  2.72   55

Simplicius
  ad Cat.
  80a4   34

Speusippus
  Fragments (Tarán)
  Fr. 28   148 n.24, 150 n.27, 162
  Fr. 29a   162 n.45, 166
  Fr. 30   148, 166
  Fr. 32   162 n.45
  Fr. 33   166
  Frs. 33–6   162 n.45
  Fr. 34   166
  Fr. 37   166
  Fr. 42a   149, 150 n.27
  Fr. 43   148–9, 150 n.27, 160
  Fr. 44   150 n.27, 160
  Fr. 47a   159
  Fr. 58   149

Fr. 59	149	1.93	34
Fr. 61a–b	160	1.98	34 n.21, 127
Fr. 73	166	1.98, part	127
Fr. 75	153, 156	1.99	27 n.1, 32
Fr. 77	146 n.21, 153, 158, 159 n.38, 163	1.102, part	127
		1.111	27
		1.135	176
Fr. 78a	154	1.136–8	176
Frs. 78a–c	146 n.21	1.141	56
Fr. 78b	154	1.160	174 n.57
Fr. 78e	145	1.171	106
Fr. 78d	146 n.21	1.182	119
Fr. 79	146 n.21	1.201	110
Fr. 80a	152–3	1.230	107
Frs. 80b–e	152	2.35	29, 106
Fr. 81b	152	2.54	64 n.18
Fr. 83	152	2.65, part	64
Fr. 84	153	2.205	38
		2.300	174
Stobaeus		2.341	58 n.7
Ecl.		2.381, part	34
1.1	149	2.509	112
1.8	34	2.776	106
1.19	27 n.1, 32	2.836, part	56
1.29	170	2.1013	118 n.27
1.106.20–3	112	2.1027	106
1.136	36 n.24	2.1077	177
1.177.21–1.179.17	64, 66 n.20	3 Apollodorus 6, part	34
2.7.18	154	3.16	119
2.59.4–7	110	3.85	111
2.64.20–2	110	3.169	109
2.73.16–74.3	57 n.4	3.394	107
2.75.12	28		
2.77.16–27	119	Tertullian	
2.85	108	*Apol.*	
2.86.17	109 n.15	21	174 n.57
2.86.17–18	108–9		
5.906.18–907.5	108	Theodoret of Cyrrhus	
		Gr. aff. cur.	
Stoicorum Veterum Fragmenta		5.19	156
1.55	55, 59, 67		
1.59, part	55, 61	Theophrastus	
1.60, part	59, 67	*Meta.*	
1.61	59, 67	2a18–26	152
1.65, part	36 n.24	6a23	149
1.66	121		
1.72	106 n.11	Cod. Neapolitanus	
1.73	105	2 D 22, sent. 18	169 n.52
1.75	29 n.4, 31		
1.85	34 n.21	FHS&G	
1.90	34 n.21, 174	461	169 n.52
		476	169 n.52

479	169 n.52	Fr. 123	156
481	169 n.52	Fr. 126	156
493	175 n.60	Fr. 133	149
497	175 n.60	Fr. 134	149
498	175 n.60	Fr. 142	144
		Fr. 150	145
Xenocrates		Fr. 151	144, 146
Fragments (IPD)		Fr. 153	159
Fr. 2	150, 155	Fr. 154	144
Fr. 14	149	Fr. 158	144
Fr. 20	149	Fr. 165	153
Fr. 23	149	Fr. 166	145–6
Frs. 85–117	149	Fr. 171	144, 156
Fr. 110	150	Fr. 177	155–6

www.ingramcontent.com/pod-product-compliance
Lightning Source LLC
Chambersburg PA
CBHW062225300426
44115CB00012BA/2217